What Is This— Some Kind of Joke?

MORDECHAI SCHMUTTER

What Is This— Some Kind of Joke?

MORDECHAI SCHMUTTER

Copyright © 2016 Mordechai Schmutter
ISBN 978-1-60091-458-4

All Rights Reserved

No part of this book may be reproduced in any form
without written permission from the copyright holder.
The rights of the copyright holder will be strictly enforced.

Book design by:

vividesign
SRULY PERL • 845.694.7186
mechelp@gmail.com

Cover Illustration by: Yishaya Suval

Proofreading by E.M. Sonenblick
esonenblick@gmail.com

Published and distributed by:

Israel Bookshop Publications
501 Prospect Street
Lakewood, NJ 08701
Tel: (732) 901-3009
Fax: (732) 901-4012
www.israelbookshoppublications.com
info@israelbookshoppublications.com

Printed in the USA

Distributed in Israel by:
Shanky's
Petach Tikva 16
Jerusalem
972-2-538-6936

Distributed in Europe by:
Lehmanns
Unit E Viking Industrial Park
Rolling Mill Road,
Jarrow, Tyne & Wear NE32 3DP
44-191-406-0842

Distributed in Australia by:
Gold's Book and Gift Company
3-13 William Street
Balaclava 3183
613-9527-8775

Distributed in South Africa by:
Kollel Bookshop
Northfield Centre
17 Northfield Avenue
Glenhazel 2192
27-11-440-6679

DEDICATION

This book is dedicated to all the people who, when I told them I wanted to be a humorist, laughed at me.
Thanks.

TABLE OF CONTENTS

Acknowledgments...11
Introduction..13
About the Title..31

SECTION I: A RABBI, A PRIEST, AND A BISHOP
(OR "SOCIAL SITUATIONS")

Talking Small..39
Magic Words...45
You Never Call..51
Early Polls..57

SECTION II: TAKE MY WIFE. PLEASE.
(OR "MARRIAGE MADE EASY")

Home Economics..67
All the Trimmings...72

SECTION III: POP CORN!
(OR "DAD JOKES")

Untapped Buffet..81
What Did I Say?..86
Noisy Toys...92

SECTION IV: SEVEN ATE NINE!
(OR "FOOD FRENZY")

Supper Ideas...103
Charred, but Raw...108

Trying New Things..114
Some of the Samples at This Year's Kosherfest Had Bugs...121

SECTION V: NO SOAP RADIO!
(OR "ANIMALS AND US")

If It Looks Like a Duck and Sounds Like a Duck,
    It's Probably a Baby..132
Not an Exact Science..140
No Flies Were Harmed in the Making of This Article..........146

SECTION VI: TO SEE TIME FLY
(OR "SIMPLE ENTERTAINMENT")

Not to Be Used as a Flotation Device...............................157
Having a Ball...162
Wanna See a Play?..167
Here "for the Kids"..172

SECTION VII: HE HAD NO BODY TO GO WITH
(OR "BEING BIG BONED")

How Drunk Are You?..183
Trimming the Fat...188
Bee Happy, Bee Healthy..193
This Year's Ig Nobel Prize Winners Are
    Wearing Two Pairs of Socks......................................198
A Shot of Soda..204

SECTION VIII: TWO PARACHUTES
(OR "PLAYING THE ODDS")

You Win Some, You Lose Some.......................................213
No Weights!..218

SECTION IX: WHY THE LONG FACE?
(OR "AGING GRACEFULLY")

Look at This Clown! 227
Physically Ill 232

SECTION X: CHICKEN ON THE ROAD
(OR "TIPS FOR TRAVEL")

Look, Ma! No Hands! 241
Day Trips 247
Plain and Simple 253
Get Lost 259

SECTION XI: ORANGE YOU GLAD I DIDN'T SAY "BANANA"? (OR "PROTECTING YOUR HOME")

Questions and Answers 269
Extreme Weather 275
Too Much Energy 280

SECTION XII: CHANGING A LIGHT BULB
(OR "POWER STRUGGLES")

What to Do during a Power Failure 289
Sandy Weather 295
Grinding Halt 307

SECTION XIII: IS YOUR REFRIGERATOR RUNNING? (OR "TECHNOLOGICALLY SPEAKING")

To Continue in English, Keep Reading 317
Remember the Omer! 323
Look Out, World! 328
If It's on the Internet, It Must Be True 333

Walk-ins Welcome?..338
Overcharged..342

SECTION XIV: WHERE DOES A FISH KEEP ITS MONEY? (OR "COLD CASH")

Many Happy Returns..355
I Don't Work Here..360
Weighed Down..366

SECTION XV: A MAN WALKED INTO A BAR. OUCH. (OR "TRAGIC ACCIDENTS")

Harmful If Swallowed..375
Lost and Found...381

SECTION XVI: ONE WAS A SALTED (OR "CRIMINALS EVERYWHERE")

The Weirdo on the Bus Goes "Snip Snip Snip"..............391
All the Amenities of Home.......................................397
Fair and Balanced...403

SECTION XVII: BLACK AND WHITE AND RED ALL OVER (OR "WRITING FOR A NEWSPAPER")

Another Book? By Mordechai Schmutter?....................413
How to Publish a Book in Twelve Months
    or Less, Jewish Time..418
Your Turn...424
The Mailbag...432

ACKNOWLEDGMENTS

I would like to thank the *Ribbono Shel Olam*, Who deserves more than a passing mention in my books, for creating the very concept of humor to help us get through all the other craziness that life throws at us.

I would like to thank the following people, places, things, and abstract nouns, without whom this book would not have been possible: my wife, my parents, my in-laws, Adina, Daniel, Heshy, Gedalyah, Israel Book Shop, *Hamodia*, Aish.com, all the other publications that run my articles, my readers, the people who stop me on the street to tell me that their grandmother likes my articles, their grandmother, Chaim Kaufman, Yishaya Suval, Folgers, the makers of Advil, any siblings of mine who call my parents less than I do, pickles and ice cream, the wedding industry, dad jokes,

WHAT IS THIS — SOME KIND OF JOKE?

your momma, toys you get so that your child can pretend that he's doing whatever *you're* doing so he'll stop touching your stuff, Kosherfest, *milchig* grills, tiny annoying dogs, new fruit, old fruit, shopping bags made out of sackcloth, free-range chickens, soap radio, sweatpants, mini Queen Esther impersonators, magic marker moustaches, healthy alternatives, my Purim robe, bubble wrap, Uncle Moishy, Cousin Nachum, Siddur plays, *Chumash* plays, Gemara plays, *Mishnah Berurah* plays, Rabbi Flam *a"h*, cholent belts, Obamacare, the Ig Nobel Prizes, Slurpees, Chinese auctions, Brad the workout guy, Cookie the clown, Areyvut, the elderly, my PCP *a"h*, Morris Kenneth Schmutter, Myron Hyman Schmutter, Melvin Clarence Schmutter, the occasional cow, the Amish, covered bridges, Yossie Schachner, The Sukkah Outlet, corded phones, the Kellermans, the Spiras, the Bergers, the Lobls, the *eruv* hotline, *yahrtzeit* candles, the Herskovitzes, my little MEEP car, post-Pesach tax deadlines, brown Shabbos shirts, hotel amenities, and everyone I'm forgetting. Especially the relatives.

INTRODUCTION
"WHAT <u>KIND</u> OF JOKE?"

One of the most annoying things about being a humor writer, aside from people constantly telling you that you used to be funnier,[1] is that when you tell people what you do for a living, they all have the same basic reaction.

"Oh, you write jokes?" they ask. "Tell me a joke."

There's no other profession where people expect you to do your job, for free, standing on the street or at a *simchah*, right after you meet them, while they stand there and do not pay you. Except maybe a *magician*. Or a *dermatologist*. It's not like if you told

---

[1]. Even people you've just met.

WHAT IS THIS — SOME KIND OF JOKE?

someone you were a teacher, he'd go, "Oh, you're a teacher? Teach me something." And then he'd stand there expectantly, and if you don't tell him something he didn't know, he won't value you as a teacher.

I can say this firsthand, because I'm also a teacher. I teach high school English, and no one says, "You're a teacher? Teach me something." In fact, I walk into class and the students say, "Oh, nuts! You're here. Please don't teach us anything today."

But that's it. Even if you say you're a doctor, at most, people will tell you to look at something. They generally don't tell you to operate on them in the middle of a wedding.

"I don't know; there's a washing station right over there, with pitchers, and these forks look pretty clean. You can just lance it."

No, at most they just ask you to look at things, because everyone else they try showing these things to makes excuses to leave or just throws up.

But no other job. Really.

"Oh, you're a barber? I have this hair..."

"Oh, you're a waiter? Can you get me a drink?"

"Oh, you're a boxer? Can you punch someone for me? Professionally?"

"Oh, you're a judge? Who's taller — me or *this* guy?"

"Oh, you're a dog walker? Can you take my kids out for a few minutes?"

"Oh, you're a babysitter? Hold this one."

"Oh, you're a librarian? Can I borrow money?"

"Oh, you're a lifeguard? I just dropped my hat in the river."

"Oh, you're a tailor? Listen, I split my pants. Would you mind joining me under the table for a second?"

"What Kind of Joke?"

"Oh, you're a dentist? How's my breath? Relatively speaking."

"Oh, you're a chess master? Can you pass the salt? ...What's taking so long?"

"Oh, you're a *shochet*?"

Or maybe people *do* say things like that with other professions, which is why, when you ask most people what they do for a living, they just say, "I'm in business."

"Oh, you're in business? Can you... Nah, I can't think of any freebies. I don't even know what that means. *Everyone's* in business."

That's basically like saying:

"What do you do for a living?"

"I do things for a living."

"Really? *Baruch Hashem*."

But I shouldn't complain. It could be that these people are just looking for clarification as to what I do.

In fact, some people ask me straight out. They go, "What do you mean, 'humor'? What do you *do*? You write jokes?"

And I'm like, "Yeah, I write jokes."

What am I *supposed* to say? *Technically* they're jokes, but not in the way most people think of jokes.

So they say, "OK, tell me a joke."

That puts me on the spot, because the vast majority of my jokes don't make sense out of context. Most of them are parts of articles about 1,500 words long, that take, on average, about six minutes to read.

"You got six minutes?"

WHAT IS THIS — SOME KIND OF JOKE?

And I can't really tell them a single joke, because I can't take a line out of my articles. The lines don't work that way. Half the jokes in my columns require you to have to read the beginning of the article. So should I recite the first paragraph of an article?

"Tell me a joke."

"Sure. 'Elul is a time to work on our *middos*, and there is no *middah* that we need to work on more than that of respecting other people's feelings. And if you don't think that's the biggest *middah* we have to work on, then too bad on you, because it's *my* humor column.'"[2]

"What?"

This isn't something they were expecting. They were expecting me to say something like, "A rabbi, a *rebbi*, and a rebbe walk into a *beis medrash*..." If that's what you're looking for, then what I say doesn't even sound like jokes. It sounds like I'm just complaining about my life.[3] My jokes aren't really made-up stories. They're more like things a stand-up comedian might say. But imagine a stand-up comedian had to do his routine one-on-one with a stranger in a huge social setting while yelling over the noise.

"So tell me a joke!"

"OK, um... What's the deal with the black box on airplanes?"

"I don't know! Stop changing the topic!"

"Take my wife! Please!"

"What? I just wanted a joke!"

---

2. Then, if there's a footnote, I can say that in a different voice.
3. "Oh," you're just now saying. "The jokes already started? I thought this was the intro."

"What Kind of Joke?"

"I want to die peacefully in my sleep, like my grandfather! Not screaming and yelling like the passengers on his bus!"

"Can we do what *I* want first? I feel like if we do *your* thing, we won't get to mine!"

People tend not to get comedy when you're yelling it in their faces.

So sometimes, I try a different approach.

"What do you do?"

"I write comedy."

"OK, so tell me a joke."

"No, I *write* comedy."

But I can't say that anymore these days, because I also do stand-up. To crowds only.

But maybe this is all an excuse I use because my mind goes blank. The truth is that when someone says, "Tell me a joke," I suddenly forget every joke I've ever heard in my entire life. For goodness' sake. This is why I write them down!

It doesn't help that I don't actually look like a funny guy. People expect me to be a real-life cartoon character with huge eyes and no nostrils, walking around, going to weddings, and funerals, and so on. But I'm just a regular guy. My nose doesn't even make noise when you honk it.

Nor does it help the situation that I keep saying that I write "humor." The word *humor* is probably the least funny way to express the concept of humor. Also, most of the time, no matter which way you spell it in your head and whether or not you pronounce the

WHAT IS THIS — SOME KIND OF JOKE?

"h," the other person won't understand you, because he probably pronounces it differently.

"Oh, you mean *hhyoumor*, right?"

I don't know. I do this for a living, and I pronounce it yoomer.

Also, some Europeans, for example, spell it "humour,"[4] and I'm not even sure how to pronounce that. Is the second half pronounced like the word "our"?

So this is why people ask me to demonstrate.

Or maybe the reason they ask me to demonstrate is that they're like, "That's a job? Can't *anyone* tell a joke?"

Maybe. There are a lot of jobs where people are like, "Can't *anyone* do that?" but if I bring any examples, I'm going to get hate mail. So I might as well say *mailman. Anyone* can be a mailman. It's really just a question of having enough time. And seven pairs of shorts.

So generally, when people ask me for a demonstration, I hand them an article printout and walk away. Or else I hang out over their shoulders, and whenever they laugh, I say, "What part? What part?" This is why people don't come up to me at parties.

OK, so I don't do that anymore. These days, if people ask me to demonstrate my comedy, I give them the whole *shpiel* that I just gave *you*.[5] And then they go, "Forget it. So *don't* tell me a joke," and they walk off to find someone who *will*, because after all, anyone can do this. They don't actually realize that that *shpiel was*

---

4. HUMOUR: (n.) really, really dry humor.

5. Even though I should probably just ask them what *they* do for a living, and then tell *them* to demonstrate it.

"What Kind of Joke?"

the joke, and I was working off their setup. They were just looking for a story involving three racially-diverse characters changing a light bulb on a plane.

Because when most people think of jokes, they picture a short story — generally a pretty stressful, *tense* story, sometimes involving a tragic death — which goes on for a while, and then suddenly there's a funny line, and then the story just stops. That's the end of the story. What happened *after* that?

"Well, it's not important."

"So the whole point of the story was that this funny line happened?"

"Yeah."

"But I got invested in the characters. You got to the best part — there were only two parachutes. What did they do next?"

"I don't know. Nothing. The guy died; it was funny!"

"Oh. OK."

Because in a good story that's NOT told as a joke, that's the part where they put their heads together and come up with an ingenious plan to either land the plane or have everyone get out safely. Like they timeshare the parachutes, or attach both chutes to the plane and slow down its descent, or use the chutes to swing out and fix the plane in midair or something. Didn't the Polish guy used to be a mechanic?

I don't love anecdote jokes. Especially if the joke is written down, where you see exactly where the punch line is, and you *know* there's only one punch line, so you're like mentally counting down — "We're getting closer to the punch line... OK, almost... This

WHAT IS THIS — SOME KIND OF JOKE?

is going to be good... Here goes!... What? Oh, I wasn't really paying attention to the setup."

And then I have to read it again. So I'm like, "One second. OK, let's picture this. A man walked into a grocery store..." And I'm picturing: man, grocery store. Man, grocery store. "And he says..."

"I heard it was a hardware store."

"It didn't really happen!"

This is why I like to insert multiple punch lines into my comedy. That way, you never know when it's coming. It's like a pop quiz, so you have to pay attention.

On the other hand, anecdotes might be better for social situations, because they're easier to shout in someone's face. I don't automatically know that, because I'm not very social. So maybe I should write some anecdotes. Am I allowed? No one actually knows who writes these kinds of jokes. There's never a name attached. Especially if the joke is offensive. People just kind of find them and pass them on.

This isn't a new thing. Traditionally, anecdotes don't have names attached. I'm not sure why. We're not bringing the *geulah* to the world over here.

So I don't know anybody who writes them and I don't know anybody who even changes them into these different versions that people argue about. Sometimes you'll tell a joke, and someone else will say, "I heard a different version." And then he'll *tell* the different version, and the punch line will be the same, of course, because otherwise it would be a different joke, so no one is going to laugh when he gets to the end, even if his version is better. He's just repeating the joke to the same people one minute later. It's

"What Kind of Joke?"

like he's doing the version that someone stole and changed minor details to protect himself from copyright lawsuits.

"No, your joke was about a barber. Mine was about a hair stylist."

But not all jokes are anecdotes. There are actually a lot of different kinds of jokes: riddles, one-liners, blonde jokes, bathroom jokes, dining room jokes, slapstick, cartoons, situational comedy, satire, dry humor, moist humor, juvenile humor, senior citizen humor, big-boned jokes, prank phone calls, sarcasm, parody, anti-jokes, non-sequiturs, cookies, and that thing where someone lies and then they say, "I was just joking."

"Really? You were joking? No one laughed. Not even you."

Some jokes are even offensive, if you can imagine. Ethnic jokes, for example.

I'm not so big on ethnic jokes. I think Jews have been persecuted long enough that we shouldn't really be persecuting other people.

But for example, there are a lot of jokes out there that make fun of people from Poland for being intellectually inferior. Though I don't think that's fair. Is this even actually based on anything? Are Polish people actually dumb?

"Hey, you know how Polish people are always forgetting their parachutes?"

So there might be a difference between making fun of Polish people for being dumb and making fun of Jews for being cheap.[6] Jews actually *are* cheap. But there's a reason behind it. We have a lot of kids, yeshivah tuition is expensive, and Yamim Tovim add

---

6. Famous joke: Why do Jews have big noses? Because air is free.

WHAT IS THIS — SOME KIND OF JOKE?

up.[7] You have to save money wherever you can. Whereas Poland, I just read, has one of the highest average IQs of any country in Europe. And Marie Curie and Copernicus were both Polish.

Ethnic jokes are sometimes OK if you're making fun of the people persecuting you, as long as you look over your shoulder first. It's a method of coping. Though I'm not going to *pasken* whether or not it's *nekamah*. If it is, it's way too small. So it's just to make *ourselves* feel better.

"They may have taken our houses and all of our possessions, but I came up with a good line about it."

Once upon a time, Jews used to be allowed to make Polack jokes because the Polish people persecuted them. But nowadays, most of those people are dead. Primarily from lack of parachutes.

On the other hand, I also read something that said that the idea that Polish people are dumb actually came from Nazi propaganda. They told everyone the Polacks were dumb so they'd have public support for taking over Poland, and then they killed the educated Polish class to make the Polish intellectually inferior. So it's OK to believe Nazi propaganda if it's about other people? If anything, we should be making jokes about how *Nazis* are dumb.

Wait. Is that what blonde jokes are?

On the other hand, a recent survey in Poland showed that about two-thirds of the Polish population believe there is a Jewish conspiracy to control the banking and the media. So maybe they're *not* so bright. Or they believe propaganda, like we do.

---

7. For most Yamim Tovim, you're spending money for either crackers, plants, seat rentals, or food baskets for everyone you've ever met in your life.

"What Kind of Joke?"

I'm sorry, but if there's a whole Jewish conspiracy, why have I not been invited to a single meeting? Is it the whole "humor" thing?

And speaking of jokes about persecutors, there's also dad jokes. OK, so dad jokes aren't jokes about dads; they're corny jokes that dads *make*. The people who they make them *to* are the ones persecuted.

Dad jokes are very corny. Some popular dad jokes are:

"Hi, hungry. I'm Dad."

"Dad, where are we?" "In the car."

"Could we start this Rosh Hashanah meal already? I haven't eaten all year!"

"Yeah, I'm calling to let you know that your phone is ringing."

"Well, if you're scared of escalators, you should really take steps to avoid them."

"Poof! You're a sandwich."

"I bought your mother a fridge. Her face lit up when she opened it."

"Hi, sandwich. I'm Dad."

Some fathers are *extremely* into dad jokes, and they, for example, schedule all their dentist appointments for two thirty. Despite that midafternoon is the worst time to book appointments.

And I make dad jokes too. In fact, I'm both a dad and a teacher, so I have twice the amount of corny jokes bubbling up inside me all the time and I can't even use them in my articles. So I use them in real life. This could be why my students are never happy to see me. Sure, they tell me it's the classwork, but I think they're trying to be nice.

My wife *also* doesn't laugh at most of my jokes. Though it could

WHAT IS THIS — SOME KIND OF JOKE?

be because she can predict me by now. Or it could be because she's blonde.

In general, kids absolutely hate their dads' dad jokes, but as it turns out, most of the really annoying ones are the kids' fault. The jokes kind of stem from a combination of the dad in question:

1. working all day every day to support his family and not having time to get out there and have new adventures, and seeing as most of his interactions involve talking, most of his jokes are some form of word play,

2. not being sure which jokes his kids are old enough to get yet,

3. getting the same joke setups from the same kids over and over when his mind is otherwise occupied ("Dad, I'm hungry. I'm hungry. Stop trying to earn money so you can buy me food and feed me already.") and

4. being annoyed enough at them to just want them to stop bothering him.

So yeah, dad jokes are annoying. But you annoyed us first.

Speaking of annoying, another popular joke format is riddles. (And by "popular," I mean popular among people who tell them, not among people they tell them to.) In a riddle, you ask a question that has a logical answer, and most of the time, that logical answer makes the question moot.

"How many members of a certain demographic group does it take to perform a specified task?"

"I don't know. One. Unless the group is like fish or something."

But the logical answer is not the punch line. The answer that they're looking for is even *more* ridiculous.

"What Kind of Joke?"

"No, the answer is: a finite number — one to perform the task and the remainder to act in a manner stereotypical of the group in question."

There's also the kind of riddle that's *not* funny and that you have to think about for hours and there's a complicated logical answer. They're not jokes at all, but they're called "riddles" anyway, so when someone starts telling them to you, you assume they're going to be a joke.

The guy says, "Do you want to hear a riddle?"

"Sure."

"OK, this guy has a fox, a chicken, and a large amount of corn, and he gets to a river..." And you're smiling, and thinking, "Ooh, the rule of three! This is going to be funny." And then he gets to the question,[8] and you say, "I don't know. *How*?" like you're expecting there to be a funny answer. And then he says, "*You* figure it out." And that's it. And you're left grinning like an idiot, and you now have homework. That's the joke, I think. It's a joke on *you*. He made you grin and listen, and now you have to spend hours solving other people's problems.

I try to solve them, despite the people in the riddles being almost definitely dead by now, but these questions always leave me with more questions. First of all, how much corn do you have that you're willing to make an extra trip across the river? When I go to the grocery, I could buy a hundred bags, and I'm carrying them

---

8. It's a famous question: A guy is traveling with a fox, a chicken, and some corn, and he gets to a river. There's a boat, but it can only fit two of them at once. If the guy leaves the fox and the chicken together unsupervised, the fox will eat the chicken, and if he leaves the chicken and the corn unsupervised, the chicken will eat the corn. How does he get everyone and everything across the river without teaching the fox to row a boat?

WHAT IS THIS — SOME KIND OF JOKE?

all in from the car in one go. You really can't fit the corn on the boat with you? How much corn do you have that it takes up as much room as a fox? And how fat is your chicken? And if you really *do* have that much corn, can the chicken really eat all of it in the time you bring the fox across? It's a chicken! Also, why can't you put the corn on a high branch? And isn't the corn in a sack or something? Can't you seal it? Chickens aren't that strong. Or how about this: Pour all the corn out of the sack and into the boat, and put the chicken in the sack. Or... Wait. Why do you have a fox? Also, how did you get the chicken and the fox and the corn to the river in the first place? Do you have three hands? I can't even get across the street holding three kids! I have to do this whole logic puzzle where I have to decide who I can trust to leave with whom while I go get the other ones.

And actually, a *lot* of these riddles have ridiculous premises. Like take the riddle where there are two doors, one leading to life and one leading to death, and there are two guards, one of them a liar and the other one a truth-teller. Seriously? How do you know this about them? Who told you this, and why do you believe them? Because seriously, who only lies? That's impossible. How does he ever have a conversation? Or does he always give people headaches? Is that why they gave him a job where he has to stand alone and not talk to anyone all day except for the occasional traveler trying to solve a riddle? "Hey, we have this guy with a severe mental disorder where he only lies; why not leave him guarding a room that may have an alligator pit? Also, is it weird that there's no word in our language for someone who only tells the truth? A *"truth-teller"*? Really?

And a lot of times the answers aren't even fair. Take the famous riddle about St. Ives:

"*As I was going to St. Ives, I met a man with seven wives.*

"What Kind of Joke?"

Each wife had seven sacks; each sack had seven cats; each cat had seven kittens. Kits, cats, sacks, wives, how many were going to St. Ives?"

The answer, officially, is, "One, because it says that YOU were going to St. Ives. You just met these other people on the way. They were coming FROM St. Ives."

OK, so first of all, who says they weren't going to St. Ives? Just because you met them? Maybe they're going to St. Ives too, but they're moving a lot slower than you because of all the cats and the sacks. Or maybe you're coming from different places, and you actually arranged to meet them on the way, at a rest stop or something, and you're going together. I don't know why you'd specifically arrange to travel with a Mormon cat family, but I guess there's safety in numbers. And why are they keeping the cats in sacks anyway? Are they crossing rivers? Also, the guy has forty-nine sacks, and he's making each wife hold seven? Who figured out the math on that one? What's *he* holding, exactly?

Joke riddles are kind of the same, except that they're all based on puns, and the teller never gives you anywhere near enough time to figure it out. He just says the answer quickly. And then he asks, "Get it?" and *then* it's your turn to answer.

It's always a good sign when you have to ask "get it?" to make sure the other person is still breathing.

I actually try to figure out the riddles before they answer, because I'm corny like that, and I'm usually like a word off and it's not a crucial word and the person corrects me anyway.

"What did the _____ say to the _____?"

"Well, seeing as I have about zero information about either

WHAT IS THIS — SOME KIND OF JOKE?

of them or their situations or their history together, I'm going to assume you want a pun here."

Because I've read a lot of jokes in my time. A lot. And here are some things I learned:

1. A chicken doesn't cross the road unless he has a good reason. (Such as that he's practicing for a river.)
2. A *lot* of things in this world are black and white and red all over. They're like the most common colors.
3. Restaurants have flies in their soup basically all the time. This is why they started with health ratings.
4. Bars are hilarious.
5. Everyone has to change a light bulb eventually. One way or another.
6. Even in the 21st century, there are an insane number of desert islands out there. Why are there no explorers anymore?
7. Planes never have enough parachutes.
8. Hair color is directly related to intelligence.
9. A surprising number of people don't check their apples for holes before taking a bite.
10. Joke scientists are always trying to cross things with other things, to mixed results.
11. Genies are everywhere, but they're very literal. Like Amelia Bedelia level. They're thousands of years old, so even if they magically know English, they don't understand modern expressions.
12. Bartenders will let you bring an animal into a bar if you can prove that it talks.

"What Kind of Joke?"

13. Parrots will memorize the one most embarrassing line you've ever said and spout it at the least opportune moment.
14. If you die and go to Gehinnom, they let you pick a room.
15. Poland has a space program.
16. It's really easy to get a dumb person out of a tree.
17. If you're in the jungle and encounter a primitive tribe, their first reaction will be, "We should probably eat this guy, no?"

Anyway, the point of my writing, in general, is to share this kind of knowledge with you. But mostly, I make observations about life that I then write down so I don't have to tell you in person. The book you're holding in your hands is a collection of some of my humor columns, plus additional material such as footnotes[9] and section intros and a few columns that have never appeared in print before. The columns are grouped together by topic, and each section is named after a popular...sorry, a *famous* joke. They're not popular, just famous. Most of them are groaners.

The idea, hopefully, is that the famous jokes will keep the traditionalists happy — the ones who just want to hear a joke they've heard before. You want jokes you've heard before? Jokes you can identify with? OK, why did the chicken cross the road?

"Hey, I can identify with that! I cross the road too!"

"Why?"

"I don't know."

So we're going to go through those jokes and see if we can't analyze why those jokes specifically are famous, whereas I have

---
9. Hi.

WHAT IS THIS — SOME KIND OF JOKE?

to work the word "joke" into the title of my book to attract readers and let them know that it's a joke book so they don't think it's a kid's story just because there's a cartoon on the cover and a lot of bookstores keep filing it away in the kids' section.

ABOUT THE TITLE

For most of my previous books, I had people write in with title ideas, which worked out nicely except for the people who wanted me to get sued, and sent me titles such as "Humor for the Soul," "Jewish Humor for Dummies," "Let My People Laugh," "Reader's Indigestion," "Partners in Humor," "Megillas Mordechai," and "Mordechai Schmutter and the Something of Something."

This time, though, I decided to come up with my own book title, based on a famous joke. The cover is actually what's called a *meta-joke*, which is a joke about jokes. I mainly came up with it so I could have a joke about jokes with the word "joke" in it. In case anybody didn't realize this was a joke book. You know, so I can pull in new readers. Like the ones who don't quite get what I do. Or so I can have something to hand them at parties when they ask.

I also did this to wake up the bookstores. A lot of the bookstores

WHAT IS THIS — SOME KIND OF JOKE?

out there keep filing my books in the kids' section, for some reason. Just because they have cartoons on the cover. Nothing against bookstore stock people, but they didn't get the job because they read all the books in the store. They're like, "Ooh, a picture on the cover. Let's put it in the kids' section."

You're a bookselling professional. You don't know not to judge them by the covers?[10]

I also happen to like giving my books titles that people have to repeat.

"Do you have *Cholent Mix*?"

"What? This is a bookstore."

"No, it's the name of a... You know what? I'm going to go check the kids' section."

So in that tradition, I've selected a title that is not only guaranteed to cause misunderstandings, but people won't even be sure whether to say it with a question mark after every time they mention it. And the fact that the title is split doesn't help either.

You walk into the bookstore and say, "I'm looking for *Some Kind of Joke. Some Kind of Joke?* I'm not sure how to say it."

"Well, what KIND of joke?"

"No, there's a book called... *What Is This? Some Kind of Joke?*"

"No, it's not a joke at all. I'm trying to help you."

"No, that's the title of the book."

---

10. There's nothing in the book that is inappropriate for kids, as far as I know. But I'm pretty sure that no adult looking for a book for himself or a fellow adult is looking in the kids' section.

About the Title

"*What's* the title of the book?"

"No, *What Is This?* is the title of the book."

Or maybe people will just call the book *What Is This?*

"I'm looking for... *What Is This?*"

"It's a bookstore. What is *what*?"

Apparently I'm willing to hurt my book sales and annoy readers and book sellers just for the sake of a joke I'm not even going to be there for. Or maybe booksellers will stop hiding the book so people can stop asking for it. That'll be an idea. This is why I had to have the word "joke" in the title in the first place.

The title is also designed to pull in customers who don't even know about the book, and come into the store not knowing what they're looking for.

"Yeah, I'm looking for some kind of joke book."

"Oh! Come to think of it, we happen to have a book called *Some Kind of Joke?!*"

"Sold! I'll take twenty!"

The question mark in the title doesn't help either. Because you don't say, "I'm looking for *Some Kind of Joke*," you say, "I'm looking for *Some Kind of Joke?*" Like you're a teenager who ends every sentence with a question to let the other person know that the conversation isn't over.

And they say, "I don't know; *are* you?"

"I am!"

"What are you looking for?"

"*Some Kind of Joke?*"

WHAT IS THIS — SOME KIND OF JOKE?

"Yes. OK, a rabbi, a priest, and a bishop walk into a bar. And the bartender goes…"

"Wait, why would a rabbi go into a bar?"

"It's a salad bar."

This was the publisher's thing. They didn't want an actual bar on the cover of their book, even though my argument was that doing so would probably keep the bookstores from putting it in the kids' section. So I came up with some choices:

1. **The bar at a *simchah*.** There's a *simchah* in the background, but there's still a bartender and maybe some stools up against the bar, though that last thing is not something I've seen at *simchos*. Maybe we can start something.
2. **A salad bar.** This was the option they went with, as it allowed for a bunch of cute visual jokes, and maybe this idea would also keep the book out of the kids' section. Kids have no interest in salad bars.
3. **A bagel store.** This isn't a bar at all, but bagels are very Jewish, at least according to irreligious comedians. Mostly we eat them on fast days.
4. **A coffee shop.** This is the modern-day bar anyway, where people get together to compare religions or whatever.

Then the publisher told me that they weren't crazy about putting a priest on the cover either. So I decided to replace it with everything and the kitchen sink.

Anyway, that's the book. I hope you enjoy it, because when you're done, you still have nineteen more copies to get through.

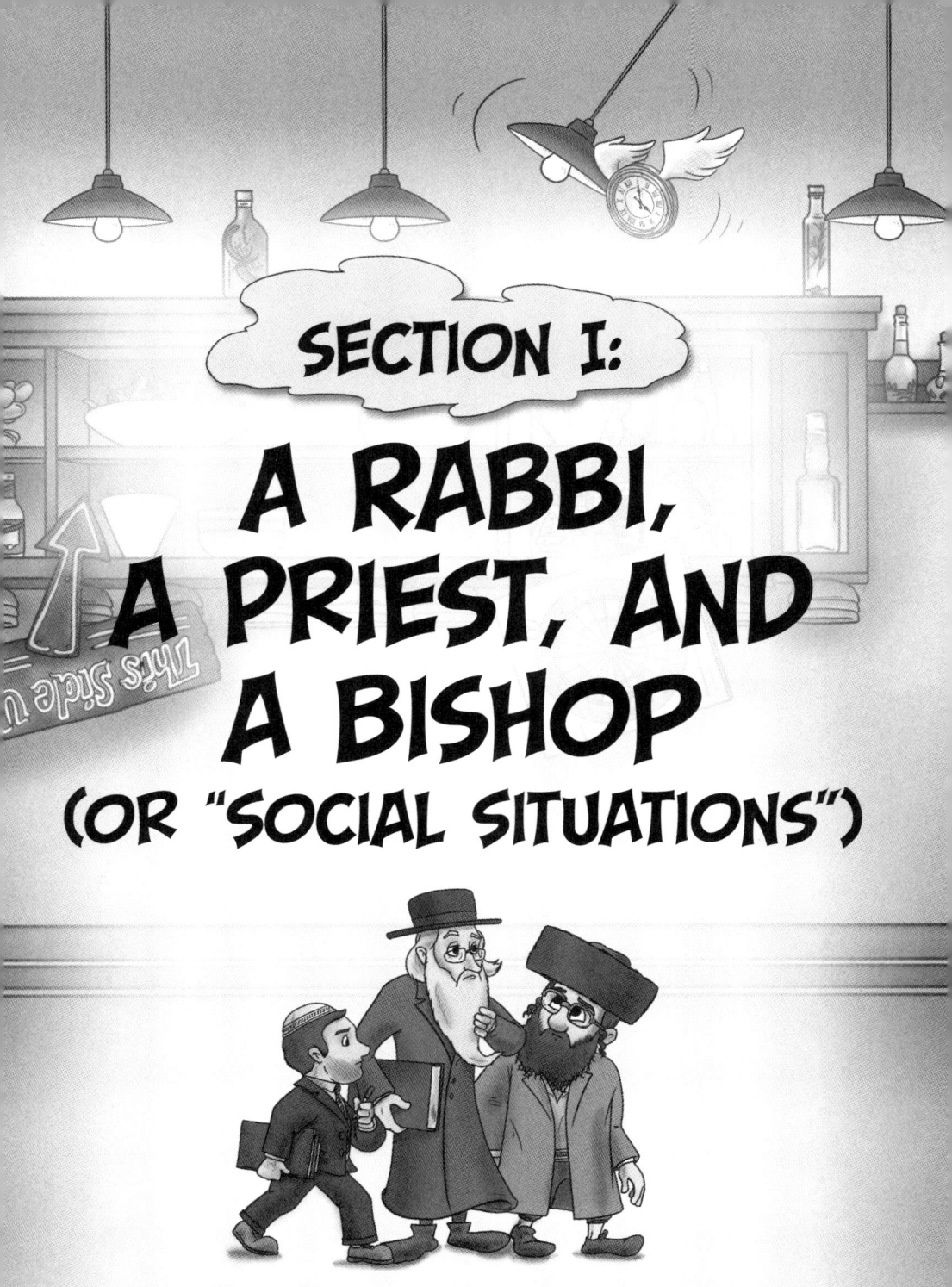

SECTION I:
A RABBI, A PRIEST, AND A BISHOP
(OR "SOCIAL SITUATIONS")

There are many versions of this joke: A rabbi, a priest, and a bishop (or possibly an imam, or possibly a minister, or — if your publisher doesn't want priests and bishops on their book covers — three rabbis) walk into a bar, and they each say something unique to their religion, and the rabbi is hilarious.

Though I always wondered: Why are these three people hanging out together like this? And why in a bar? Imams don't drink, and a rabbi probably wouldn't either in a non-kosher establishment, even if the drink was kosher. Are there kosher bars? Is this a bar at a wedding? A salad bar? A bar mitzvah?

I mean, I guess a bar is a decent irreligious meeting place. In the old days, bars were where people got together to talk honestly. So maybe it's also where religious leaders got together to debate religion. In a peaceful manner, without the beheadings. They didn't have coffee shops back then, and there weren't a ton of kosher establishments. So this is an old-timey joke format.

On the other hand, it's not like there was less anti-Semitism back then. Every joke is about the rabbi outwitting the other two. I think this might have *caused* the anti-Semitism.

And it's not always a bar. Sometimes the three of them are just shmoozing. They play golf, they go on hikes... Sometimes they're at a funeral.

Point is, sometimes for one reason or another, the religious leaders needed to go somewhere so they could discuss how their respective communities can co-exist in the same society, and also to learn about each other's cultural differences, such as, say, the difference between a priest and a bishop. I don't actually know the difference between a priest and a bishop, except that a priest can't get married, and a bishop can only move diagonally. That makes it tough when the bar is crowded.

Point is, rabbi or not, it's important to be social, and it's important to get out of the house once in a while. The following articles are about doing just that.

TALKING SMALL

I think I might be antisocial. It's not that I don't *like* people; I just don't like making small talk with the ones I don't know.

This is why I usually bring my kids to *simchos*. That way, I can pretend that I'd really love to shmooze, if only I didn't have to deal with my kids. If my kids can't make it, I have to make a whole show of going off to get some more food. Also, what I find a lot of guys do is they suddenly announce, as soon as they get bored, that they have a *shiur* to go to. And then they just disappear, probably to learn in the car.

I guess the main problem is trying to come up with a topic that you can easily discuss with someone whom you don't really know well enough to subject to a personal rant about how everyone in your family is insulted at each other. That's a privilege you save for your close friends. So you try to talk to him about *small* things,

WHAT IS THIS — SOME KIND OF JOKE?

such as how everyone he knows is feeling. But if they're all feeling fine, the conversation dies down pretty quickly.[1]

For a while, I told myself, "I'm a writer: I should be able to think of conversation topics." After all, that is basically what I do in this column every week. If you had to describe my entire weekly column in two words, they would be "small talk."[2] But on the other hand, I have to come up with at least fifty of those topics every year. And most of those topics are conceived through last-minute panic two days after my deadline. So there's no way I can come up with even *more* topics for an audience of one person that I barely know, and even when I do, I'll probably think of the topic a day or two after the party.

It shouldn't be this hard. I get the feeling, listening in on other people's small talk in shul after *davening* while pretending to look something up in a *sefer* that a lot of small talk is about following up on previous topics. Like if the last time we were in an elevator together you mentioned that your son was going for his high school interview, this time I would ask you how it went.[3] But *my* problem is that I can never manage to jumpstart a topic that *first* time. I'll ask someone, "How is your son — the one in eighth grade?" and he'll say, "Good."

Thanks, that's a great story. Next time I'm going to have to follow it up with: "So how's your son? Still good?"

---

1. And they're all going to be feeling fine. Social protocol dictates that you never answer, "How are you feeling?" with how you're actually feeling. That's something else you save for your close friends.

2. If you could use four words it would be "one-sided small talk."

3. Especially if the last time we spoke was so long ago that you don't even remember how it went.

Talking Small

I hope the elevator doesn't get stuck.

I also think that maybe my problem is that my questions are too general. Like sometimes I go to my parents' house, and I find that they, let's say, got a new car.

So I'll ask, "Why didn't you *tell* me? I speak to you three times a week!"

And they'll say, "You didn't ask."

And I'll say, "Yes I did! I asked, 'What's new?'! You could have said, 'A car!'"

Some people say that if you don't have anything to talk about, you can always discuss the weather. My feeling is that even people who *do* know each other don't talk about the weather, unless it relates to their plans for something *else*. Otherwise, you should only be able to talk about the weather if it's *extreme* weather, such as a major blizzard or a heat wave. ("I can't talk to you right now. It's too hot.") Weather is boring.

And that's the other issue. Some people, usually the people you get stuck talking to, tend to gravitate toward the most boring conversation topics. Here are some of the topics they find fascinating:

The recent changes to their child's nap schedule. If there's anything more boring than kids sleeping, it's listening to people *talk* about kids sleeping.

("Yeah, so my day was messed up because the baby fell asleep at 11, and she usually falls asleep at 10 and then again at 3, and... Are you falling asleep?"

"Yeah. I just changed my nap schedule.")

WHAT IS THIS — SOME KIND OF JOKE?

The route they took to get here, and why. ("Really? You hit traffic? What is *that* like?")

Describing, in great detail, what they ate at a chasunah. ("Look, it's too late. I can't go to that *chasunah* anymore. It's over.")

The issue with these topics is mainly that you have nothing to add, so you're stuck waiting for the other person to finish talking. Or you can scrape the bottom of the barrel for follow-up questions. ("I see. And did it come with potatoes?")

What I generally do, because I don't like being impolite (I don't like making small talk, but I don't like being impolite either; it's a horrible combination), is I space out about something else, and I nod my head a lot. I have also trained myself so that, when I subconsciously hear certain types of pauses in the other person's monologue, I can insert the appropriate comments, such as, "Really?" or, "Yeah, whatayegonnado."[4] And if the speech ended with a question mark, I shrug my shoulders and say, "I don't know," and then magically it starts up again. And apparently I'm really good at doing this, because these people have no idea I'm not listening. They can go on for hours.

Also, sometimes people start telling you a funny story — and you know this, because they introduced it by telling you that it's a funny story, which is why you're even listening in the first place — and they keep getting bogged down by minor details that don't matter at all.

"So one time — it was a Sunday, I think... No, it was a Tuesday...

---
4. I picture people reading my columns the same way.

Talking Small

Wait, it *was* a Sunday. I remember, because I had just driven carpool... No, wait. It was Yom Kippur."[5]

Also, some people just don't know when to end a conversation. I have this one relative who calls several times per day,[6] whenever she (or he) has the tiniest thought about anything. So you'd think that each conversation would take about two minutes, right? Wrong. Because when we're done, we stay on the phone for a while saying things like, "So...," and, "Uch, my computer is so slow today." And I'm too polite to end the conversation. But I do try to drop hints.

GENERAL PHONE TIP: If you're ever talking to someone, and that person says that he has a lot of stuff to do, it's because he has a lot of stuff to do. It's not because he wants to get into a whole conversation about how, "Hey! I *also* have a lot of stuff to do! Isn't that funny?" No. Can we get off the phone? I want to go do my stuff!

And then there are the people who, whenever you see them, talk about the same one or two topics. For example, I'm a high school language arts teacher,[7] and if there's anyone that teenagers find boring, it's their teachers. Look at it from *their* perspective: Every day this guy comes in, and he talks about grammar. Grammar

---

5. TRUE STORY: I was at a bar mitzvah the other day and I ran into a distant relative of my wife's, who is also an entertainer, and he told me a joke, and then I told him a funny story, and then he told me a story about his wife that took about ten minutes for him to tell, and I could barely hear him, because of the music, but I just kept nodding along and doing that short laughing sound every few seconds, and after ten minutes, I realized that the story was actually tragic and involved ongoing headaches for his entire family and I felt like an idiot. See? Tragic endings at the end of long footnotes aren't fun either.

6. See? I mentioned you.

7. I introduce this every time it comes up, because if there's one thing that I've learned as a high school language arts teacher, it's that I have to.

WHAT IS THIS — SOME KIND OF JOKE?

grammar grammar! I get it! I don't even talk to my *own* friends about grammar! Doesn't he ever talk about anything else? And imagine if you went to a party every day, where someone talked to you about the same topic that completely bored you, and then every time you were bored to the point where you started tuning out, he announced that there's going to be a test on what he just said.

So yes, I go to school every day, where I get the feeling that I'm boring, and I see boring people who don't even *know* they're boring, and I'm like, what if *I'm* one of those people? So I'm afraid to initiate small talk.

Speaking of which, I should go. I have a lot of stuff to do. In the meantime, feel free to clip this article[8] and share it with certain key people in your life, as sort of a hint. Don't worry, you won't be insulting them. They're not going to get what you're trying to do anyway.

---

8. Or this chapter, if that's something you do. I realize it's a book.

MAGIC WORDS

Elul is a time to work on our *middos*, and there is no *middah* that we need to work on more than that of respecting other people's feelings. And if you don't think that's the biggest *middah* we have to work on, then too bad on you, because it's *my* humor column.

One way to show people that you respect their feelings is to be polite. Unfortunately, people these days are afraid to be polite, because the truth is that what's polite in one culture isn't necessarily polite in another. For example, let's say you run into a Japanese person. Now, normally when you meet someone, you stick out your hand, because in our culture, the polite thing to do when you meet a stranger is to wonder why his palms are sweaty.[9]

---

9. Unless you meet someone of the other gender, in which case the polite thing to do is fake a cold. But if the person is the same gender as you, you shake his hand even if you *have* a cold.

WHAT IS THIS — SOME KIND OF JOKE?

Meanwhile, in Japanese culture, everyone bows, and whoever bows the lowest gets the most points to be redeemed later for valuable prizes.[10] So *he* bows, *you* stick out your hand, and you basically end up slapping him in the face.

I don't know if that's polite in *any* culture.[11]

So some people are just so afraid that they don't bother being polite to *anyone*.[12]

I'm reminded of a joke about a reporter doing a story on a global meat shortage. He goes over to an American and asks, "Excuse me, what is your opinion on the meat shortage?" And the American says, "What's a shortage?"

Then he goes over to someone from India:

"Excuse me, what's your opinion on the meat shortage?"

The man replies, "What's meat?"

Then the reporter goes over to a Chinese person:

"Excuse me, what's your opinion on the meat shortage?"

"What's an opinion?"

The poor reporter is getting nowhere.[13] Finally, he sees an Israeli:

"Excuse me, what's your opinion on the meat shortage?"

So the Israeli looks at him: "What's 'Excuse me'?"

(I can make this joke, because I'm one-third Israeli.)

---

10. Generally *Hello Kitty* merchandise.
11. Except maybe France.
12. It's called *dan l'kaf zechus*.
13. Plus we have deadlines.

— 46 —

Magic Words

And it's not always easy to be polite. Like, for example, if you're opening a door and someone is coming up behind you, being polite means that you hold the door open for him, instead of waiting for him to be halfway through and then launching it at his face like a slingshot. And likewise, if someone is holding the door open for *you*, you should try to get through the door as promptly as you can, so as not to keep him waiting. That's fine. But sometimes you'll have some stranger standing there, holding the door open for you, and you're still halfway down the block. And because you don't want to keep him waiting, you end up jogging all the way to the door, which is a lot harder than just opening the door for yourself in the first place.

And then you have to say "thank you," on top of that.

But "thank you" is a big one. The easiest ways to be polite are saying the simple words that show that you're taking the other person's feelings into account — words like "Thank you," "You're welcome," "Please," "I'm sorry," "Pardon," "Excuse me," and "Come again."

"Thank you."

"Excuse me?"

"I'm sorry?"

"Pardon?"

"Come again?"

"I said, 'Excuse me.'"

"Oh. I said, 'Thank you.'"

"*Please*. You're welcome!"

WHAT IS THIS — SOME KIND OF JOKE?

Of all of those phrases, "I'm sorry" is probably the hardest to say. But I find that the easiest way is to yell it.

"I'm sorry! Are you happy?"

Although usually, they are not. What do these women *want*?

Of course, the thing about niceties is that you have to be very careful about how you say them. Yelling "I'm sorry!" is not any more of an "I'm sorry" than saying "puh-leaz" is a way of saying "please." I also find it scary that our society in general is so impolite that we've found a way to turn the most polite sayings into the most aggressively impolite things to say:

"Thank you!" means, "If anyone asks, this is totally your fault."

"Puh-leaz!" means, "I can't believe you won't stop lying to me."

"ExCUSE me?" means, "Come *here* and say that!"

"You're WELCOME," means, "I can't believe you didn't say 'thank you.'"

"I'm SORRY?!" means, "Say that again, and *you'll* be sorry."

Of course, there are some situations where polite words aren't necessarily the best course anyway. I'm a high school teacher,[14] and whenever I want my students to sit down, I say, "Everyone, please sit down." And most of the time, to my complete and utter shock, no one sits down that wasn't already sitting for some *other* reason, such as that they were doing homework for another class.

Now, I've discussed this issue with countless people, and they all told me the same thing: Basically, as far as my students understand, when I say "please," it means that if they want to do me a favor

---

14. In case you've forgotten since the last chapter.

Magic Words

more than they want to continue what they are doing, then they can stop what they're doing and sit down. So, after thinking about it, most of them choose not to do me this favor. Their logic is: "OK, so I'll listen to him and sit down. But will that make him happy? No! He's going to want me to *keep* sitting for the next forty minutes! So why on earth would I stop what I'm doing?"

So what everyone tells me is that I should stop saying "please" because it implies that my students have a choice.

I've since tried their advice, but somehow most of the time I accidentally say "please" anyway. (I totally blame my upbringing.) Even if I correct myself and take out the "please" the second time (don't worry; there's *always* a second time), by then it's too late.

But should I really train myself to stop saying "please"? Personally, I don't think this is my fault. I think that some people are just so not used to using the word "please" on a regular basis — they mainly use it when they're asking their parents for more money — so they think I'm begging them, totally at their mercy. And for goodness' sake, I just asked them for the same favor yesterday! So I think that if they learned that "please" was just another part of the language, they wouldn't even notice that I'm saying it, just like *I* don't always notice when I'm saying it.

But therein lies the question: if I don't notice that I said "please," and the person I'm *talking* to doesn't notice that I said "please," is there even a point to saying "please"?

That's like asking, "If a tree falls in the forest, and no one is around to hear it, should it still say 'excuse me'?"

But my wife and I have been trying to teach our kids to say these things. Our kids will ask, "Can I have a lolly?" and we'll say,

WHAT IS THIS — SOME KIND OF JOKE?

"No," and they'll say, "Why not?" And we'll say, "Because you didn't say 'please.'" So they'll say, "OK, can I *please* have a lolly?" And we'll give it to them. The ironic thing is that if they would have said "please" the first time, we probably would have said "no." "Please" is not a magic word; sometimes there are other reasons not to give a kid a lolly at four o'clock on a Wednesday. So I'm pretty sure that I've taught my kids that they can get pretty much anything they want if they first ask for it without saying "please," and then ask again and say "please." But the truth is that they're little kids. There's nothing that they want that we so badly don't want them to have that we're willing to pass up the opportunity to teach them to be polite.

"Totty, can we have ices?"

"How do we ask?"

"Twice. The first time without 'please,' and the second time *with* 'please.'"

"Very good. You may have ices."

So I think we need to start rethinking some teaching methods here. But it's not the worst thing to teach a kid. In real life, no one is listening the first time you say something anyway, so I think it's more important that you insert your manners the second time you say it.

Those are my feelings on the topic. You don't have to respect them.

YOU NEVER CALL

I never call my parents.

At least that's what my *parents* believe. About half our conversations are about just that.

"You never call us," they say.

"I just called you!" I say. "We're on the phone right now! As we speak!"

"You were supposed to call *yesterday*," they say.

I blame my sisters. I have two married sisters, and they both speak to my parents way more than *I* do. My sister Raizel, for example, literally never gets off the phone with my mother. When I call my parents, my mother has to hang up on her to talk to me.

"I have to go," my mother says. "It's Mordechai. He *never* calls."[15]

---

15. I recently asked my sister about it. "I *so* don't call every day," she told me. "First of all, I don't call on Shabbos. I call on Friday, of course, and I usually visit them on

WHAT IS THIS — SOME KIND OF JOKE?

I also suspect — although my parents don't seem to believe me — that girls in general speak to their parents more often. To prove this, I went around polling random people in shul after Ma'ariv, and I found that most men speak to their parents about once a week, unless they're going to their parents for Shabbos, in which case they count that as their phone call. In fact, they figure that if they call their parents the previous week to invite themselves, that takes care of *two* weeks' worth of calls. And if they sleep over until Sunday, that's three weeks. But when asked how often their wives call *their* parents, most men reply, "Every day. Sometimes more than once."

In general, I try to call my parents three times a week, even when I have nothing to tell them. It's not like something new and mind-blowing happens to me three times a week. But sometimes I forget to call. Sometimes I'm lying in bed on a Friday night, and I ask myself, "Did I call my parents today?"

TIP: If you're not sure whether you called your parents, you didn't call them.

So these days, my parents have apparently decided to reward me with information based on how often I call. Like if I call three times a week, they won't tell me anything about their own lives — they'll just ask me if there's anything new in *mine*. If I call four or five times, they'll tell me who's not feeling well. If I call ten times, they'll tell me about anything major, like if they moved.

"You changed your phone number? Why didn't you tell me?"

"You didn't call."

Sunday for like a half hour. And between Monday, Tuesday, Wednesday and Thursday, I only talk to them like three or four times."

You Never Call

On the other hand, even though my wife talks to *her* mother at least once a day, her mother rarely tells her anything important. Like my mother-in-law will sometimes call us five times in one day, and then my wife will find out later — from her sister — that my father-in-law is away on a business trip. So my wife will call her mother (of course):

"Abba went on a business trip?" she'll ask. "You told me the same Wal-Mart story five times,[16] and *this* you couldn't tell me?"

"Why do you think I spoke to you five times?"

But aside from my in-laws, no one ever calls us. Basically, the unspoken rule in my family is that it's up to the younger generation to call the older generation. That makes sense. It's not like I'm going to get on the phone with my grandparents and go, "How come you never call?"

Actually, I'm never sure *what* to say to my grandparents on the phone. Grandparents are generally better in person.[17] So our phone conversations usually revolve around trying to invite them for Shabbos. Only the thing is that they would never come to us for Shabbos, and not just because it's easier to cook for two seniors than to remember to pack everything into a couple of suitcases which they would then have to shlep. But the main reason they won't come over is that the other unspoken rule in our family is that, with the occasional exception of parents, the older generation does not go to the younger generation for Shabbos.

I don't know why that is. I think the older generation is afraid

---

16. She returned some shoes. I think. I stopped paying attention halfway through every single time she told it.

17. Without technology in the way.

WHAT IS THIS — SOME KIND OF JOKE?

that the younger generation doesn't know how to cook. Or maybe the older generation knows exactly where all of the younger generation's recipes came from,[18] and why travel all that way to eat the exact same foods?

Personally, I think it's like when our six-year-old comes home from school with a plate of cookies that he made himself, and he offers us some, and we look at it and see some weird discolorations that look like maybe the teacher didn't make sure the kids washed their hands before they started. Or else it's hand soap. So we tell him, "No, it's OK. You don't have to give us." Or we take one and pretend to eat it.[19] The point is that when a kid finally does grow up, the older generation still can't get those streaked cookies out of their minds, so they're hesitant to be subjected to a whole Shabbos of pretending to eat their grandchildren's food.

"Was that play-dough?"

So if we want to spend Shabbos with my grandparents (or aunts and uncles), they would have to invite *us*. Only they won't, because they'll never *call* us. Of course, these days my wife doesn't want to go anywhere for Shabbos anyway, because at this stage in our lives it's easier to cook for kids who refuse to eat than to pack clothing for them for every possible weather.

It's amazing how quickly we turned into my grandparents.

So as a result, we're always the last to find out anything that happens in our family. But anyway, I find that everyone, no matter

---

18. This is the other good topic for Bubby phone calls — asking for recipes. It's flattering, and you don't actually have to make the recipe ("Wait. I have to grind the wheat myself?"), but it makes her feel good.

19. Like he does with his vegetables. What goes around comes around.

how often they speak to family, will always say, "You know? I'm always the last person to hear everything!"

I think that's why my mother's side of the family started a quarterly newsletter. Actually, it started off as a monthly, until we all realized that even though we'd originally felt like no one was sharing anything, it turns out that nothing actually happens over the course of the average month. But because the newsletter goes to everyone at once, no one is the last to know anything.

Basically, what happens is that every issue, the editor reminds everyone to send in his news, and everyone sits down and realizes that he cannot for the life of him remember what happened over the last three months, but everyone *else* is submitting news, so he has to come up with *something*. So a lot of the newsletter is about how many teeth came in or fell out over the last three months. (As of the last newsletter, my family currently has 2,196 teeth.)

Also, sometimes the newsletter can get kind of repetitive — especially when it comes to all twenty-five nuclear families recounting what they did over five days of Chol Hamoed. (This comes out to 125 days of Chol Hamoed.) Also, when there's a wedding in the family, the *chassan* and *kallah* send it in as their news, and their parents send it in as well, which I guess is OK. Then one aunt sends in, "We had a lot of fun at the wedding!" and another uncle says, "We spent Tuesday night at the wedding!"[20] Basically, we get to read about the same wedding twenty-five times, and this is a wedding we all went to anyway.

But now, thanks to the newsletter, we have less reason to call each other.

---

20. Also, the editor mentions it on page 1.

WHAT IS THIS — SOME KIND OF JOKE?

"So what's new with you?"

"We went to a wedding."

"I know, I read about it. And I was there!"

"I know. I read about that."

In fact, I'm thinking that if we just put in a classified section where people can invite each other for *Shabbosim*, no one will ever have to call *anyone*.

But here's the thing: Calling your family is not really about news. Your family doesn't really care if you have news for them; they just want to hear the sound of your voice. It's like when you're sitting around the dinner table, and you ask your kids, "What did you do in school today?" and they say, "I ate lunch."

Wow. Maybe we should put that in the newsletter.[21]

At the end of the day, it doesn't really matter *what* they say. It just matters that they're talking.

"Wait, he had lunch? I'm always the last to know *everything*!"

---

21. This is actually good news, though, as it turns out because my kids don't always eat their lunch. Most of the time, they're shlepping 20–30 old sandwiches back and forth every day.

EARLY POLLS

I don't want to get into politics, but it's almost Election Day.

"*Again*?" you're asking. "Didn't we *just* have an election day, like two years ago?"

Close. It was last year.

But I do know the feeling. When I was a kid, I distinctly remember learning in school that elections are held once every four years. Then I found out that those were the *presidential* elections. There are also gubernatorial, mayoral, senatorial, house of representorial, and shul *gabbai* elections. So we're basically voting every November. And then I bought a house, and I started getting flyers in the mail, and it turns out that, at least in this country (New Jersey), we have at least some sort of election like every other Tuesday.

WHAT IS THIS — SOME KIND OF JOKE?

It's like, "Enough with the voting already! Can't these politicians make their *own* decisions for once?"

But it's very important that we all exercise our right to vote — a right that our forefathers fought and died for. (In the old days, voting was punishable by death.) Unfortunately, these days, people don't even exercise their right to *exercise*. And voting is even *more* of a pain, especially since it comes up more often. First you have to go down to the polling place and stand in a long line of people who are not sure what line they're supposed to be standing in. Then you get to the front of the line, where a poll worker takes your driver's license and asks you for your name no less than five times — like you maybe accidentally gave her the wrong name the first four times — while leafing desperately back and forth through a ledger that should be a breeze to look through because it's arranged alphabetically.

"*What's* your name again?"

"It's on my license. You still have it."

When she finally finds your name, you have to sign your name *again* in at least two separate books, and then you're handed a receipt that you have to give to *another* poll worker that is sitting literally three feet away.

"Do you have a receipt?" he asks.

"You just saw me get one!"

The second worker then takes your receipt and ushers you into a little voting booth, where you pull the curtain shut behind you and are expected to find the name of the candidate you want to vote for WITH NO HELP. There's also a little area at the bottom where you can type in the name of a friend, because as history

Early Polls

has shown us, most United States presidents never actually ran for office — they were all typed in by their friends, usually as a prank. ("But I don't *wanna* be president!" "Sorry, we all typed you in.")

But I really do think it's important to vote, which is why I signed up as a poll worker for last year's gubernatorial Election Day.

OK, that's not why. I did it for the money. But I also wanted to see if I could assess the problems in our current voting system through close observation. And, if nothing else, being a poll worker for a day gives one a lot of time to sit in one place and assess things (and also, in my case, to polish off an entire bag of chocolates). One of the things that one can assess, for fourteen hours, is how much one is actually getting paid per hour, after one factors in setting up and taking down the polls, as well as the mandatory training session. Not enough, as it turns out. So I'm becoming more knowledgeable *already.*

For starters, the poll workers have to be there literally all day. Not only do we have to stay until about nine o'clock at night, but we're expected to have the polls open by six in the morning just in case someone comes to vote that early, which no one really does. And according to our training session, in order to be open by six, we have to be at the site by five fifteen to start setting things up.[22] So after spending an entire day as a government worker, I believe I have discovered why the government moves like it's half asleep and annoyed about something.

Sure, we were allowed to take breaks. In fact, we were allowed to take a full hour's worth of breaks, which we could split up however we wanted, although that hour did include travel time. So I used

---

22. Setting things up takes about five minutes.

WHAT IS THIS — SOME KIND OF JOKE?

mine for Shacharis.[23] Then I was stuck in the one room for the rest of the day.

And if there's anything worse than getting up really early to do something boring and repetitive for fourteen hours, it's having to deal with the public on top of it all. For every voter who knows what he's doing, there are five people who step into the voting booth, forget to close the curtain, and go, "Hey! I can't find *Obama's* name!"

Yeah, don't worry about it. Just type it into the bottom. I'm sure he wouldn't mind, on top of all of his duties as a president, also being the governor of New Jersey.

Also, the general public in *general* does not listen. Every person thinks that *he's* the exception. You explain the voting procedure to the person in line in *front* of him, and the person in line *with* him, and there's a sign right next to him that *says* the procedure, and he's been standing there for quite a while facing the sign because for some reason, everyone on line in front of him has to take the absolute maximum time in the voting booth, like he wants to get his money's worth, and then he gets to the front of the line and goes, "So what do I do here?"

And then there was a woman who, after I motioned for her to step into the booth, walked right past it and followed me *behind* the booth, where she just stood there, like she thought she was supposed to whisper her vote in my ear or something.

"You're supposed to go *into* the booth," I told her.

Thankfully, I didn't spend the entire day as the usher. If I had,

---

23. I'm glad voting is on Tuesdays, and not Mondays or Thursdays. I bet this is why.

Early Polls

then by the end of the day I would have been ushering people into an empty elevator shaft. But things weren't much better when I was looking up people's names. There were actually two of us looking up names — one for names beginning with the letters A through K, and the other for L through Z. This system did not take a rocket scientist to figure out, and everything was clearly marked. There were two signs next to me that said, "L–Z," in case someone blocked one of them, and if it turned out that there were people blocking *both* of them, there were also two signs next to my co-worker that said, "A–K." But about half the people somehow ended up on the wrong line anyway.

"My last name is *Frank*."

"That's A through K. The book I have is only L through Z."

"Oh. I didn't see the sign. Is that 'first name' or 'last name'?"

"It's 'last name.' Why, what's your first name?"

"*Frank*."

So in conclusion, poll workers in general are in a bad mood because they've woken up at four thirty in the morning to come in forty-five minutes early and put up signs that people don't read and set up voting booths that people are apparently taking naps in, all for a bunch of voters that don't really start coming in until about eight thirty anyway, then drop off in middle of the day, and then all come at once an hour before the polls close; and the vast majority of voters are bumbling around with no understanding of the concept of how booths work. ("So wait. I'm not supposed to stand *behind* it?") I blame the emergence of cell phones for that.

My point is that if we all voted more often, we wouldn't be as clueless, and the poll workers would be in a better mood and on

WHAT IS THIS — SOME KIND OF JOKE?

the ball enough to remember the order of the alphabet.[24] It's all about practicing. Maybe that's why they're holding elections so often these days.

But it also wouldn't kill the government to open the polls at a more earthly hour, such as noon.

---

24. I have to sing it every time. I can never remember what comes first — Q or LMNOP.

SECTION II:
TAKE MY WIFE. PLEASE.
(OR "MARRIAGE MADE EASY")

This joke plays better with a crowd. It starts with a comedian saying something like, "Some people always have to be right. Take my wife. Please."

At least she taught you how to say please.

This is a famous line, made popular by the late Henny Youngman — a famous Jewish comedian who apparently did not like his wife.

He also said, "I take my wife everywhere, but she keeps finding her way back."

Comedy is borne of pain.

Of course, this doesn't necessarily mean he had a bad marriage. He also said, "I've got all the money I'll ever need. If I die by four o'clock." So maybe he was trying to cut expenses.

(Unfortunately for him, he lived to the ripe old age of ninety-one. So much for dying by four o'clock.)

But this is a very famous line, even though it's specific to the English language. It doesn't make sense if you rephrase it.

"For example, my wife. Take her. Please."

Because apparently, there's nothing funnier than starting the audience thinking that you're just bringing an example to what you were talking about previously, and then ending with a punch line about spousal kidnapping.

Anyway, this section features articles about how to get along with your wife and how to get married on the cheap.

HOME ECONOMICS

A recent survey shows that the average family spends about four days arguing every year. (Extra points if you can guess which days. I'm guessing they're in April.) I can definitely believe that, although the reason I do is none of your business.

But as my readers know, I am a very big advocate of *shalom bayis*, and I occasionally like to use my column to resolve a lot of these arguments, at least on weeks when there's nothing good in the news. The basic idea is that I can provide helpful insights into *shalom bayis* problems because:

1. I am an objective, professional writer, and the truth is that most marital arguments, when looked at objectively, turn out to be pretty silly, and usually center on the topic of who started the argument. Also:

2. Since I am *writing* my opinions, rather than saying them out

WHAT IS THIS — SOME KIND OF JOKE?

loud, no one is going to interrupt me, so long as I can finish this column before my wife gets home.

Experts say that most husband/wife squabbles stem from some kind of misunderstanding. They say that the best thing to do is to keep the lines of communication open. But you have to wonder why these people are calling themselves "experts" in the first place. Is it because they never argue with their spouses, or because they always "win"? Or do they always "lose," and they're experts in the sense that they have a lot of time to lie on the couch and think about things they *should've* said?

Either way, they're wrong. It turns out that men and women are so fundamentally different that even a simple, vague piece of advice such as "keep the lines of communication open" can lead to fights. Here's what will happen:

1. What *women* will take from it is that they should tell their husbands everything that happened to them every day, including what their plans were, what they actually did, why they didn't do what they'd planned to do, who they ran into, what *those* people's plans were, why *they* didn't do what they'd planned to do, and so on. But the truth is that a husband doesn't really *want* to know every single thing, which is why he goes to work in the first place. So he'll try to block out most of it, and keep an ear open for key words that involve either him or the car. And of course he'll miss something, and his wife will have to repeat herself, and that will lead to a fight.

2. What *men* will take from this is that they should only tell their wives things that they absolutely need to know, so that there's nothing for her to block out. And consequently, she will accuse

Home Economics

him of not sharing his feelings, when the truth is that he really only has one feeling, and that is: only tell her what she needs to know.

So I've come to the conclusion that most things that men and women fight about, including how much to communicate, can be boiled down to one thing: men, in general, are more economical.

Take cooking, for example. I can cook an entire four-course meal, and in the end there will be maybe two pots in the sink, and, depending on my mood, a fork. Whereas my wife can decide to make herself a single omelet, and I will later come into the kitchen to find every bowl, pan, cup, and spatula that we own, all piled up in the sink. I picked up a lot of my cooking skills from yeshivah, where I lived in a *dirah*[1] with five other guys, and between the six of us, we had exactly one pot. (The general consensus was that it was *milchig*.) If we needed to stir something in the pot, we used a plastic fork from the yeshivah dining room, and when the fork was sufficiently melted, the food was probably done, at which point we put the cover back on and strained out as much water as we could, using a yarmulke as an oven mitt. So yes, I'm pretty sure this is a man/woman thing.

I've noticed a similar thing when it comes to leftovers. When faced with leftovers, a woman will put it all together and whip up a casserole. Men don't think in terms of casseroles. I have never, in all my years of hanging out with men, heard one say, "You know what I can sure go for right now? A casserole!" A man will eat a casserole for one reason only, and that is to avoid an argument. If a man is faced with leftovers, he will make himself a sandwich. This is the ideal man food, because it doesn't involve heating anything

---

1. DIRAH (*n.*): An apartment that smells vaguely of feet.

WHAT IS THIS — SOME KIND OF JOKE?

up, or taking out more pots, and he can eat it cold and with one hand. He doesn't even need a plate.

But sometimes, being economical can actually get men in trouble. Let's take the area of leaving the house. When a woman leaves the house, even to go to the supermarket, she will set off with a whole caravan of belongings in case somehow, on the way there, she gets stuck on a desert island. Her pocketbook alone weighs more than most of her kids. But if she calls her husband to tell him to meet her there with the baby, the husband will get into the car with just that: the baby. Even if he's meeting her at her parents' house for an eight-day Yom Tov, he will bring: the baby. No diapers, no change of clothes, and nothing for the baby to spit on.

"It's OK; I have two undershirts."

But that's part of being economical. Men don't like carrying a lot of stuff. That's why we like having gadgets that do more than one thing, such as phones that take pictures and send text messages and store "to do" lists. (TO PACK: *Tallis*, Undershirts, Baby) The Swiss army knife, for example, was definitely invented by a guy whose wife asked him to set the table:

"There. Happy? Everyone gets one of these."

"How about plates?"

"We're having sandwiches!"

But the key is to remember, before you yell at each other in increasingly higher tones until you're having an argument that only dogs can hear ("What are they saying?" "They're saying, '*I'm* not arguing, *you're* arguing!'"), that these traits are built into our very natures. Men hunt and women nest. Have you ever seen a bird

Home Economics

build a nest? It takes a confusing mass of millions of sticks and turns it into a home. And it's always the female bird that does this. If it were the male's job to build a nest, he would show up with maybe one twig. Then the female will go out of her way to work his twig into the nest among all *her* twigs, and then one day he's going to go crazy looking for it. "Honey, have you seen my twig?" And she's going to go, "It's there! Move stuff around!"

Men, in the meantime, hunt. And when you're squatting in the woods and charging after animals, you don't want to do it with a diaper bag and a wheelie suitcase in one hand and a packed stroller with your dry-cleaning slung over it. You want to hold *one spear*. And you also want that spear to be able to take pictures and receive text messages. ("OMG 8°! It's a buffalo! Stay low and be very quiet. LOL!")

But what do we do because of these differences? We argue. And even *that* doesn't go smoothly. Usually, about ten minutes into the argument, the husband suddenly finds himself thinking: "How did we get to the subject of laundry? I thought we were arguing about toothpaste!" Because that's where *women* economize. Instead of having three separate arguments, they have all three at the same time, and jump back and forth between them.

So that's what it boils down to. Maybe if we understand that, we can "get" where the other party is coming from in any given argument, and hopefully have less of them. Or at least have them all at once, and get it over with.

ALL THE TRIMMINGS

So you're making a wedding. Mazel tov! And by "mazel tov," I mean "good luck," as in "good luck paying for all of that."

Weddings these days are a multi-million dollar industry. *Each*. But as the person paying for the wedding, if you even mention the word "money," everyone will look at you as if you'd just announced that you wish it were someone *else's* child getting married.[2]

So perhaps you're looking for ways to save on the wedding that you can actually get away with. This isn't easy. Firstly, you don't really want to cut out things that matter to the *chassan* and *kallah*, because this is their big day, and no one wants theirs to be

---

2. It is. To *yours*.

All the Trimmings

the wedding where the *chassan's* father decided there would be no band because he and his friends were reasonably OK at a cappella.

Also, many wedding tips that you read in magazines are not entirely thought out. For example, one article I read said that instead of buying bouquets and centerpieces, you should find a field of wildflowers and put together your own. What a great idea! Although the article didn't really say *when* you should do this. Don't flowers have to be picked relatively close to the wedding? Who's running out into a field the morning of the wedding and trying to figure out how to weave flower stems into a circle? ("Check your phone!" "OK, my phone says that this is poison ivy.")

But there are definitely ways to save money that won't hurt anybody. Or give them major rashes. (Not that it matters, because you didn't hire a photographer anyway.)

1. REPHRASE THE INVITATIONS — Let's put it this way: Most of the people that you invite to the wedding, you invite only so they shouldn't be offended that they weren't invited, and they show up only so that *you* won't be offended that they didn't. If you have such a close relationship with them that you're willing to pay over $50 a plate for their meal (and you don't even pay $50 for your own plates at home that you get to *keep*), then why aren't you close enough to talk to each other and straighten this out?

Of course, the answer is that you really don't have time to do this with each person you invite, because you're busy putting together a wedding for five hundred people so none of them will be offended. But the main problem, I think, is the invitation itself. Most wedding invitations are copied word for word off three-year-old invitations that are for some reason still on your refrigerator, and which, in turn, were copied from older invitations that were

WHAT IS THIS — SOME KIND OF JOKE?

on *those* people's refrigerators, so that all invitations are basically phrased exactly the same, except for the occasional typo. (Mine said "the twenty-seventh fo February." And finding typos after the fact, by the way, is a good way to save on wedding invitations.) Every invitation says that the hosts "request the honor of your presence," or that you are "cordially invited" — the implication being that you'd better be there unless you have a really good excuse, such as that you're dead. So I think that invitations should be rephrased to be a little less forceful:

Mr. and Mrs. Bob Finkelstein
and Mr. and Mrs. Sam Weinberg
cordially invite you
to be aware

that
Becky
and
Dave
will not be available to come to any weddings
that you may be throwing
on Sunday, the thirtieth fo June,
because they will be otherwise engaged,
and then married
at one p.m.
at Temple Beth Shalom.
So don't be offended.
Although you can come
if you really have nothing else going on that day.

All the Trimmings

But having a cheaper wedding is not just about cutting people out. Here are some other tips:

2. CUT DOWN THE MUSIC — I'm not saying you should cut down the *band*. But cutting down on the *volume* definitely won't hurt. It must save money *somehow*. I recently attended the wedding of my wife's second cousin or something, and I looked over at the band and noticed that every musician was wearing earplugs. Do you know how, when your ears are covered, you tend to speak louder? So I think a good way to save some money would be to: A. Stop buying the band ear plugs, and B. Make the volume a little lower. My father-in-law, who himself was wearing earplugs, like the band, suggested that instead of blasting the music, they can just give all the people at the wedding a pair of headphones and let them set their own volume. So I told him that I didn't think this would save a lot of money, especially once you factor in the wire tanglage of a few hundred people walking in circles for an hour.

3. GET RID OF THE PROGRAMS — We've all been to weddings where various friends and relatives walk down the aisle, and you know it's going to be one of those weddings when they hand out a program beforehand, like it's a high school play. But why waste money printing programs? Does anyone see people walking down the aisle and go, "Who on earth is *that*? That's not the *chassan*!" No, we can figure it out. "That's someone's grandmother, flanked by someone's little brother." The only people who might need programs are the photographers, so they don't go taking pictures of anyone who comes running down the aisle because he got to the wedding late and all the open chairs are in the first row.

"Smile!"

"No, I'm not part of this!"

"You're not (*checking program*) the flower girl?"

4. SHORTEN THE CEREMONY — No one likes a long *chuppah* ceremony. And all those extra people walking down just makes it take more time, which also means that the band and the photographer are going to end up charging for more time, because everyone walks slowly, stops for the camera, and isn't sure which way to go when he gets to the end because there are no signs or anything. It would be far more efficient, if you want to save money, to just have everyone race down at once, with maybe a special prize going to the winner.

5. MAKE FEWER DESSERTS — The caterer usually makes enough dessert for everyone, but not everyone's there for dessert, such as, for example, the people who have to get home to their babysitter because they don't want to pay her overtime just so the whole entire wedding could walk down the aisle two at a time and then cram themselves onto the stage like they're getting into the *teivah*. Maybe you should mail all the guests programs in advance when you send out the invitations, so they can let you know if they'll still be there come dessert. You should also write what you're serving for dessert, so they can make an informed decision.

These are just *some* ideas. But if you pull them off, you will definitely save a ridiculous amount of money.

"This is all we saved?" you will ask no one in particular. "That's ridiculous!"

SECTION III:
POP CORN!
(OR "DAD JOKES")

"Pop corn!" is the answer to the riddle, "Who is the father of corny jokes?" The truth is that *every* father is the father of corny jokes. That's what a dad joke is.

The idea of the popcorn joke is that it in itself is a corny joke, probably made up by this "Pop Corn" person.

A corny joke is defined as a joke that is not actually designed to make people laugh — a joke that is purposely designed to make people groan. In other words, whereas most jokes are told to help you make friends, corny jokes help you get people to unfriend you.

I wonder if it would be possible to find out who was the first person in history to tell a corny joke. The *grandfather* of corny jokes, I guess. It was probably the joke about why someone threw a clock out the window.

So this section is articles about parenting. I was originally going to call it "Your Momma," after the popular style of joke in which one person insults another person's mother by calling her, for example, extremely unintelligent, though he doesn't do it to her face, because he's nevertheless scared of her. But I decided not to, because "your momma" jokes are designed to upset people. Like the popcorn joke, but in a different way.

Sure, some "your momma" jokes are funny, but not to the person you're telling them to. To them, it's like, "I have to respect my momma, but you can make fun of her?" "Your momma" jokes take the fact that the listener won't make fun of his own mother and combines it with the fact that all kids are secretly embarrassed of their parents.

And most "your momma" jokes revolve around the momma in question being overweight, even though the person telling the joke has not had seven kids and then had to take care of them instead of spending her days jogging while some nanny raises them, and maybe we'll see how fat *you* are when you're *my* age!

"Your momma is so fat, that when she sits around the house, she sits AROUND THE HOUSE!"

"You think I sit around the house?!"

Also, most people who tell "your momma" jokes have never actually met the other person's momma. They just have this image in their heads. So the joke reveals more about the speaker than the actual mother.

But I have to say that one thing that I've noticed about being a corny father is that there's nothing more awkward than accidentally telling your kids a "your momma" joke.

Especially if your wife is around.[1]

Even if you insist you were kidding. She's going to think there was a kernel of truth to it.[2]

---

1. That said, I hope you didn't take any of the marriage advice in the previous section to heart. They were written by the same guy who accidentally says "your momma" jokes in front of his wife.

2. That was a popcorn joke. I retain my title.

UNTAPPED BUFFET

My youngest child, Gedalyah, is about to start crawling. But he doesn't know it yet. He's at this stage where we put him down on the floor near his toys, and he lies down and sits up and lies down and sits up, and all of a sudden he's nowhere near them. Sometimes, we find him in a different room entirely, and he's very upset, because he has no idea how he got there. He doesn't realize that he's traveling, and we're not about to tell him, because, as parents, we're torn between wanting to see our kids develop normally and not wanting to have to babyproof the house again.

This is the difference between first-time parents and experienced parents. First-time parents think that the entire house, including the pull-down attic and the detached garage, needs to be babyproofed

WHAT IS THIS — SOME KIND OF JOKE?

months before their child is born, as if it's going to come from the hospital, stand up, and run into the coffee table.

True story: A few years ago, a car stopped in front of our house, and a young couple got out and asked if they could use our garden hose. So we gave them the hose, and the husband opened the back door of the car, picked up a pacifier off the floor of the car, and held it out so his wife could wash it. Then they popped the pacifier into their child's mouth, thanked us, and drove off.[3]

But actually, I don't know if they were first-time parents. *Real* first-time parents would have thrown away the pacifier. *Second-time* parents are the ones who wash *off* the pacifier, and third-time parents just wipe it on their shirt. ("What?! It's a clean shirt!") By the time your fourth child rolls around, you don't care *what* he puts in his mouth, so long as he doesn't choke on it.

That's the real fear — choking. You know how, when you lose a contact lens, you get down on your hands and knees and crawl around until you find it? Well, babies are on their hands and knees *all the time*. Imagine what they're seeing down there.

And whatever they do see, they put in their mouths. Most babies' main goal is to fit the entire *world* into their mouths. That's why they have such big cheeks.

But they're not trying to misbehave; they're just curious. "What's this? I've never seen it before! Is it hard or soft? Does it make noise? Can I eat it? Does it make *noise* when I eat it? Does *Mommy* make noise when I eat it?"

So pretty soon, Gedalyah is going to figure out that he can crawl,

---

3. Maybe the car was a rental.

Untapped Buffet

and we're going to have to spend a large part of our days fishing around in his mouth and pulling out soggy things and trying to figure out what they were.

"Is that a contact lens?"

It's part of being a parent. You're sitting there, doing whatever it is you need to get done, when it suddenly occurs to you that you haven't seen or heard from the baby in about five minutes. So rather than enjoy the peace and quiet, you get up and look around. You even start calling the baby's name, like he's going to respond. Finally, you see his legs sticking out from under the couch. He doesn't even notice you're there, because he's happily doing something that maybe involves a faint crinkling noise. So you grab his leg and gently pull him out, and he looks up at you, with a long piece of hair stuck to his face, and he smiles, because the truth is that he really had no idea how he was going to back out of under there, and he hadn't considered an escape plan before he went in. And in that smile, you notice that he's definitely chewing on something.

The first time this happens, it doesn't register. You start to turn back to what you were doing, but then it occurs to you: "I haven't actually given him any food, yet he's *chewing on something*." So you dive down and hook your finger into his mouth, and the baby turns his head away to fight you, and he starts whimpering, but finally you get it, and you triumphantly pull your finger out of his mouth to find: part of an old cookie.

I always feel so bad when that happens. Sometimes I find myself apologizing to the baby. "Oh, I'm sorry. Here, you can have it back." And then I put it back in his mouth. And he looks at me, like, "I don't want it *now*! Who *knows* where your fingers have been!"

WHAT IS THIS — SOME KIND OF JOKE?

There is a bright side to this whole crawling thing, of course: We won't have to sweep under his high chair anymore. In general, there's always a humongous mess of food under the high chair. We don't actually put it there; we put it on his tray, and he's supposed to eat it. But here's how it gets distributed:

44% — on the floor under his high chair

20% — on his seat, directly underneath him

10% — on parts of his face other than his mouth

8% — on parts of his head other than his face

7% — on his clothing

5% — *inside* his clothing

3% — *inside* his diaper, somehow

1% — in his mouth

(The final 2 percent is never found.)

So as you'd imagine, he's very hungry between meals, which is why he's always trying to eat sneakers and soggy pieces of paper and tiny little rubber tires. So maybe he'll start crawling into the dining room and eating his leftovers.

But we're going to have to get on top of the other kids about cleaning up as well. They're still very excited about the baby; they think that we got them a new toy. They're always making him laugh, and lugging him around, and once in a while I come downstairs and yell, "Hey! Who drew on the baby?" But now, having a baby brother is going to mean picking things up, like art projects and lone crayons and Polly Pocket shoes (which are smaller than contact lenses), and those tiny little rubber balls that *rebbis* give as prizes that bounce really high and then immediately get lost. And wait until he discovers the pile of knapsacks near the front door. There's always food in *those*.

Untapped Buffet

And let's not forget Band-Aids. My kids believe that any boo-boo, no matter how small, needs a Band-Aid. It doesn't matter if it's not bleeding, or if there's not even a visible scrape — as soon as they fall, they go right upstairs to get a Band-Aid, and of course they leave their wrappers lying around. And then, a couple of days later, I find a Band-Aid stuck to the floor. In my kids' view, a Band-Aid isn't a patch to stop blood from getting on your clothes; it's a sticker you get for falling down.

It's very important that we clean all this up, because Gedalyah is definitely the curious type. He sits on my lap when I'm working and tries to type. He picks up the phone on a regular basis, starts pushing buttons, and then, when he hears someone say "hello?" he puts the phone in his mouth. And when I wash him off in the kitchen sink between meals (I actually sometimes consider running him through the dishwasher), he takes the opportunity to play with the things that are drying on the drain board. With his dirty hands.

But curiosity is fine; it's a sign of a healthy baby. Basically, Hashem created tiny babies with no immune systems, and they have only about three years to get their immune systems in top shape before we drop them off to spend a day in a room where, at any given moment, approximately 90 percent of the kids have runny noses. So He made it that babies crawl around and pick up random things with their filthy hands and put them in their mouths. Band-Aids, for example, have got to be great for the immune system. Except in my house, where they're probably the cleanest thing on the floor.

WHAT DID I SAY?

I was in the supermarket the other day, waiting in line for the register and trying to ignore the candy, and I overheard a little boy asking his mother for just about every kind of candy in the general vicinity. After the mother shot down several choices, the boy pulled one last bar off the shelf.

"Oooh, Mommy! Mommy! MOMMY! Is this one kosher?"

"No!" the mommy snapped.

I probably don't need to tell you that we were actually in a kosher supermarket. Apparently, everything in the whole store is kosher except for the candy that they keep near the register. Nevertheless, I'm not judging this mother, because what she did was a lot easier than taking a knee and explaining the real reason she didn't want to buy it for him with a bunch of impatient people waiting in line behind her:

What Did I Say?

"Look, if I buy you one, I'm going to have to buy one for all the other kids, because you can't keep your mouth shut. Or else I'm going to have to explain to each kid individually why you get to have chocolate and he doesn't, and frankly, I don't actually know the answer to that one. And then the next time you ask me, not only am I going to have to go through this again, but I'm also going to have to come up with a reason that I said it was OK *this* time, but not *next* time. Or else I'm going to have to spring for chocolate bars for everyone in the family, *again*."

And it's not like none of us ever stretches the truth with our kids. We're not proud of it, but we tell ourselves that it's just easier this way.

For example, a lot of people tell their kids that coffee stunts their growth. In fact, parents have been telling this to kids for generations, and our society has come to believe that it's true. But there's no research that proves it. Nevertheless, parents say it anyway, because they don't want their children drinking coffee — the reason being that parents drink coffee in the first place so they can keep up with their kids. They don't even want to think about how much coffee they're going to have to drink if their kids start drinking coffee too. But this isn't really something we want to explain to our kids, so we play on the fact that they want to grow big and strong, and combine that with our mutual lack of scientific knowledge.

"If you swallow the seeds, you're going to have a watermelon growing in your stomach."

"Like you, Totty?"

This is also why we tell them that if they eat their vegetables, they're going to grow up to be big and strong. Is this true? I think it

WHAT IS THIS — SOME KIND OF JOKE?

has more to do with genetics and exercise. And even if they don't eat any vegetables, chances are they'll still grow up to be bigger and stronger than they are now. In fact, you're not really sure *what* vegetables do. You yourself eat them so you *won't* grow bigger. Are they magic? All you know is that your doctor keeps telling you to eat vegetables, so you eat vegetables.

"But why?"

"I'm the doctor. That's why."

There are many other things that we tell our kids that are not necessarily as true as they could be, such as, "I'm not going to say this again."

Yes you will. We all know you will.

But the biggest is what we say when we're trying to discourage our kids from lying:

"If you tell me the truth, I won't get mad."

No, you'll get even. Most of us have had this conversation with our parents at some point:

"Aren't you going to go easier on me for telling the truth?"

"No! Not after what you did!"

As parents, we find ourselves saying a lot of things to our kids, and most of these are things that we don't *want* to have to tell them, or don't want to have to tell them *again*, or never thought we'd have to say to another human being *ever*.

"Don't lick the floor!"

(Seriously, you've never told your child before that he couldn't lick the floor. How was *he* supposed to know?)

Indeed, there are a lot of rules that we make up on the fly after

What Did I Say?

our children have already broken them. For example, one rule that we have in our house is that we're not allowed to go into the living room during meals. We made this rule because our son Daniel tends to run into the living room between bites and leap headfirst onto the couch, and his face is usually covered in food, although, to be fair, by the time he comes back to the table, it's *not*. Our couch is basically a giant napkin. We bought it only few years ago, and it already looks like we pulled it out of the Gulf.

There are also a lot of things that we say to our kids that, upon closer examination, don't quite make sense:

"What part of 'Don't hit your brother' don't you understand?"

Well, the "Don't" part, obviously.

We'd always hoped we'd never have to say any of these clichéd parental things, but now we feel like it's all we *ever* say:

"Don't wipe that on me."

"Close your mouth and eat your food."

"No, it's not *muktzeh* to flush."

"Don't hit your brother while he's sleeping."

"What would you like with your ketchup?"

"How would you like it if I spit in *your* soda?"

"Your shirt is not a napkin."

"Why do you always get boo-boos *after* your bedtime?"

"Don't eat ketchup with your fingers. At least use a spoon."

"No, you're not old enough to pour milk."

"How do you know you don't like it if you haven't even *tried* it?"

WHAT IS THIS — SOME KIND OF JOKE?

"Of *course* you're not going to like it now that you've *said* you're not going to like it!"

"Don't just stand there crying! Clean it up!"

"I said, 'Don't lick the floor!'"

"All right, that's it. I'm counting to three."

I find myself counting to three way more often than any healthy person should. For a while, my son Heshy wasn't even sure what number came after three. We'd watch him count his toys. "One, two, three... five... s-seven? Fourteen, fourteen, fifteen..." So we started counting to ten. And it's not like this really gave him more time anyway, because when we count to three, we stretch it out as long as we can. (I'm surprised he wasn't counting: "One, two...two and a half...two and three-quarters...") To this day, my kids have no idea what's going to happen when we get to three, but they have no desire to find out. Neither do I, because I'm pretty sure it will involve getting up.

Also, about once a day, you have the following conversation with one of your children:

"You're crying; you must be tired... Now you're *denying* it; you must be tired... OK, now you're *admitting* to it; you must be tired..."

It's like you're having a conversational chess match they can't possibly win.

"No, Mommy! *You're* tired!"

"Yes. Yes, I am."

Adults aren't afraid to admit that they're tired. All we want is for the kids to go to bed already so we can start doing all the things we need to do, and maybe we'll get to sleep sometime before the end of the week. That's why we give kids such early bedtimes. Because

What Did I Say?

honestly, who on earth really *needs* to go to sleep at six thirty? Do you have any idea what time you wake up if you go to sleep at six thirty?

"For goodness' sake, it's still dark out! Stop fighting with each other and go back to bed!"

I don't know if I have a point. I guess my point is that our kids keep blindsiding us with questions and requests every minute of the day, and we don't always have time to weigh all of our options. So we say whatever we can to try to turn them into decent human beings, and to get it over with before the *next* kid blindsides us with something.

But don't worry as you tell your kids that you're the mommy, and everything you do hurts you more than it hurts them,[4] and someday they're going to thank you for this.

Really? That's going to be an awkward conversation.

---

4. Maybe you should eat more vegetables.

Noisy Toys

It's hard to figure out what to get really little kids for Chanukah. In the past, I've written Chanukah articles about chemistry sets and board games and play-dough, but as a lot of the more experienced parents will attest, these are maybe not the best things for babies. Babies like to explore the world by tasting everything, and as it turns out, most board games taste pretty much alike.[5] And play-dough is way too salty.

(The things I do to research these articles.)

I remember the first Chanukah that I bought my daughter a present. It was her first Chanukah, actually. In fact, she was *born* on Chanukah. So I ran out while my wife was still in the hospital (I was really excited to have an excuse to buy toys again.) and I bought

---

5. Besides maybe *Operation*.

Noisy Toys

her a piano. OK, so it was a *toy* piano, but this is as opposed to my youngest child, who, for *his* first Chanukah, got a winter hat. And he only got that because the other kids had stretched out all the other baby hats playing dress-up. Because after a certain amount of kids, you come to realize that your baby, in his first year, doesn't actually know that it's Chanukah anyway. But *you* still do, and you feel like you should get him something, especially if:

A. He's your first child, and you're convinced that he's a genius who does indeed know that it's Chanukah (in which case I'd suggest a chemistry set), or

B. He's *not* your first child, and you have other children whose presents he will otherwise try to eat, because, let's face it, he's no genius.

But what does he want? Unlike your older children, babies rarely tell you what they want. They *do* cry, but that's hardly informative. Does he want a bottle? Does he want to be held? Does he want to be passed back and forth while people shout, "I don't know what he wants!"?

Of course, some baby experts say that babies have different cries depending on what they're looking for. OK, Mr. Expert, so which cry means, "I would like something that makes noise when I shake it, please," and which cry means, "I was thinking more along the lines of a toy with a suction cup on the bottom so it won't keep falling off my high chair"?

And you can't even tell which toys you should get based on the pictures on the box, because those are very obviously taken by the people who are trying to sell the toy. These are not candid shots. There's always a nice picture of a baby who is staring in sheer delight at a bunch of balls spinning around in a fishbowl, or at cups

WHAT IS THIS — SOME KIND OF JOKE?

that can go inside each other, but can also stack. Those are some very mundane things to be delighted about. There's no way that's not photo-shopped. You've taken your kids for professional photos, and you happen to know that babies don't pose on command. So how many pictures of the baby did they have to take before they got that shot, and what are the chances that the toy was even in the room when they were doing it? The box should be more honest. Like it should show the huge mess of pieces that you're going to have to clean up, and then it would show the baby off to the side, eating the box.

So here are some helpful ideas, with the names of some popular toys highlighted in bold. Like this:

Bold

One thing you can get your kid is **a toy that plays music**. This is just about every toy out there. The basic idea is that if your baby's not crying, then you want to hear what he's doing, because if you don't hear anything, then you can be sure that he's off somewhere pulling out ***sefarim***. So now, every toy you buy plays essentially the same three songs, on rotation:

"Baa Baa Black Sheep,"

"Twinkle Twinkle," and

"ABC."

And they're all the same song! Someone should look into this.

The other thing about musical toys is that they never die. When the battery is low, it won't stop playing songs altogether, it will just play the same song over and over again until you smash it

Noisy Toys

with a **hammer**. My son has an **activity center**[6] in his crib, and sometimes he pushes the button on a Friday night, and it keeps playing the whole Shabbos. We'd get rid of it, but we like having it there, because that way we can tell from all the way downstairs when he's woken up from his nap. Or, alternatively, when one of the other kids has climbed in there *with* him.

ME: "Wait. The baby doesn't know how to push that button yet. He's two months old. ARE YOU IN THERE WITH HIM?"

MY OTHER KIDS (IN UNISON): "No."

ME: "Hang on. How many of you are *in* there?"

Another category of toys that makes a lot of noise is **musical instruments**, such as a **toy piano** or maybe a **xylophone**. I don't know what it is with toymakers and xylophones. I have never actually seen an adult playing a xylophone.

And then there's the **Fisher Price Corn Popper**, which is by far the most annoying toy ever. It's a stick that makes noise when it moves. There's nothing good about it. It's the kind of toy that you buy only for *other* people's kids. Someone bought one for us, and it lives on top of the *sefarim shrank*. What useful life skill does it give your children? Is someone at Fisher Price going, "Well, sometimes I want to take a walk, but I also want to make popcorn!"

There are also a lot of **toys you get so that your child can pretend that he's doing whatever *you're* doing, and he'll stop touching your stuff**. This includes fake **pots** and **pans** and **tools** and **cash registers** (because that's a job we want to prepare him for) and **fake keys** that he can lose and even little

---

6. Depending on how loosely you define "activity."

WHAT IS THIS — SOME KIND OF JOKE?

toy **vacuum cleaners** that make noise. My kids are scared of the *actual* vacuum cleaner noise, so why would they want to play with *that*? Also, once they're making noise, why not just give them a *real* **vacuum cleaner**? Let them get some housework done. What's the worst that can happen? They'll accidentally clean up their toys?

Another make-believe toy that's very big with girls is **tea sets**. Does that classify as a "make-believe" toy? My wife hasn't been to an actual adult tea party since I've known her. Occasionally the yeshivah hosts something called a "tea," but it's not the same thing.

Also, a lot of kids love **riding toys**. When I was a kid, the law was that every Jewish family had to have one of those little red cars with the yellow roof — the "**Cozy Coupe**." And boy, was it cozy. The way you'd play with it was you'd all pile in and fight over whose turn it was, and then you'd drive around with all of your friends hanging off the roof. There are also lots of other riding toys that look like a cross between a car and a bike, and even though the manufacturers rigged them so that they make a lot of *vroom* noises, the vast majority of them do not have functional steering wheels. If you want to turn, you have to stand up and aim the car in the direction you want to go.

I had a *real* car like that once.

You can also get your child a **book**. There are lots of books for little kids, and most of them are either plush or made of cardboard. Or they're waterproof, so your child can read them in the bath. (Do I want baths to take *longer*? I'm kneeling in a puddle!) Most of these books have a picture on each page, with a word underneath describing the picture. Who are these descriptions for? Is there a

Noisy Toys

baby who can read the words? Or are there parents out there who honestly don't know what these things are?

"Wait... Oh, it's a duck."

But you should definitely read them to your kids.

"Let's see... Car, duck (*turn the page*), ball, xylophone (*turn the page*). Wait a minute. Is this a *catalogue*?"

SECTION IV:
SEVEN ATE NINE!
(OR "FOOD FRENZY")

You know the joke:

Q: Why was six afraid of seven?

A: Because seven ate nine!

OK, I was wrong. *This* is the father of corny jokes.

It's like, "Why was two upset after playing dreidel? Because two won zero!"

It helps to know why people feel the way they do, so you can get to the root of their problem.

Though the first time I heard this joke, I was like, "Six *what* was afraid of seven *what*?" I'm still not sure. The numbers? The actual number seven ate the number nine? Wasn't the eight in the way? Also, why weren't 1–5 afraid of seven?

Also, how could something smaller eat something bigger? Is that like Pharaoh's dream about the seven skinny cows and the seven fat cows, and the number seven ate the number nine but didn't end up any fatter? And why am I trying to attack this joke with logic?

OK, so let's assume that all these numbers are alive, and they have emotions, such as fear. This is a joke about cannibalism! *Why was six afraid of seven*, you ask?! Because seven was a cannibal! And six always had to stand right next to him! Poor six — he has to stand next to seven in every line up, seven's big open mouth is facing him, and breathing, and six is terrified. Because seven ate nine! Even though nine is right there.

Six is like, "Don't eat me, eight is right next to you and he's clearly fatter! He's shaped like a snowman!"

Six is thinking, "Well, if seven ate nine, he's gonna want to eat me too.

I look just *like* nine. Maybe when he comes for me, I can stand on my head and confuse him. He'll be like, 'I thought I already *ate* nine!'"

There has to be something that six can do to avoid having seven eat him. Apparently, hiding behind eight doesn't work.

In fact, arguably, I would say this whole thing is eight's fault.

Point is, we as a society will eat anything. Nothing is safe. We keep finding new things to eat. So the following articles are about eating.

SUPPER IDEAS

I have a great idea for a business venture. It came to me while I was trying to figure out what to make for supper. Which I'm still trying to do, by the way.

Yes, I sometimes make supper. Basically, my wife has agreed (although I don't think I was *at* this meeting) that *I* will make supper on nights that I'm home, and *she* will make supper on nights that I'm not. Or else she'll warm up leftovers from the nights that *I* made supper. And even though I am, for the most part, unemployed, I do teach on most days from 4 to 6 p.m., which *baruch Hashem* is the exact time that supper needs to be made. But on the other hand, I don't teach during the summer.

In general, I don't really mind *making* supper; it's the *planning* supper that I mind. (I do want to point out, though, that I'm talking about *supper*, as opposed to *dinner*. Your children's yeshivah,

WHAT IS THIS — SOME KIND OF JOKE?

for example, invites you to a *dinner* every year. There's no "31st Annual Supper." The difference, as far as I can tell, is that dinners have speeches and centerpieces and sometimes dancing, and frankly this is a bit over the top when it's just us and the kids on a Tuesday night. On the other hand, they say that families who have dinner together have stronger relationships and are better adjusted. So maybe we should think about dancing.)

The easiest days to plan suppers, hands down, are fast days. ("Let's see... We'll have bagels and spreads, soup, baked ziti, and eggplant parmesan. And then a half hour later we'll have *fleishig*.") Sometimes I'll spend the entire second half of the fast making supper.

But in general, I'm hesitant to make anything that will take more time to prepare than it will to eat (besides for Shabbos and Yom Tov, when meals are longer to begin with; also, those technically classify as "dinners"). For example, chicken on the bone takes five minutes to prepare, after which it pretty much cooks itself. And it takes more than five minutes to eat, assuming you use a knife and fork. Blintzes, on the other hand, have numerous steps. You have to make the crepes and the filling SEPARATELY, and then you have to roll them together (what's *that* about?), and you have to stand there while they heat up, *twice*. And they take much less time to eat than chicken does, especially if you keep noshing on the ones that are done while you're waiting for the others.

But it's really the deciding what to make that people don't like. People hate having to make decisions. And this is a decision that comes up every day, and you have to come up with an answer *that day*, and no matter what you decide, you will have to decide again the next day. That's why so many times people give up.

Supper Ideas

"Forget it! Let's just go out to eat!"

"OK, so where do we go?"

"I don't know; where do *you* want to go?"

And then when they get there, they spend a half hour staring at the menu.

"Everything looks so good. What do you recommend?"

"I don't know; what do *you* recommend?"

So now that's *two* decisions they have to make. It's almost easier to just stay home.

On the other hand, if you're eating at home, you want to try to make a supper that everyone will eat. For example, there may be someone in your family who doesn't like eating *fleishig* during the week, because she has this huge fear that, for the six hours after she ate, she won't be able to eat approximately half the foods in the house. So instead, she puts up this wall, and, for most of her life, doesn't allow herself to eat the *other* half of the foods in the house.

You also might want to satisfy the people who, like me, don't want to eat the same thing two nights in a row. The funny thing is that if you'd ask me, on any given day, what I'd had for supper the night before, I wouldn't remember. But if you made it again, I would say, "Hey! We just had this *last* night!"

My wife, on the other hand, doesn't care as much. If it were totally up to her, she would cook supper once at the beginning of the week, and keep serving it every night.

But that's only assuming it's something the *kids* will eat. Children, for the most part, only want to eat foods that their parents really should not be eating. And they also want to be part of the decision process. Sometimes, when my wife and I can't decide what to make for supper, one of us will suffer a momentary lapse of judgment and say, "Let's ask the kids what *they* want." And they always ask for pizza. So essentially, saying, "Let's ask the kids," is the same as saying, "Let's have pizza." So much for not making decisions.

I'm not sure why kids love pizza so much, but I could make pretty much anything and call it pizza, and our kids will eat it. I like pizza, but not more than any other food. I like it a healthy amount. But when I was a kid, I couldn't get enough of it. I could not for the life of me figure out why pizza shops bothered offering anything else. Who would have soup when they could have pizza? (I have a similar question nowadays with fancy weddings. Who would pick salmon when they could have the prime rib?)

(People who are afraid of becoming *fleishig*, that's who.)

But it's totally normal. Kids want pizza at every opportunity, but they don't always get it. So when they become teenagers, they eat pizza approximately 150,000 times per week. Whenever the yeshivah serves a bad meal (defined as "any meal that is not pizza"), they will go out and buy pizza. I'm a high school teacher,[3] and even though the official school policy is not to eat in class, at any given moment there are at least two people trying to pretend they're not eating pizza.

But eventually, they get sick of it, and when they become parents, and their kids suggest pizza every single time they're asked for their opinion, they roll their eyes and try to convince the kids that chicken tastes better. It's the circle of life.

So we can't have pizza every day. But I do think we should at

---

3. Really.

Supper Ideas

least make one thing per meal that the kids are willing to eat. My wife, on the other hand, is into trying to convince them to eat foods that they're not normally willing to eat by not making anything else. Like sometimes she will make quiche for supper. Just three different flavors of quiche. Now, my wife makes really good quiche, but you'd only know that if you were willing to try it. Which my kids are not.

Maybe we should start calling it "pizza."

So how do we figure out what to make? For a while, I had this strategy wherein I would close my eyes, open up a cookbook, and put my finger on a random page. But after a few nights of "blonde brownies" and "homemade popsicles," I realized that maybe this wasn't the greatest strategy. Although it was a big hit with the kids.

Which brings me to my business idea: I think there should be a service that we can sign up for, wherein we'd give them all of our information, such as allergies, food-gender phobias, wash-*bentch* phobias, and the ages of our kids, and then we can call them any night of the week, and a person — preferably someone who's been fasting all day — will tell us what to make for supper. There will be no decisions on our part.[4]

This would definitely be a great business idea for you if you're the type of person who enjoys

1. money, and

2. receiving millions of phone calls during supper.

In fact, I urge you to set this business up today. Let me know when you're done, so I can call you for supper ideas.

---

4. Unless someone opens a competing service.

CHARRED, BUT RAW

The thing I love most about barbecues is that you can invite people over to celebrate pretty much any occasion, such as the beginning of barbecue season, the end of barbecue season, and any week that meat is on sale. Last year, I had my whole family over to celebrate the fact that we bought a barbecue. We didn't do this when we got a new stove.

"This food is so good! What's your secret?"

"I used the oven timer."

Nor would we invite them over if we got a dishwasher.

"This food is even better than last time! What's your secret?"

"Clean plates."

Men, in particular, love to barbecue. This is partly because when men actually cook supper, we want the whole neighborhood to

Charred, but Raw

know. Also, the truth is that men don't really mind cooking, but they only like making things that look pretty much the same going into the oven as they do coming out, like chicken or roast potatoes. They very rarely make cakes or kugels or basically anything they can't nosh on to "see if it's done." When it comes to a barbecue, not only can they nosh on the food to "see if it's done," but since each piece of food gets heated at a different rate, they can taste *every single item on the grill*. If a man were making a barbecue just for himself, he would be finished eating before he puts out the fire.

So yes, I love to barbecue. Just last week I barbecued twelve chicken wings, a basting brush, and two oven mitts. You probably smelled it.

HOSTING A BARBECUE
STEP 1: BUY A GRILL

I'm not talking about a George Foreman. A George Foreman is not a grill; it's a waffle iron for meat. If you invite people over for a barbecue, and they show up to find you hunched over a George Foreman, they're going to leave. It doesn't matter how much they like you:

"Hey, come back! Bubby!"[5]

There are basically two kinds of grills: charcoal and gas. With a charcoal grill, you have to pour in a load of briquettes, and it's much safer than a gas grill because you generally can't get them to light. They're *little bricks*, for goodness' sake. At most, you'll get them to start smoking, and wind up engulfed in a plume of smoke,

---

5. She probably saw you using your fingers.

WHAT IS THIS — SOME KIND OF JOKE?

trying to guess when your food is done and where on the grill it is exactly.

At our house, we have a propane grill. Basically, you buy a tank full of flammable gas, and you try not to think too much about the fact that you're leaving it unattended in your backyard all year. But it's pretty easy to use. You open the valve, push a button, and then you thank Hashem that there was no explosion. (I also have my kids stand by with the garden hose.)

I love my grill. I'm thinking of getting one for *milchig*.

On the other hand, a propane grill can run out of fuel with no warning. This happened to me just this week. I had my whole family over — parents, siblings, nieces, and nephews — all waiting in the living room for me to finish cooking, and suddenly, my brother, who was outside helping me because there was nowhere left to sit, said, "Hey, did the fire go out?" And I said, "That's ridiculous! It lets off some kind of warning! No?"

No.

So we came inside nonchalantly and headed straight for the kitchen, holding all the stuff we didn't get to make yet. Everyone was like, "You're inside; does that mean the food's done?" and we said, "Almost!" all the while hoping they wouldn't see us boiling the frankfurters. Thank goodness we'd already done the shish kabobs, or they would've walked into the kitchen to see us holding them over a burner.

STEP 2: FIGURE OUT WHAT TO GRILL

The most common foods that people barbecue are hot dogs and hamburgers, which are both pieces of meat that look nothing like they did when they were in the animal, and we're pretty sure

Charred, but Raw

that if you take them out of an animal, it wouldn't even notice they were missing. Hot dogs are particularly popular, because you can fit about five hundred of them on your grill to make up for the fact that they're constantly rolling onto the ground. Whenever that happens, I pick it up with the tongs, very gently, and put it back on the grill.

No, I'm just kidding. I throw it over the fence into my neighbor's yard. My neighbor has a tiny annoying dog that is constantly barking, especially when it smells meat, and I find that throwing hot dogs over the fence gets it to stop.

Another fun thing to make is shish kabobs. Shish kabobs are great, because they allow you to serve something that is not just hot dogs or hamburgers without actually coming out and buying everyone a steak. Basically, you're giving each person like three bites of meat, except that no one is saying, "He only gave us like three bites of meat." They're all saying, "Ooh, shish kabob!" The name "shish kabob" is specifically designed to sound appetizing, coming from the word "shish," which means "stick," and "kabob," which means "that is on fire." My sticks always catch fire, and I can never quite put them out with the tongs, so most of my guests end up eating some shish.

You should definitely also add some vegetables to the grill, so you could tell people, "*What*?! I'm also making vegetables!" Like corn, for example. (Corn on the *cob*, we mean. We won't make *that* mistake twice.)

STEP 3: PREPARE YOUR MEAL

1. Make sure to set up your skewers ahead of time. It takes a lot

WHAT IS THIS — SOME KIND OF JOKE?

more time than you'd think to thread pointy sticks through hundreds of pieces of meat and vegetables.

2. About ten minutes before the guests show up, yell, "Oh my goodness! I forgot to take the chicken out of the freezer!"

3. Take the big block of chicken cutlets out of the freezer and wonder how on earth you're going to thaw it. Put the entire block on the grill.

4. While the chicken is thawing, shuck the corn. Put that on the grill.

5. If a corncob rolls off the grill, pick it up with your tongs and throw it over the fence at the little barking dog. If you do this correctly, you will hear a slight "BONK!" and the dog will stop barking.

6. Yell, "Oh my goodness, I forgot to make the hamburgers!" Go inside and make patties.

7. Come back outside, take the corn off the grill, and check on the big block of chicken. The part touching the grill should be black, and the other side should be frozen solid. Flip it over.

8. Put the burgers on the grill and keep them there until the middle is no longer pink. But don't poke them open to check, or the pieces will fall through the grate.

9. Look at your chicken. It should now be black on both sides and frozen in the middle. Flip it back onto the other black side and hope for the best.

10. Put the shish kabobs on the grill. If any of the sticks catch fire, put them out with the hose.

11. If you want your food to cook faster, close the lid. If you want

Charred, but Raw

it to cook *even* faster, go inside for a few minutes. You won't believe how fast things cook when you're not watching.

12. When the neighborhood smells like it's burning down, run back outside to see smoke billowing out from under the lid. Open the lid and get blasted by a cloud of smoke.

13. Come inside, your face black and your eyebrows missing, and announce that the food is ready.

STEP 4: ENJOY THE COMPLIMENTS

"What happened to my skewer?"

"Why are the burgers wet?"

"What is that big black rock in middle of the table?"

"These frankfurters are great!"

"You like them? He made them on the sto — Ow! Why'd you kick me?"

TRYING NEW THINGS

I generally spend Rosh Hashanah at my parents' house. This works out very well for me, because our *minhag* is to eat pretty much all the symbolic foods in the *simanim* booklet, and I have a bunch of little kids who refuse to try anything new.

"Eew! What's that?"

"It's a new fruit."

"Oh. I don't *like* new fruit."

So there's no way the kids are going to eat any of the foods that they don't come home with a song about, such as black-eyed peas, and that leaves just me and my wife, and neither of us are crazy about black-eyed peas either. And it's not really worth boiling two peas.

Maybe we should just swallow them with water, like a pill.

So we go to my parents' house, where between us and my siblings, there are about twenty people. That way, my kids are free

Trying New Things

to spend the meals sitting way down at the end of the table and sticking their fingers in the honey, and the adults are free to huddle together at the other end of the table and try really hard not to think about it. By the end of the meal, we have to throw out the table.

But if you're actually making Yom Tov on your own, and are not sure how to prepare beets or find leeks or get your hands on a fish head (very carefully, is my advice), I've prepared a field guide to help you. I have some time on my hands, because I don't have to cook.

BEETS

There are two parts to the beet. There are the leaves, which are kind of like spinach, and there is the root, which is kind of like a horseradish without the radish. (It's just *horse*.) You can also buy beets in the form of a liquid called "borscht," which tastes exactly like it sounds.

BEET FUN FACTS

In the old days, the root part was used as a medicine. You know how nowadays, a lot of medicines taste like bubble gum? Before bubble gum came along, they tasted like beets.

In Australia people put pickled beets on their hamburgers. In America we use pastrami.

According to my Encyclopedia Britannica (1957), "The Romans spread beets throughout the Roman Empire." This is probably what led to their downfall.

POMEGRANATES

Pomegranates are great, because they have a very long lifespan,

WHAT IS THIS — SOME KIND OF JOKE?

so you can buy a bag of them once and pretty much be set for life. It is said that there are pomegranates in Europe that are over two hundred years old.

I'm not actually sure how to eat one, though. I've always sucked off the seeds and spit them out, but then someone told me you're supposed to *swallow* the seeds. They should come with instructions.

POMEGRANATE FUN FACTS

Another name for a pomegranate is a "Chinese apple" because "pomegranate" is really hard to spell.

In China, of course, they just call it an "apple." And on Rosh Hashanah, they bring in "American apples" and they say things like, "How do we eat this? There are almost no seeds!"

This is not true. China is actually the biggest grower of regular apples in the *world*. But I have no idea what they call them.

Also, in Australia the term "Chinese apple" is used to refer to the riberry (some kind of berry, I'm guessing[6]), and in Holland and Germany, the term refers to oranges. "That's like comparing apples to *Chinese* apples," is a common German saying.

Pomegranate juice stains like you wouldn't believe. There are currently stains in Europe that are over two hundred years old.

SQUASH

Squash is another one of those foods that tastes exactly like it sounds. There are over a hundred varieties of squash. It's like

---

6. Or a place where they make ribs.

Trying New Things

at some point they ran out of names for vegetables, so they said, "OK, from here on out, we're going to call every new vegetable *squash*."

The easiest way to get squash — even easier than going to the supermarket — is to plant it in your backyard, because squash is the easiest thing to grow. You can plant a single seed, even by accident, and before you know it, your entire property will be covered in gourds, and you will be, as they say, "squashed."

SQUASH FUN FACTS

The word "squash" actually comes from the Native American word "*askutasquash*," meaning "*green thing eaten raw.*" Obviously, the Native Americans hadn't discovered kugels.

Most men have nothing against squash, but left to their own devices, they would never actually think to eat it on their own.

LEEKS

A leek is basically a scallion that has grown completely out of control.

"Whoa! You should have picked that scallion *months* ago."

The way to eat a leek is to put it in your soup, and then everyone sits around making leek-related puns. (Such as: "Hey! My bowl has a *leek* in it!")

HONEY

There are several ways to get honey, and many of them are dangerous and irresponsible. You can grow it in your backyard, for example, and then go outside in one of those funny outfits with

WHAT IS THIS — SOME KIND OF JOKE?

screens on it whenever you want to, say, pick up a squash. Just bear in mind that you also have screens on your *house*, and once in a while a bug gets in. So imagine if those screens were inches from your face.

Alternatively, you can buy one of those bottles that are shaped like a bear. Why a bear? I don't know. Better a miniature bear than an enormous bee.

HONEY FUN FACTS

Honeycomb is the only cereal named after a honeycomb.

September is National Honey Month. I have no idea what this means. But it's also National Rice Month, National Potato Month, National Chicken Month, and National Self-Improvement Month. I wish I were making this up.

Honey is a preservative, so you can make a honey cake, and it will be good for years. ("Good" is a relative term.) My mother-in-law once made a honey cake for her son to bring to yeshivah at the beginning of the year, and he found it behind his bed before Pesach. It was still soft.

HEADS

I'm actually not sure how to get a ram's head, but my parents usually buy a fish head. And I'm not even sure how to get *that*. I think they walk into the store and ask for the whole fish. So if you're in the market for a ram's head, just walk into the store and ask for a whole ram.

To prepare the head, open up the paper wrapping, gasp, and run screaming from the house. Then come back in and say things

Trying New Things

like, "I feel like it's staring at me." You can cover the eyes with pieces of carrot.

A lot of people are not too crazy about fish heads, so when I go to my parents, I bring along a beef tongue. A lot of people don't like the thought of eating tongue, but I say it can't be any worse than eating a hot dog. Nevertheless, before you serve tongue to innocent people, you should first give some thought to the kinds of things that cows lick.

NEW FRUITS

Spotting a new fruit is easy. You just look around the fruit section until you see a fruit that you've never seen before, and that's your new fruit.[7]

My brother usually buys the new fruit, and every year he tries to top himself. Last year he came home with this hairy thing that we weren't totally sure was a fruit; we thought maybe it was some kind of creature that had come into the country *with* the fruit, and the supermarket had decided to charge him for it anyway. But we peeled it and peeled it and peeled it, and in the end, we were left with a delicious, juicy, fruity thing that was maybe the size of a grape.[8] So you should always get more than one kind of fruit, just in case.

OTHER FUN FACTS

Black-eyed peas are also called "China beans." I don't know if anyone consults China before they come up with these names.

---

7. New fruits are subjective.

8. I later found out it was called a *rambutan* (formerly Buy.com).

WHAT IS THIS — SOME KIND OF JOKE?

Orange carrots get their color from beta carotene. That's why they're called *carrots*. Wow.

There are a lot of facts about leeks, but none of them are fun.

Fun Facts aren't as much fun as they sound. They're actually a lot of work.

SOME OF THE SAMPLES AT THIS YEAR'S KOSHERFEST HAD BUGS

The first thing I noticed, when I walked into Kosherfest this year, was how crowded it was. People kept coming in and going, "Boy, there are a lot of people here this year!"

"Yeah! And now there's one more!"

I don't know if it's that the kosher industry has grown, or if we, as a society,[9] are just bigger around the middle. I know *I* am. Or it could be that more and more people are coming to this thing every year, and it doesn't help that writers like me keep calling it a kiddush. (Imagine if every kosher food manufacturer in the world got together and threw a massive joint kiddush. Wouldn't *you* go?)

But it's not really a kiddush. It's actually a food industry trade show that, like *every* trade show, has booths giving out samples. It

---

9. And especially those of us who work in the food industry.

WHAT IS THIS — SOME KIND OF JOKE?

just happens to be that the food industry is swimming in food, so that's what they give out.

Basically, the way it works is that the manufacturers come in and set out a bunch of samples of their products, and you walk around and stop by their booths and eat things such as chicken wings, and then you go over to people and shake their hand and talk to them about factors like variety and distribution while they stand there wondering what that was on your hand.

It's all about marketing. Basically, every booth has some kind of interesting display, or samples of their product, and when you stop to look, they say, "Here, have some! You're skin and bones!" (Even though, as I pointed out, *no one* there is skin and bones. It's just something you say when you're trying to conduct business.) This is how I ended up eating three baby food samples.

So you pick up a sample and you start chewing it,[10] and the guy walks over to your side of the booth and starts talking about the product, and you can't interrupt him to say, "No, I'm just looking," because your mouth is full of — What *is* that in your mouth? It's definitely not what it looked like.

While I'm eating samples, I generally have people telling me the product's entire history, because when I go to Kosherfest, I wear a badge that says "Press." That's what it says. It doesn't say "Humor Columnist." So a lot of people assume that I'm a serious journalist. So I have to act interested, *and* they expect me to ask intelligent, journalist-style questions.[11] So instead of listening to their story, I'm

---

10. Or, in the case of baby food samples, smearing it on your chin.
11. With my mouth full.

Some of the Samples at This Year's Kosherfest Had Bugs

racking my brain to come up with an informed question, such as, "So how do you get the vegetarians into the hot dogs?"

Besides for food, a lot of companies were giving out cloth bags. Cloth bags are very in nowadays, because they help save the environment. Apparently, making bags out of sackcloth is good for the environment. Or maybe having five thousand cloth bags all over your house is good for the environment. I'm not sure; I'm not an environmentalist. But the bags had the companies' names on them, and the strategy was that people would walk around loading samples into their bag, and everyone would see the bag, and the company would get free advertising. The thing is, though, that there were so many companies giving out bags that people were using their bags to carry their *other* bags. So basically, the company with the roomiest bag got all the advertising. Not that it worked anyway, because the average person doesn't read. I had a lot of people come up to me, look at my bag, and go, "Oh! Which company is giving out bags?"

"Um... The one whose name is on the bag."

But I wasn't there to advertise. I was there to ask hard-hitting questions (such as, "What did you say this food was, again?") and write about trends. And the main trend this year seems to be: healthy food.

Let's see if it lasts.

Once upon a time, most foods were either healthy or edible. If a food was edible, it wasn't healthy, and if a food was healthy, it wasn't edible. Some foods were neither. The only foods that were healthy *and* edible were the foods that were all natural, such as produce and water. And now we realize that those were the foods that had bugs, because, as it turns out, bugs *also* like healthy foods. This is why I mainly stick to candy and soda.

WHAT IS THIS — SOME KIND OF JOKE?

So for starters, there is now a whole industry of pre-washed, pre-checked fruits and vegetables. Some of these companies had booths at Kosherfest, where, in between eating chicken wings and cold cuts, you could eat a sample of lettuce. One company was giving out little slips of paper with lettuce bugs laminated onto them, so people could see how small these things are. It's like they were checking their lettuce, and someone said, "No, don't throw those bugs away! We can give them out at Kosherfest!"

Seriously, though, I have no idea how they managed to do it. If *I* would try laminating bugs onto little slips of paper, they would throw me out of Staples.

But there is also a trend of companies who are trying to break the barrier and produce foods that are both healthy *and* edible. For example, a lot of manufacturers keep coming up with healthier ways to make potato chips, and a lot of them are pretty good. I think the only real difference between their products and regular potato chips, if you want to get technical, is that their products taste nothing like regular potato chips.

There were also companies selling various types of granola. Granola is those little brown chips that they put down in the playground so no one will get hurt. It turns out that if you make the chips small enough and add raisins and brown sugar, people will go, "Ooh, granola!" The calories you burn chewing the wood chips helps to balance out the calories put on by the brown sugar. Wood chips are also very healthy in general, because they're high in bark.[12]

There was also an inordinate amount of booths selling some sort of fish. Fish is very healthy, and it's rich in Omega-3, which,

---

12. Like hot dogs.

Some of the Samples at This Year's Kosherfest Had Bugs

as I understand it, is a very healthy amount of Omega. So there were companies selling frozen sushi, Moroccan fish balls, and even some kind of gefilte *meat*, which sounds like a really cool new idea until you realize that it's meat loaf.

So some of the fish wasn't actually fish. But maybe it *seemed* like there was a lot of fish around, because of the smell. There was one booth that had a guy sautéing trout, and you could tell that it was really fresh because people could smell it from three aisles away. But the thing about fish is that even if you love fish, if you're not eating fish at the moment, you don't want to be subjected to the smell. Most people eat fish *despite* the smell. Even the fish themselves aren't crazy about it. They're always swimming up to each other and going, "You can't *smell* that?" That's why they're always making that face.

"Seriously. Take a bath."

"Where? We're in a river!"

And the health craze is extending even to babies. People even want their *babies* to be healthy, if you can believe it.[13] So there were several companies offering organic baby food. "*Organic*" is a word that manufacturers use because it sounds like it could mean "healthy," even though, according to the dictionary, it means, "of or relating to an organism or living entity." So in other words, anything that comes from a plant or animal is technically organic. So organic chicken, for example, is made out of chickens, and regular chicken is made out of...well, something *else*, apparently.[14]

---

13. "Look at all that baby fat! All you do is lie there! And look at your cheeks. Check out how much cheek I can get between my fingers! Great, now you're crying. Don't just cry; do something about it!"

14. Free-range chicken, meanwhile, is chicken that is free to cross roads and such.

WHAT IS THIS — SOME KIND OF JOKE?

There was even one company offering *gourmet* organic baby food, in such dishes as shepherd's pie and pasta bolognese.

Really? My baby eats things off the floor. And it's not even always food.

And speaking of things with nutrients, there was also a *chalav Yisrael* baby formula. I'm a little disappointed that they weren't letting us drink any samples, because that would have made for an interesting article.

SECTION V:
NO SOAP RADIO!
(OR "ANIMALS AND US")

Three elephants are sitting in a bathtub. The first one says, "Can you please pass the soap?" and another one says, "No soap radio!"

I know people who still don't get this joke. And one of them was around back when soap operas actually played on the radio. And those people are probably expecting me to explain it here. But I don't know if I should. I don't want to ruin it. But you should know that it's a really dumb joke designed to embarrass people, and it's not worth getting it. In fact, I would say that the funniest part of that joke is that there are three elephants in a bathtub. That is just a hilarious mental picture. Much better than numbers eating each other.

First of all, there are elephants in a bathtub. I'm not even sure how that made it past the censors. How do you get three elephants into a bathtub? My guess is you lather the sides heavily with soap. That's why there's none left for radio. Whatever that means.

On the other hand, seeing as we live in an age where if you don't understand a joke, you can probably look up the explanation pretty easily, I might as well do it here:

The real "*chapp*" is that it's not a funny joke. There is no punch line, and it doesn't make sense. It's nonsensical enough that it sounds like it *might* be a punch line, and everyone who's laughing is actually in on it, so the one person who doesn't get it gets to feel stupid, and either laughs to pretend he gets it or is ridiculed for not being in on the joke. For not having been at the meeting earlier, I guess. So no one has ever actually laughed at this joke. It's a joke designed to exclude people, unlike the elephants themselves, who agreed to get three of their kind into a bathtub.

In fact, the whole scenario doesn't make sense. First of all, the first elephant did not ask for *soap radio*. He asked for *soap*. So why respond about soap radio? Was the first elephant named "Radio"? You never mentioned that. Was this a catch phrase back in the days of soap radio that I'm not getting?

Second, why does there have to be *three* elephants in the bathtub? The third one doesn't seem to have any dialogue. Why not give the middle guy something to do? Is he just a background character? Is his head under the water?

Also, why are the elephants even in the bathtub? Don't they use their trunks to shower? It doesn't seem worth the hassle of getting them up the stairs is all I'm saying. Maybe a bath *house* would be better. Is it funnier if they were at the *mikvah*?

And why do they have to be elephants?

You know, I'm slowly deciding, based on these famous jokes, that if you want your joke to be really really famous, it has to not be funny. At all. Like people have to wonder how you even intended for it to be funny. Do people just like jokes about animals?

Yes. Yes they do. Animals represent things we want to make fun of about human beings, the only exception being that if we make fun of animals, they don't write in and threaten to stop buying our books. Elephants, for example, are big boned and have long noses. We all know someone like that.

This is why there are a lot of

famous elephant jokes, many of them involving the elephants hiding in strawberry patches. Take this string of jokes, for example:

Q: How many elephants can you fit into a Mini Cooper?

A: Four: two in the front, two in the back.

Q: How many giraffes can you fit into a Mini Cooper?

A: None. It's full of elephants.

Q: How do you know there's an elephant in your refrigerator?

A: There are footprints in the butter.

Q: How do you know there are *two* elephants in your refrigerator?

A: You can hear giggling when the light goes out.

Q: How do you know there are *three* elephants in your refrigerator?

A: No soap radio!

Q: How do you know there are *four* elephants in your refrigerator?

A: There's an empty Mini Cooper parked outside.

But sometimes after hiding in a strawberry patch or the fridge all day, they need a bath. At least to wash their feet.

IF IT LOOKS LIKE A DUCK AND SOUNDS LIKE A DUCK, IT'S PROBABLY A BABY

Purim is here,[1] and it's about time you gave some serious thought to the subject of costumes.

But not *too* serious a thought. I have a friend who takes pictures of his kids in costume sometime before Purim, develops the pictures, makes several copies, and attaches them to his *mishloach manos*, which is *also* themed to match the kids' costumes.[2] Whereas *I'm* not quite organized enough to remember to take pictures of the kids in their costumes *on* Purim. Sometimes I have to do it *after* Purim.

---

1. I don't know when you're reading this book exactly. But Purim was here at some point.

2. I'm not sure why, but I feel the need to point out that he's a therapist. And so is his wife.

If It Looks Like a Duck and Sounds Like a Duck, It's Probably a Baby

"All right, everyone, back in your costume! We forgot to take a picture!"

"But I'm missing half the outfit!"

"Stand behind the others; you'll be OK."

"We can't *all* stand behind each other!"

Kids.

But what kind of costumes do you need? I guess it depends on your kids. Little boys generally want to be something that ends in the letters *M-A-N*, such as a policeman, fireman, mailman, Superman, Haman, etc. (But they don't want to be what their father does for a living. Not a lot of kids want to be a lawyer or a humor writer, even though being a humor writer means you get to wear sweatpants and drink a lot of coffee.) In fact, boys will decide what they want to be, and if it doesn't actually end in *M-A-N*, they will *make* it end in *M-A-N*. One year when I was a kid, I told my mother I wanted to be, quote, "a magic man."[3] Also, a lot of kids say they want to be a workerman, like everyone else doesn't work. The only guys who work are the ones you see at the side of the road, taking four months to patch up a tiny piece of highway, and every time you drive by, they're taking a break. *Those* guys are workermen.[4]

Another thing little boys want is to be able to carry a gun. For most of us, our daily lives require very little use for a gun, except maybe to open the front door when we forget our keys. So if the kid can be, say, an army man (for some reason the word "soldier"

---

3. Then I grew up to be a writer.
4. They drink coffee *without* the sweatpants.

WHAT IS THIS — SOME KIND OF JOKE?

escapes him), that's a double bonus. But if boys had to rank it, the thing they'd want to be most is a fireman.[5]

Why do little boys have such an obsession with being a fire fighter? I guess it's because you get to wear boots when it's not snowing and put your hat on backward and charge *into* a building when everyone else is charging *out*, and you get to slide down poles and climb ladders and play with water and hang from the back of a truck going really fast down city streets.[6] Actually, I guess that *does* sound like fun! Why am *I* just a humor writer?

Little girls, meanwhile, want to be Queen Esther.[7] Their class has a Purim party a few days before Purim, and there are like twenty-four Queen Esthers. It looks like a mini-Queen Esther convention.

If they're not Queen Esther, then they want to be a *kallah*. I can't help but notice, though, that there are so many little *kallah*s on Purim, and so few *chassanim*. It's like a mini *shidduch* crisis. I think it's because when little girls go to a wedding, what impresses them most is the *kallah*. When little boys go to a wedding, what impresses them most is the guy in the middle of the dancing circle with his hat on fire.

Babies, meanwhile, usually get dressed up as some kind of animal, with a hood that looks like the animal's head and a little

---

5. Preferably one with a gun. For getting into burning buildings without keys.

6. Garbage trucks are fun too, but they go like three miles per hour and they keep stopping at every house.

7. Queen Esther was the heroine of the Purim story, who, at great personal sacrifice, married the most *powerful* anti-Semite in the world and stood up to him and the most *cunning* anti-Semite in the world to save the Semites. Even *Queen Esther* didn't want to be Queen Esther.

If It Looks Like a Duck and Sounds Like a Duck, It's Probably a Baby

button on the baby's chest that makes animal noises.[8] Not that the baby has any idea why everyone is laughing and pointing at him. One year, my wife and I got our newborn a costume that looked like an ice cream cone. It had a little cherry hat, and instead of two separate legs, both of the baby's feet went inside the pointed cone. It was very cute until we realized that there was no way we would be able to strap him into his car seat.

But generally, what really determines what your kid is going to be is whether you're buying the costumes or making them yourself. Because there are certain costumes that are easier to put together. It's just a question of convincing your kids that this is what they really want to be. We'd suggest adding an *M-A-N* to its name in your argument.

"Don't you want to be a bakers-man?"

Bakers are a popular option with mothers who put their own costumes together, because they're pretty easy.[9] You just make a hat out of cardboard, put on a huge apron, and maybe draw a curly moustache on the kid's face, because apparently, most bakers have huge curly moustaches, so they have something to scratch their noses with when they have both hands in the dough.

Another popular option with mothers is to dress their daughter as an old lady. It's the same as a regular lady, but with a cane. (Like all old people use canes.) Also, they put a kerchief on their head instead of a snood. Yes, snoods have been around for like thirty years, but if you're a little old lady, there's no way you bought a

---

8. But does not make the costume laundry safe.
9. For starters, the kid doesn't actually have to bake anything.

WHAT IS THIS — SOME KIND OF JOKE?

new head covering since the '80s, right? And you're still wearing the same enormous glasses you got as a little girl.

Also, a lot of mothers like to dress their kids up as clowns, even though research has shown that over 100 percent of children don't like clowns. Clowns act weird; they have big, floppy feet; they squirt water at you; their hair looks like they slept in it; and they try to fit too many of their kind in a car. They're like teenagers, but smiling. Is that what you want your kid to be? Never mind trying to put a full face worth of makeup on an excited child. And good luck getting those face prints off the couch cushions.

Another popular option with mothers is to get a cardboard box out of the recycling, and do something with *that*. If your kid is willing to wear a cardboard box, he can be a *pushke*, a box of cereal, a computer, a sukkah, a gift, a pair of shoes, a robot, a jack-in-the-box, a garbage can, a coffin, a stove, a running refrigerator, and a cardboard box from the recycling.

Whereas if you're buying the costumes, it really depends on what sort of costumes were on sale at the beginning of November.[10] Because there's no reason to pay full price for an outfit that the kids are going to wear for one day.

Not even one day. They'll wear it for a couple of hours in the morning, and by the time you're back from delivering *mishloach manos*, the mask will be gone forever. The mask is the first thing to come off, because mask-designers have no idea how far apart a kid's eyes are, so after a few tries at blindly stumbling out of the car and tripping over the sidewalk, the kid just decides "forget it," and the mask disappears into somebody's *rebbi's* house. If there's

---

10. Do gentiles go shopping for costumes the day after Purim? I should look into that.

If It Looks Like a Duck and Sounds Like a Duck, It's Probably a Baby

no mask, the *beard* is the first thing to come off. (Fake beards are incredibly itchy. This is why so few rabbis have fake beards.) Then a short while later, the gloves will come off, then the jacket, and by the time you get to the *seudah*, you aren't even able to tell what the kid is supposed to be.

"What are you?"

"I'm Haman! Can't you see the moustache?"

And it's not like the kids can even really wear the costumes the next year. Most costumes are so cheaply made that you're afraid to wash them, so you put them in a box in the attic, as if twelve months of being crunched up in a ball will get rid of the sweat and the spilled juice. And the attic smell.

And then there's the question of whether anyone will see the costume in the first place, especially on a year like this one,[11] where Purim is very early. (It basically falls out Chanukah time.) There's no way that these flimsy costumes are going to keep anybody warm, so most kids will end up walking around glumly with coats on over their costumes.

"I'm Haman! Can't you see the moustache?"

The good thing about being a grown-up, though, is that even if it's blustery cold, you get to decide if you're going to wear a coat. Like a few years ago, I decided I wouldn't wear a coat. And boy was I wrong.

Purim was on a Friday that year, and I wore what I usually wear on a Friday Purim — a bathrobe over rolled-up pant legs, a towel around my neck, flip-flops, and a shower cap. The basic joke is that

---

11. 2010, I think.

WHAT IS THIS — SOME KIND OF JOKE?

I'm in middle of getting ready for Shabbos.[12] But one year it was very cold, and of course, since it was Friday, a lot of people weren't home,[13] so I spent a lot of time standing outside and waiting for people to not answer their door so I could leave their packages for them to come home to after Shabbos, weather permitting.[14] My feet and legs were dark red, and I barely had time to ACTUALLY get ready for Shabbos afterward. My wife was like, "I don't understand. You've been wearing that bathrobe all day."

The first year that I wore my robe, it wasn't a Friday. I was in yeshivah, and I'd had five minutes to come up with a costume using only things I could find in my dorm room so that we could leave to go collecting already. And it was either wear the robe or wear all of my clothing backward, which I did not want to do because I had no idea how I would get my button-down shirt buttoned.

Most of the other guys had costumes that they had bought piecemeal at the local thrift shop — a pair of pants for two dollars, a jacket for a dollar fifty, etc.; the basic message being, "Look at me! I'm wearing different colors than I usually wear! I hope this was cleaned before I bought it!" Because who *knows* what kind of people wore those outfits firsthand. The kind of person who pays full price for these things *new*, who walks into the store and says, "Hey, this is a great suit! Orange and corduroy! I'll sit down on my couch, and no one will even know I'm there! This will go great with my flip-flops!"

---

12. I don't know what's up with the shower cap. I have to take it off when I get up to my hair.

13. When Purim is a Friday, everyone eats supper in the morning.

14. Everything that was supposed to be refrigerated was *fine*. It was cold.

If It Looks Like a Duck and Sounds Like a Duck, It's Probably a Baby

But when it comes to adults, there are basically two schools of thought. There is the school of men whose costumes consist of a tie with a palm tree on it, or else they wear their wife's old *sheitel*.

"You spent four figures on this. *Someone* should get some more use out of it."

And then there are the men who ascribe to the "There's no rule against grown men dressing up" way of life. Because there isn't. But they *should* bear in mind that while it's cute to see a kid dressed up, I think the media doesn't publicize Purim as much as they could. This is something one of my friends, who lives in Manhattan, realized on Purim as he, dressed as a hobo, got onto the subway with a little shopping cart piled with some nicely-wrapped food baskets featuring wine. No one wanted to sit next to him.

And do you have any idea how hard it is to drive in an inflatable costume?

Women, for the most part, don't dress up; their job is to stand around looking embarrassed for their husbands, or to carry around the *mishloach manos* that their husbands can't hold because they need their hands free for their costumes: "I can't hold the cane *and* all the *manos*!"

The interesting thing, though, is that the boys are all dying to be "men," and the men are trying really hard to be boys. Purim sure is backward.

NOT AN EXACT SCIENCE

Welcome to our latest installment of "What Are Those Kooky Scientists Up To *Now*?" where we look in on scientists around the world and try to figure out what on earth they're doing, in an effort to study the drawbacks of sitting around a lab all day and squinting at things that are either too small or too far away.

Our first story today comes from Iran (by camel), where scientists are making tremendous advances in the field of sending tiny confused creatures up into space.

"Iran has scientists?"

Yeah! Apparently so!

A short while ago, they sent up a ten-foot spaceship containing a mouse, two turtles, and a handful of worms. Personally, I wonder why they decided on those creatures specifically. It's like they put

Not an Exact Science

in the mouse and the turtles, and they were like, "There's still room in the rocket. Oh, look! Worms!"

Iranian officials, in an effort to explain this to the world, said that this experiment shows that Iran can defeat the west in a battle of technology.

Yes, it definitely does. You're exactly where *we* were seventy years ago, when we were putting dogs and monkeys into test rockets.

They also say that the experiment was a success, and that the animals got back down safely, although this hasn't actually been proven. For all we know, there are little tiny worms floating around in the atmosphere.

Iranian scientists say that in about ten years, they will be able to put a man into space. They weren't specific about which man, but logic tells us it's Ahmadinejad.[15]

United States defense experts, meanwhile, are saying that there was no scientific purpose in the Iranians sending these creatures up into space, because they're nothing like humans. They say that, most likely, the Iranians are developing rocket technology so they could, in ten years, use it to fire missiles. But Iranian scientists are claiming that these creatures are indeed providing them with valuable data, presumably because their humans share more in common with rodents, reptiles, and worms.

And in the meantime, United States scientists are saying that in about ten years, space tourism will be the biggest thing. So it's nice

---

15. Ahmadinejad was the leader of Iran for a while. He was in the news, claiming the Holocaust never happened, and then media just stopped talking about him. So he probably never happened.

WHAT IS THIS — SOME KIND OF JOKE?

to know that when we do get up there to our bungalow colonies, there will be mice.

But it's not like the Iranians are the only ones experimenting with mice. NASA scientists recently succeeded in getting a mouse to float up in the air, using a magnet that was powerful enough to counteract the pull of gravity. The scientists said that they want to simulate the conditions of outer space, and figure out what would happen to humans.

No they don't. They just want to see if they could get a mouse to float. Be honest. If they wanted to use test subjects that were closer to humans, they would be levitating monkeys. The truth is that the scientific community has *always* been experimenting on the mouse community, but this goes largely unnoticed because the mice don't speak up. For example, look at these recent headlines, absolutely none of which I am making up:

"MICE CLONED FROM FROZEN BODIES"

"SCIENTISTS BRING SIXTEEN-YEAR-OLD FROZEN MOUSE BACK TO LIFE"

"SCIENTISTS GROW REPLACEMENT TEETH IN MICE"

"SCIENTISTS TRIGGER HAIR GROWTH IN MICE"

"JAPANESE SCIENTISTS CREATE FEARLESS MOUSE"

"SCIENTISTS CREATE MICE WITH HUMAN BRAIN CELLS"

"GENETICALLY-ENGINEERED SUPER MOUSE STUNS SCIENTISTS"

(That last article was about a mouse they created that can run nonstop for five hours, live longer, have children well into old age, and eat more without getting fat.)

Not an Exact Science

Is that what we need? Super-fast, super-smart, tremendously-hairy mice that have extra teeth and are not scared of us? Floating around in our kitchen? And then we need to clone *more* of them? What are we going to do with all of these mice?

Maybe we should send them to Iran as a gift for their space program.

Sure, once in a while the mice are used in a study that can directly benefit humanity. For example, scientists in Florida have recently discovered — based on extensive experiments wherein they exposed mice to cell phones for two hours per day for about nine months — that cell phone radiation is not only not harmful to the brain, but it can actually help cure maladies such as Alzheimer's. But of course, to get the same results in humans, you'd need years of exposure and an *enormous* cell phone. Like one from the '80s.

But why do they conduct all these other experiments on mice? Why not an animal we can actually *use*, such as sheep?

OK, so they do conduct the occasional experiment on sheep. For example, a recent study in Scotland, concluded in 2009, reveals that some sheep are shrinking by 3.5 ounces every year.

I don't know about you, but I'd like to know what prompted them to do this study. Was someone going, "Yeah, they're definitely shrinking! You don't see it? It's got to be at least a thousandth of an ounce per day! Just look! Don't blink!" But I'm assuming they conducted the study to benefit humans. "How can we get *humans* to lose three and a half ounces every year?"

What they eventually discovered, after spending twenty-four years weighing and cataloguing all the sheep every summer, one at a time, was that, because summers are getting longer and winters

WHAT IS THIS — SOME KIND OF JOKE?

are getting shorter, the sheep don't have to beef up as much to survive the winter, and the smaller sheep are actually living longer and having more children. In the twenty-four years of the study, the average sheep went from 66 to 61 pounds.

I know, right?

Sadly, though, I don't think this study will really benefit humans, because even *smaller* humans generally survive the winter, due to the fact that, even during the winter, we have supermarkets. Unfortunately, thanks to supermarkets, there are no longer any smaller people. So that's twenty-four years well spent.

In other science news, Osama bin Laden[16] has recently released a tape in which he said, based on his intense scientific research of sitting around in a cave in middle of the desert, that global warming is real, and that it is all the United States's fault.

Wow! What are the chances that he'd actually get something *right* for once? We *know* it's our fault! We've been saying that for *years*! Not that he has anything to complain about. It's going to be much hotter where *he's* going.

Also, there is still plenty of room to say that global warming is a myth. Florida, for example, is currently having their coldest winter ever, with temperatures plunging to 36 degrees. They have to go out and buy coats and ice scrapers and everything.

But the ones really having a hard time are the animals. There are a lot of iguanas down there who like to climb trees because they're sick of people almost stepping on them and then running

---

16. Osama bin Laden was a terrorist mastermind who would, from time to time, broadcast videos from his cave in Afghanistan, whereas I can't get my cell phone to work in certain parts of the house.

Not an Exact Science

away screaming. But it turns out that when the temperature drops below 40 degrees, iguanas go into a sort of hibernation, where they basically freeze solid and fall asleep. And rain down from the trees.

As you can imagine, this isn't very pleasant for the *people* either. Maybe we should figure out how to levitate the iguanas.

In fact, according to a news article, one man was driving around, picking them up, and throwing them into the back of his station wagon so he could sell them as pets without having to go through the ordeal of trying to catch them. But it turns out that the interior of his station wagon was warmer than 40 degrees, and all the iguanas suddenly came back to life while he was doing 65 on the interstate. And they weren't very happy.

So it turns out that global warming might not actually be a global phenomenon, and we have to question what gave Osama the idea that it *was*. Maybe he noticed that all of his sheep were shrinking.

NO FLIES WERE HARMED IN THE MAKING OF THIS ARTICLE

This week, I would like to write about a topic that is weighing heavily on everybody's mind — a topic that is so prevalent in today's society that it just begs to be addressed. Unfortunately, I can't concentrate long enough to come up with one, because this blasted housefly keeps bothering me.

He's been pestering me for three weeks. It's only one fly,[17] but whenever I sit down to work, there he is — landing on me, whooshing by my ear, going from one side of the room to the other directly through my line of vision... Right now, he's walking around on my computer screen. What does he *want*? Is he reading this? Does he know I'm talking about him? I'm going to try something; bear with me for a second.

---

17. I assume. He looks like the same fly.

No Flies Were Harmed in the Making of This Article

GO AWAY!

OK, that didn't work. Three weeks! I don't know what to do anymore.

The first couple of times this fly bothered me, I just ignored it. I thought I'd read somewhere that flies only have a twenty-four-hour lifespan. But then how do I still have a fly bothering me after three weeks? Does this mean that for the past twenty-one fly lifetimes, generation after generation of flies have been teaching their children to specifically come bother me?

"But why, Daddy?"

"Because that's what we've always done. My father did it his whole life, and his father before him. When my great-great-grandfather came to this house, he had only the wings on his back, and he went out there and bothered this guy from morning to night. And he had to fly three feet in the heat, both ways. Now be quiet and finish your garbage."

But then I looked it up, and I found that the type of fly that lives for one day is actually the mayfly, which is related to the dragonfly, so I'm glad I don't have one of *those* in my house, or there'd be a Mordechai-shaped hole in the front door.[18] Houseflies, as it turns out, can live for up to a month, even if you spray them with Raid.

Now I want to take a moment to assure you, my readers, that I do not just wantonly kill Hashem's creatures. Like most people, I have no problem with Hashem's creatures, unless they keep sitting

---

18. "Don't make a Mordechai-shaped hole in the door!" my wife would yell. "You're letting the bugs in!"

WHAT IS THIS — SOME KIND OF JOKE?

on my hand. There are only so many times I'm willing to slap myself.

It's gotten to the point that I'm even thinking about using one of my flyswatters. A few months ago, I was in my local kosher supermarket, and I found a package of three plastic flyswatters. Now my first question, of course, was, who needs three flyswatters? If you have such a big fly problem that three separate family members need to use a flyswatter at the *same time*, you should probably just call somebody. Also, I've never really believed in spending money on flyswatters when I can use whatever I have handy, such as a book or a shoe.

Before we sell our house, we're going to have to do a lot of painting and spackling.

My point is that normally, I never would have bought even *one* flyswatter, let alone a package of *three*. But the thing about these flyswatters was that they came in three different colors: red, blue, and green. And I thought it was hilarious that people need separate flyswatters for *fleishig*, *milchig*, and pareve.

I guess it kind of makes sense, though. If a fly lands on your meat, you want to hit it with a *red* flyswatter; and if it's on your cheese, you'd want to hit it with the *blue* one. Maybe you should stop leaving your food out.

But in this country, the law is that if a humor columnist sees a package of *milchig*, *fleishig*, and pareve flyswatters for ninety-nine cents, he has to buy them. So I did, and I keep them on the wall over my desk, as a reminder of how easy we Jews have it nowadays. Our fathers had to use the same flyswatter for all three genders, and you have no idea how many *she'eilos* that caused.

No Flies Were Harmed in the Making of This Article

My point, though, is that I've never opened the package, because that would ruin the integrity of the joke. So maybe I should just —

Hang on; the fly is back. He just landed on the keyboard. He's just standing there, brazenly rubbing his hind legs together. How does he do that?[19]

OK, here goes. Nobody make any sudden moves. I'm just going to remove my shoe, v-e-r-y s-l-o-w-l-y, raise the shoe over my head v-e-r-y g-e-n-t-l-y, and fglihedfuilVE98RTREGEGRDTHREFUGH6843634

Did I get it? I feel like I didn't get it.

I don't believe this. I read somewhere that a fly's average speed is 4.5 miles per hour. Why are they so hard to — What was that? Is it in my EAR?

No, there it is. It's back. Why does it keep coming back? You'd think that if someone tried to kill you with a shoe, you'd maybe keep your distance for a little while. Especially if this person had THREE flyswatters hanging over his desk.

Oh, wait, he lef — No, he's back now.

Why does he do this? He reminds me of my eleven-month-old son, Gedalyah, who just recently learned to crawl, and he is almost always under my desk. He has a whole closet full of toys at the opposite end of this room, and every single one of them is on the floor, yet he insists on sitting directly under my chair, even though he's slightly taller than the bottom of the seat. He crawls over, and I feel something on my legs, and then there's a slight BUMP! that makes my skin cringe, even though Gedalyah himself doesn't seem to feel it, and then he goes under my desk (where there's

---

19. And *why?*

WHAT IS THIS — SOME KIND OF JOKE?

slightly more headroom), sits on my foot, and pulls out wires. I have to fight him every time I want to move the mouse. When he's not under my desk, he's standing next to me, wiping his nose on the side of my pants and trying to type. And whenever I pick him up and put him on the other side of the room, he just follows me back to my desk, and the cycle starts again: Pitter patter pitter patter BUMP! Pitter patter SIT! YANK YANK TANGLE TANGLE pitter patter WIPE! TYPE TYPE — "Gedalyah, cut it out! Want to go play with your toys?" Pitter patter...

Usually, what I do with my son is I give him cookies. I keep a package of cookies on the other side of my desk, far from the mouse and just out of his reach. So when he comes over, he heads straight for the cookies, and then he stands there going "Uh! Uh!" until I give him one. Then he eats it and comes right back. He eats cookies all day long, but at least it keeps him out from under my desk.

Should I do the same thing with the fly? Should I keep some rotting fruit on the other side of the room so the fly goes there instead? If I do that, it's just going to bring in *more* flies. The strategy only works for babies. It's not like if I put cookies on my desk, I'm going to get more babies.[20]

So I really can't compare flies to babies. And anyway, the fly is far more interested in what I have going on *inside* my keyboard. It sits on the keys, trying to figure out a way to get in. There's a lot of good stuff in there, because my son eats cookies and then touches the keyboard to get my attention until I give him more.

---

20. "Where are all these babies coming from? ... Mordechai, you left the door open again!"

No Flies Were Harmed in the Making of This Article

So what do I do about it? I could wait another week for it to die of old age. Or else I can bring in something that kills flies, such as spiders. And then I'd have to bring in frogs to get rid of the spiders. And what kills frogs? Exterminators. And then I'd have a houseful of exterminators, and how do I get rid of *them*?

Cookies.

SECTION VI:
TO SEE TIME FLY
(OR "SIMPLE ENTERTAINMENT")

It's the oldest joke in the book:

Q: Why did the boy throw his clock out the window?

A: He wanted to see time fly.

The things some people will do for a little entertainment.

I've thrown clocks out the window, but it wasn't to see time fly. They were all alarm clocks. And I didn't accomplish much, because they were all still plugged in. And the windows were closed.

But that would have been my *first* answer.

This joke isn't funny, though. "To see time fly. Get it? I guess you had to be there."

Why would someone want to see time *fly*? Time flying is *bad*.

Sure, we say, "Time flies when you're having fun," but that doesn't mean that time flying is *fun*. It means the fun is *over*. You're not "having fun when time flies," "time flies when you're having fun." The time flying doesn't cause the fun. The expression means that life, and especially the fun parts, goes by too fast.

And let's say this kid was right — when time flies, you're having fun. Was *he* having fun?

"Woo hoo! My clock's flying out the window! This is so much fu — OK, it landed. It's over. That was quick... I guess time flies when you're having fun.

"Also, I need a new clock. I wonder if time flies when you're buying a new clock. I bet it does. I have no frame of reference until I get home and plug it in."

The truth is, I guess there *are*

times when you want to see time fly — when you want to *force* time to fly. Maybe the question should be, "Why did the boy throw his clock out the window *during class*?" Though chances are that if his teacher saw him throw his clock out the window, he'd get kicked out, and his wish would come true. Class would be over. For him at least.

Point is, this section is about entertainment. But don't be too entertained, or time will fly.

NOT TO BE USED AS A FLOTATION DEVICE

We're very excited about our new bathroom fixture, and here's why: it came in a LOT of bubble wrap.

People love popping bubble wrap. It's a great American pastime, like talking about losing weight and waddling around foreign countries looking for restaurants. It's the kind of thing that people can spend a good few hours doing, and then they turn around and go, "Well, *that* was time well spent."

Sure, there are other uses for bubble wrap, such as protecting things during shipping. Also, you can wrap everything in your house that is less than a foot off the ground, so that you will never stub your toe again. There are even bubble wrap displays in some art museums, and I have to say, thank goodness I don't go to art museums. I don't think I would be able to stop myself from touching those displays.

WHAT IS THIS — SOME KIND OF JOKE?

So yes, a lot of us enjoy popping bubble wrap, but none of us knows why. None of us really *cares* why either. But psychologists, who get *paid* to care, believe that it acts as some sort of stress reliever.

Like let's say you're working in an office, and you get a shipment of toner, and you're very stressed out because you've put it in and the printer still says that you need new toner. So you try turning the printer on and off and opening and closing all the little doors and taking the toner in and out a few times, and it *still* says you're out of toner.[1] So you take out the new cartridge and put the old one back in to see if it makes a difference, and it does not, so you take that one out too, and now you've forgotten which one is the new one and which is the old one, but it doesn't really make a difference because no matter what you do, the printer is still absolutely sure that neither one has toner. So you grab the printer and heave it through the window, which you did not realize was not open. And now you're stressed because you have to order a *new* printer, which probably will not have toner either. So what do you do? You pick up the little bit of bubble wrap that the toner came wrapped in, and you *pop pop pop* your bad feelings away, until all those in your office are so irritated by the sudden draft and the fact that they still can't print anything and the incessant popping noise that... Well, who cares? Let them order their *own* toner.

It's thanks to addictions like these that Sealed Air Corporation, the company that originally invented bubble wrap, has an excuse to make enough of it every year to, according to their press materials, "stretch all the way to the moon and back."

---

1. What does it WANT? You can't very well put in two toners.

Not to Be Used as a Flotation Device

Now I'm not entirely sure why they would want to do that, but I'm definitely on board with it. It sounds like a lot of fun.

Sealed Air Corporation recently celebrated the 50th anniversary of bubble wrap, which was invented by Marc Chavannes and Al Fielding in a two-car garage in New Jersey in the late 1950s. (Yes, we know that's more than fifty years ago. Hang on.) They originally invented it to be some sort of textured wallpaper.

Imagine if bubble wrap would have actually made it as wallpaper. It would be great for your kids' room, so they don't hurt themselves when they're jumping on the bed. On the other hand, if you papered their room with bubble wrap, they would NEVER go to sleep at night. You'd be lying in your bed, listening to the *pop pop pop pop pop*.

"GO TO SLEEP!!!"

"I *am* sleeping!"

So it never really took off as wallpaper. But Al and Marc were not daunted; they decided that they would figure out some kind of use for it. But what? They had no idea.

But then one day, in 1960 (see?), Marc was on a plane, landing at Newark Airport, when he noticed that the clouds were lumpy, kind of like his wallpaper, and that they seemed to be cushioning the plane, so it wouldn't get injured during travel. Then he thought about his own belongings, which were crammed into the overhead compartment behind someone's full-sized sleeper sofa and a (hopefully) deceased water buffalo that the woman in front of him had spent a half hour jamming in there after he had carefully put his stuff in. And then he thought about the clouds, and about his wallpaper. And then his ears started popping.

WHAT IS THIS — SOME KIND OF JOKE?

In those days, when people wanted to ship things, they used crumpled newspaper. Everyone had plenty of newspaper, but the downside was that you couldn't lie about when you sent things.

"Yeah, I don't know why it got to you so late. I sent it last month!"

"Are you sure? It's wrapped in yesterday's newspaper."

Also, once the shipments got to where they were going, there was nothing for the recipient to do with the newspaper besides read it, or throw it around the room like students do with their test papers. Nevertheless, to this day, a lot of people still keep piles of newspapers near their front door, in case they suddenly have to ship something at a moment's notice, and bubble wrap suddenly goes out of style like 1950s novelty wallpaper.

But what's interesting (and I use the term "interesting" very loosely) is that bubble wrap is still around, and it's used more now than ever before, what with the fact that we keep ordering tiny, expensive things by mail, plus shlepping and handling. And not only that, but even with the allure of the digital world, people still turn to bubble wrap. There is even an application that you can get for your phone or iPod that allows you to pop fake bubbles on the screen. Unless your method of popping involves putting the sheet down on the floor and stomping on it.

But my point is that if it were wallpaper, it would be relegated to the subject of humor columns by now. ("Hey, remember when people had bubbles on the wall?" "Yeah. Hanging up pictures was fun!")

People don't think about what goes into making bubble wrap. If I would work at a bubble wrap plant, I would never get anything done. I would get called into my boss's office, and he'd

Not to Be Used as a Flotation Device

go, "Mordechai (assuming that's my real name), our records show that you've made more sheets this month than anyone else here, but also that every single bubble is flat. Why is that?" And I'd go, "I don't know, sir (*pop pop pop*), but now that they're thinner, aren't they easier to ship to our customers?"

Speaking of which, how DO they ship bubble wrap? What do they pack it in? Styrofoam peanuts? That wouldn't be a good statement for their business. They probably pack it in *more* bubble wrap, but of a different-size bubble, so the customer knows when to stop unwrapping. He rips off the wrapping, throws it into the corner, and then does a double take. "Hey! Free bubble wrap!"

Personally, I think these guys were geniuses. They figured out a way to sell people *air*. Tiny plastic packages of *air*. This was way before someone figured out you could also do this with water. And what's the first thing we do when we get bubble wrap? Open as many of the tiny packages as we can and let the air free.

But the *plastic* is forever. Years from now, archeologists are going to find flat, popped sheets of bubble wrap, and they're not going to have any clue what we used it for.

I bet they're going to think it was wallpaper.

HAVING A BALL

I should have figured, when I bought my six-year-old son, Daniel, a football for his *afikoman* present, that he would want me to play catch with him.

I've been trying to avoid this day for years, and not because, as an adult (at least as far as clothing size), I have no desire to chase the ball around on the ground.

I also was not trying to avoid it because I don't want to spend time with my son. I *love* spending time with my kids that doesn't involve counting to three or telling someone to pick something up. I do homework with them; I read them books and don't complain that, out of the literally hundreds of children's books that we own, they always want me to read the same five books; and I play board games that require me to crawl under something called a "Trick-a-ma-stick"; and games that require me to collect colored pieces

Having a Ball

of fake jewelry and put them on and forget to take them off when someone comes to the door.

No, the reason I was trying to avoid playing sports with my kids was that I'd always hoped not to have to show them how much I stink.

I've never been very athletic. I did play some sports as a child, mostly in summer camp, because the rule was that if you were in camp, you had to play sports, or else the teams would be mismatched. My argument was that any team that had me on it was *already* mismatched.

When I played baseball, for example, I would always stand way out in left field, because that was a good position to play if what you wanted to do was watch airplanes. Occasionally, the ball would come near me, and I'd have to go chase it, which I dreaded, because I had no idea what to do with the ball once I was holding it. It probably would have been a good investment on the counselors' part, since they were always putting me in left field, to actually take me to the side and tell me, "Look, once you get the ball, you throw it to *that* guy." So I'd be standing there, holding the ball, and everyone would be yelling, "Throw it! Throw it!" And I would yell, "WHERE?" and no one would answer, and five or six runners would score.

In addition, I never saw the appeal of crawling through prickly bushes and under parked cars to chase a ball that I didn't even want in the first place. If you ask me, I think the ball was trying just as hard to escape and be free. So to help the ball out, I never actually threw it to anybody. I just hurled it in a random direction, and went back to looking at airplanes.

I also never understood how some guys could be so into sports

WHAT IS THIS — SOME KIND OF JOKE?

that they were willing to purposely injure themselves. Whenever I played soccer (I liked soccer, because, even though I never actually made contact with the ball, I realized that as long as I ran along with everyone else, no one would know the difference), I noticed that there was one kid in my bunk — *Natti*, I think his name was — who would bounce the ball on his head. Why did he do this? As far as I could tell, it never helped him score. Did he think that, if he ever twisted his ankle, that he could just crawl around on the field, and knock the ball with his head?[2]

It's not like my father never tried to teach me. Once in a while, he would drag me out to the middle of a field, and then he'd throw a ball at me, and I, of course, would duck. And then I'd have to run after it. Then I would throw it to him and miss spectacularly, and I would have to go off and chase it again so I could hand it to him.

"Don't *hand* it to me," he would say. "*Throw* it to me." Which was silly. It was obviously far more efficient for me to walk up and hand it to him. And actually, in my opinion, if he wanted the ball so badly, he could just keep it. (This was my opinion about almost all sports. "Why don't they just buy a second ball?" I think a lot of these games started during the Great Depression.) So it was really just a lot of my father standing in one place and me chasing the ball around until he got tired of watching me, and then I'd be free to go back to the swings.

So yes, I do a lot of things with my kids, but I was hoping that showing them how much I stunk at sports would not be one of

---

2. I should probably mention here that Natti is 1. Israeli, and 2. currently some sort of rabbi. You never know which kids are gonna be the rabbis.

Having a Ball

them. And then I went and had three boys. What were the chances that they'd all be as uncoordinated as me?

So far, chances aren't very good. Daniel, my oldest son, is incredibly into sports, and for his *afikoman* present, at his request, I got him a football.[3] And then I thought I would be done with it, and he'd stop bugging me. No way. Not more than two minutes after we got home, he started asking me to play catch with him. These kids are never happy.

I don't know what Daniel is thinking. I don't know if he doesn't care that I'm bad, or if he, like all kids, assumes that inside every adult is a person who is good at sports. We've all heard the *Journeys* song about the *rebbi* that is secretly good at sports, but keeps it under his hat (literally) until Lag B'Omer, when he wins the game for his students, and they're so impressed that they turn right around and start paying attention in class.[4] Come to think of it, maybe *my* students would start paying attention in my high school English class[5] if I could show them that I'm secretly good at basketball. I hope they aren't reading this column.

The truth is that I have a lot of knowledge of weird subjects, but this isn't one of them. I've evolved to the point where, when the ball comes toward me, I can anticipate where it's going to be and stick my hand out in approximately the correct general direction, so that, most of the time, the ball will ricochet off my hand. But I assume this is not what my son wants me to teach him. I think he wants me to teach him how to hold the ball (from what I've heard,

---

3. For the benefit of my British readers: I got him a soccer.
4. For like the last month of the school year.
5. I'm a high school English teacher, apparently.

WHAT IS THIS — SOME KIND OF JOKE?

you hold it like you hold a baby — I'm guessing over your shoulder while patting it on the back), and how to throw it so it spins (not like a baby), and where to put your fingers in relation to the stitching. I have no idea. I don't even know why, in today's day and age, the thing needs stitching in the first place. Most other balls don't have stitching. Also, all other balls are round. Who designed this thing?

Now I bet a lot of you are thinking that I'm writing this article solely so I can say to my son, "Sorry, can't play now. Can't you see I'm writing an article?" But I'm not. I actually went outside and played catch with him.

And guess what? He didn't notice that I was bad, because he's not better than me yet. And my four-year-old, Heshy, was more than happy to be my helper, and run around retrieving the ball and handing it to me. And my baby, Gedalyah, was content to sit on the sidelines and laugh whenever the ball almost hit him in the face. So, thanks to sports, I got to spend time with all of my sons on three different levels at the same time! What a great bonding activity!

Nuts.

WANNA SEE A PLAY?

I'm very excited that my son Daniel finally had his school *Chumash* play. And not because he started learning *Chumash*. He started that months ago. I'm excited that, after his two kindergarten graduations, his Pre-1A-End-of-the-Year Ceremony, his siddur play, and now his *Chumash* play, I don't think I'm going to have to go to another play of his at least until he starts mishnayos. I'm guessing.

Perhaps you feel this way too. You have nothing against school plays per se, but you've already heard all of your son's lines. You've heard them over and over again for the past couple of weeks, often at the top of his lungs, usually after he was supposed to be asleep. So why are you there? To hear the *other* kids sing?

But you go anyway, and you sit in a room full of parents who are no more interested in seeing *your* kid perform than *you* are in seeing *their* kid perform. Not that you can see anything anyway,

WHAT IS THIS — SOME KIND OF JOKE?

because all of the enthusiastic parents in the front row are standing up, so you're spending the better part of the performance staring at their backs. You do catch occasional glimpses of your child, and for some reason, even though you'd made sure he left the house in his nicest Shabbos clothes, somehow, in the half hour since you dropped him off, he managed to get stains on his shirt in at least three different colors, has a single strand of *tzitzis* poking out of his waistband, and when he sits down on the stage, he does so in a way that his pant legs ride up around his knees. Also, he's making weird faces. And you figure that all the other parents are whispering, "Who dressed that kid? And why is he grimacing?"[6]

But finally your son gets up there, and even though he has *two lines*, and even though you know he knows them, and even though you know them so well that you can get up there and pin a letter of the *aleph-beis* to *your* shirt and sing them yourself, he gets up there and does nothing. He just stands there. If you're lucky, the *rebbi* will have given each set of lines to *two* kids, and the other kid will bellow out his lines and not even notice that your son is just spacing out in the general direction of the audience. And then you, as a good parent, have to get up and take a picture of that. Or you can get up, along with the *other* kid's father, and he will take a picture and you won't.[7]

Why did your son freeze? It's your *own* fault, really. You spent weeks psyching him up for this:

---

6. Thankfully, a lot of the time, the teacher has helpfully pinned a picture or a letter of the *aleph-beis* to each child's shirt to divert the attention from his pant legs.

7. Like father like son.

Wanna See a Play?

"You're going to sing nice and loud, right? Because Mommy and Totty are going to be there, and maybe even Bubby and Zaidy."

So the kids picture in their heads that they're going to have to perform in front of an audience of maybe four people. Then they come out there and see a room full of strangers. They have no way of knowing that these people are actually the parents of the other kids. For all they know, these people just walked in off the street.

("Hey! Wanna go see a play?")

So your child stands up, in front of a sea of people he doesn't know, and decides not to sing, because he doesn't want to draw attention to himself. Only what the child doesn't realize is that the only thing the other parents are going to remember, aside from their *own* child, is the kid who refused to sing and had to be carried off the stage in tears, so that for the rest of the play, the *aleph-beis* was missing a letter.

And then each child gets called up one at a time, and his parents have to stand up to take a picture of him shaking hands with his *rebbi* and his principal and the guy who shlepped the *Chumashim* up to the stage. I'm usually pretty good about that, but this time we forgot to bring our camera, and we didn't realize until it was too late. Fortunately, phones these days take pictures, so I was able to use my phone, even though my phone in particular does *not* take pictures. It barely makes phone calls. But no one else knew that. I stood there, pointed my phone at my son, pushed a button, made a show of squinting at the screen, and sat back down. The things a parent does so as not to embarrass his child.

In retrospect, maybe I should have borrowed a camera from one of the other parents.

WHAT IS THIS — SOME KIND OF JOKE?

In all honesty, the only thing I remember from my own *Chumash* play is the nosh. Besides for being the day that I got my first *Chumash*, it was also the day I had my first cup of soda.

I had tried soda before, but I didn't get beyond my first sip, because the bubbles tickled my nose. So I was very hesitant when I came in and saw that the table was set for each kid, and that everyone had a cup of soda. Then we sat down, and we weren't allowed to touch our food until the principal finished his speech.

So I was sitting there, waiting for the speech to be over, and I saw that the kid next to me was making a face. I don't know how to describe it — it was kind of like a teeth-baring smile, except the corners of his mouth weren't turned upward *or* downward. It was like the face you make when your wife asks you to step on a bug, and you do, and then you remember that you're not wearing shoes. I kind of ignored it for a while, because parents kept snapping pictures of us, and I thought he just had a very weird smile. But then it was ten minutes later, and he was still doing it. So I asked him what was up with his face.

He told me that he'd heard that if you make this face right before you drink soda, the bubbles won't tickle your nose as much. (This is true. In fact, if you do it for an hour or more, it will probably seem like there are no bubbles at all.) This sounded like a great idea, so I did it too. And so did half our table. So any picture that was snapped of us during the second half of that speech has a bunch of kids making weird faces.

That's what I remember of my *Chumash* play. I don't remember my performance. But I *do* remember the performance at my eighth grade graduation. We performed something called a cantata, which is a Spanish word meaning "really old poem." Everyone was

Wanna See a Play?

assigned two lines of the poem, which we would try to say as fast as we could so the spotlight would move on to the next guy. My lines followed my friend Yehuda, whose lines went something like this:

"Bira dishasis minei maya — *Into the pit from which you have satisfied your thirst,*

Don't throw rocks — that's ungratefulness — one of the middos *the worst.*"

Now far be it from me to make fun of this line, because that would be in flagrant disregard to the very message of the line, which is that, if you went to this yeshivah, you can't throw rocks at their cantata. So instead I'm going to use it as an advertisement for my freelance writing business. (I also do poems for special occasions, such as occasions where someone calls me and asks if I do poems.) I mean, I understand the concept of poetic license, but that's taking your poetic license and driving it off a cliff.

But here's the thing: I don't actually remember my *own* line. I remember *Yehuda's* line, because it was embarrassing, and I remember making faces at my *Chumash* play. It's always the embarrassing stories that stick in your head for all eternity. So what I'm saying is that maybe the schools have, for example, a *Chumash* play, so that the kids will have some kind of embarrassing event, and will never forget the day they got their first *Chumash*.

HERE "FOR THE KIDS"

Guess where I went last Sunday! I went to an Uncle Moishy concert! AAAAAAAAAAH!

I'm sorry, I don't know what came over me. I think every time someone says Uncle Moishy's name (Uncle Moishy) you're supposed to scream like that. That's what all the kids at the concert were doing. (To be fair, though, some of them were crying because the lights were out.) But I think that this article would be more fun if, every time I mention Uncle Moishy, you (the reader) would go, "AAAAAAAAAAAAH!" Unless you're reading this on the subway.

In case you've been living under a rock for the past thirty-five years, Uncle Moishy is a very popular figure in the world of kosher kids' entertainment, and is responsible for many of the beloved children's songs that we all grew up on. He probably has a real name, but everyone knows him as "Uncle Moishy" (except for his

Here "for the Kids"

kids, who call him "Uncle Totty"). He wears a shirt with "Uncle Moishy" on it in big letters, so he has an easier time finding it in the laundry, and his hat has a huge white *mem* on the front so he can leave it on a hook in shul on Shabbos morning, and no one will accidentally walk off with it.

"Excuse me, I believe that's my hat."

"Are you sure?"

"Yes. Can't you see the big giant *mem*?"

"Oh. I thought this was *my* hat with a big giant *mem*."

But Uncle Moishy wouldn't get upset, because he's a warm and upbeat person, and he has an amount of patience that most of us cannot achieve without serious medication. (To illustrate my point, I ran this article by him before publication, and he was OK with it.)

I decided to go to the concert primarily because it was local, but also because my kids absolutely *love* Uncle Moishy songs, and are always asking us to play his albums. They ask us at home, in the car, around town — basically, all day long... And we will never never never eat milk and meat together, so join us, and sing the kosher song.

See? We can't get these beloved songs out of our head.

Uncle Moishy bills himself as "everyone's favorite uncle." And not the one who shows up with a bunch of funny-looking cousins that you have to sit with at weddings despite their being an entirely inappropriate age for you. Well, actually, he *is* that uncle, sort of. For example, he comes with a bunch of colorful costumed mascots who, at various points in the show, run out into the audience and try to navigate, with no peripheral vision, through a maze of excited

WHAT IS THIS — SOME KIND OF JOKE?

kids running into their midsections at top speed. It usually isn't long before they silently retreat back to the stage.

He also brought along his Mitzvah Men. I don't know why, but I'd been under the impression that the Mitzvah Men are those walking mitzvos that seem to follow him around in all his publicity photos, such as the *pushke* and the mezuzah.[8] But it turns out that the Mitzvah Men are actually the guys in the background who play musical instruments. Who knew?

I wonder how that works, though. When they're filling out forms, and they get to the part where it says "occupation," do they write "Mitzvah Man"? Does Uncle Moishy put ads in the paper:

> **WANTED: MITZVAH MAN**
>
> **MUST HAVE EXPERIENCE DOING MITZVOS**
>
> **SOME MUSICAL EXPERIENCE PREFERRED**

In addition, Uncle Moishy brought along a warm-up comedian/clown named "Cousin Nachum." I assume this guy was supposed to be his son, but I'm not sure, because I couldn't really follow the plot with all the screaming that was going on. Nachum's job was to juggle, make jokes, and fall down a lot. (The falling down bits were a big hit with the kids. In fact, I think my column would be a lot more successful with kids in the 2–7 age range if I found a way to incorporate falling down.)

Also, sometimes Nachum would drop something, such as his hat or his nose (in the field of kids' comedy, it helps to have a detachable nose), and whenever that happened, there were kids

---

8. The mezuzah is like his bodyguard, I guess.

Here "for the Kids"

who were convinced that he dropped it by accident, and started screaming at him about it en masse, which is the polite thing to do when someone gets up on a stage and his hat falls off. I mean, if your boss started giving an important speech with a little bit of lunch stuck to his face, isn't that what you and your co-workers would do — start screaming, "There's food on your face! There's food on your face!" until he notices? No wonder kids have stage fright.

But yeah, I understand that maybe I was not the target audience for the show. There are a lot of places that parents go so their kids will have a good time. You're there for the kids. It's like when people tell me, "My wife and kids love your articles. They read them all the time."

You can admit that you read them. I won't judge you.

I learned this a couple of years ago, when I took my kids to a safety fair, which also featured a clown/magic show. Obviously, the show was geared to the kids, so the adults graciously stood in the back of the room and let all the kids sit on the floor in front. But then someone had the genius idea to give out balloons with long strings, and with a mass of about twenty rows of children sitting on the floor, all the balloons lined up directly in the parents' line of vision. We could only see the clowns when they fell on the floor, which, thankfully, happened a lot. It must be the shoes.

So these shows are definitely not for the parents. But on that note, I need to say that I strongly favor some kind of corporal punishment for whoever invented that thing that entertainers do at kids' performances, where the guy on stage asks a question, and the kids all answer; and then the guy, in an attempt to make the parents feel like they're getting a longer show, says, "I can't

WHAT IS THIS — SOME KIND OF JOKE?

heeeeear you!" And the kids *always believe him*. No matter how many times he says it. So I think we should track down the original "I can't hear you" guy, put him in a room full of kids, stand on the stage, and keep saying, "I can't heeeeear you!" over and over again until the noise is enough to send dogs into hiding. Or else we can just lock him in a mascot suit and let him stumble around in the dark with no peripheral vision while enthusiastic kids run into his midsection.

Nevertheless, Uncle Moishy and Cousin Nachum tried to stick in some lines that the adults could appreciate, most of which revolved around the premise that the adults didn't really want to be there.

But it's only because of less-than-positive past experiences. For example, whenever I go to one of these shows, I end up sitting right in front of the noisiest kids in the room, and right behind an abnormally tall child who, sadly, was never taught how to sit down. Did his parents pay for a seat? They didn't get their money's worth.

And this time, I was sitting right behind a child who spent most of the concert facing the back of the room. It was very disconcerting. "Look!" I said, pointing toward the stage. "It's Uncle Moishy!"

"I know!" the kid said. And he kept on staring at me.

I also had a child sitting next to me — one of *mine*, actually — who felt the need to explain every joke to me, his humor-impaired father, right after it happened. "He didn't really trip," my son said. "He fell on purpose."

"I see," I said.

"Now he dropped his hat."

"I saw!" I said. "Look, you don't have to tell *me*. Tell it to the kid who's staring at us."

Here "for the Kids"

But all in all, it was a really entertaining concert. My kids really liked it. Especially the nostalgic songs that brought them back thirty years.

MY SON: "He means that..."

The audience *knows* what I mean.

SECTION VII:

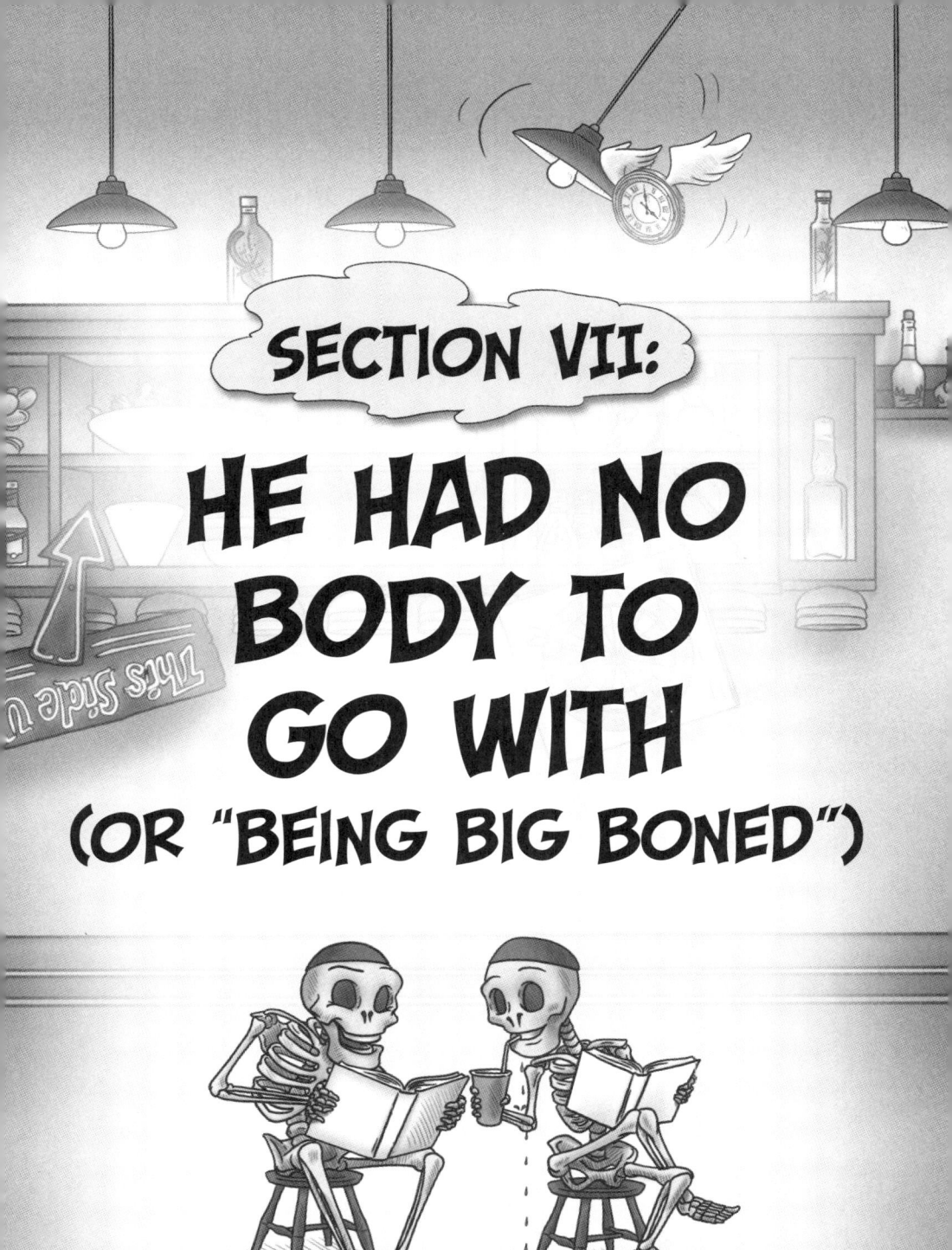

HE HAD NO BODY TO GO WITH
(OR "BEING BIG BONED")

Q: Why didn't the skeleton go to the party?

A: Because he had no BODY to go with.

Is that a first-world problem, or what?

Why does the skeleton need somebody to go with? The whole reason to go to a party is that there are people there that you can hang out with. He won't be the only person at the party. Unless he comes on time. On the other hand, maybe the skeleton was planning on *drinking* at this party, and he needs a designated driver because he can't really hold his liquor. Because he's a skeleton. Or maybe he's anti-social or subconscious about his breath, and he needs someone he knows that he can talk to. You don't want to be sitting there and you don't know anybody. It's very awkward. Especially if you're an anti-social skeleton with breath that smells like someone was *niftar*.

OK, so I understand that no BODY means no actual *body*, meaning that he's a skeleton. Because he's dead. So why does he feel obligated to go to the party? Because he RSVPed back when he was alive? The host can't understand that he died? If your host can't understand that you died, he's probably not really your friend.

Q: Why didn't the skeleton go to the party?

A: Because he was DEAD. His body was *gone*.

That's some quality humor right there.

Which brings me to the question: How many of these famous jokes end in death? All of them, I think, except the chicken crossing the road, *baruch Hashem*. In most tellings, at least. And except all the ones that are just mean, like the "your momma" jokes. People find skeletons hilarious because they're always smiling, but they're *dead people*. I guess it's probably some kind of *mussar vort* that even after you die, your bones are still smiling, but seriously, this is supposed to be a *joke*.

Anyway, if the skeleton really wants to go, I'm pretty sure he can find something at the costume store. Also, if it's a Purim party, he should be fine.

Point is, the following articles are about health. You need to keep up your health, apparently, so you can keep going to parties. And eating whatever junk they're serving there.

HOW DRUNK ARE YOU?

A Scientific Quiz[1]

Take this quiz to determine how drunk you are. If your first reaction is, "Hey, I didn't know there'd be a quiz!" then you're probably already there.[2]

1. Complete the following sentence:
   "*Arrur* _____; *Baruch* _____."

   a. *Arrur* Haman; *Baruch* Mordechai
   b. *Arrur* Mordechai; *Baruch* Haman

---

1. NOTE: This originally ran as a Purim article. Though I suppose you can use it *whenever* you think you're drunk.

2. Though, to be fair, my students say that whenever I give them a quiz.

WHAT IS THIS — SOME KIND OF JOKE?

    c. *Arrur* Osama; Barrack Obama

    d. Hey! My *brother's* name is *Baruch Mordechai*!

    e. My brother's name was *supposed* to be *Baruch Mordechai*, but his *bris* was on Purim, and my father accidentally named him *Baruch Haman*.

2. How much have you had to drink so far?
    a. One cup. But it was a *washing* cup.
    b. Just the two bottles that I'm holding in my four hands.
    c. The real question is how much I *haven't* had to drink so far! Wait.

3. Experts say that it's not good to drink on an empty stomach. (Though it's not clear if these experts are scientists, or just people who drink a lot.) What was the first thing you drank after the fast?
    a. Orange juice. Will I be OK?
    b. Schnapps. But if my stomach is so empty, where is all this vomit coming from?
    c. This is a trick question. Wasn't the fast on Thursday?[3]

4. What is the craziest thing that happened to you since you started drinking?
    a. I got hit by a parked car, tripped over a cordless phone, and fell through a window *into* a house. But I found my kids' baseball.

---

3. FUN FACT: Ta'anis Esther seems to fall on a Thursday more often than any other day. Also, Yom Kippur is basically always on Shabbos.

How Drunk Are You?

    b. I put my shoes on the wrong feet. But don't worry; it's OK. I've been walking with my left leg on the right and my right leg on the left to make up for it.

    c. I wish I remembered. What country am I in, and why am I wearing scuba gear?

5. People who drink should not drive, because statistics show that 96 percent of them cannot remember things that happened five seconds earlier, are prone to distraction, can't move in a straight line, and cannot remember things that happened five seconds earlier. What do you say to these statistics?

    a. They're *staggering*.

    b. *What* statistics?

    c. Hey! A 96 upside down is *also* 96! And a 44 upside down is two chairs!

6. Complete the saying: "Liquor before beer, never fear. Beer before liquor, _____."

    a. Never sicker

    b. Shikker quicker

    c. Wear a slicker

7. Complete the saying: "Friends don't let friends drive _____."

    a. Drunk

    b. Limos full of yeshivah guys in bunny costumes, every single one of whom is too drunk to remember whose house they left all the money in.

WHAT IS THIS — SOME KIND OF JOKE?

    c. All over town to bring them *mishloach manos* made up of food they don't really want but are going to force themselves to eat right before Pesach just so it's not in the house anymore.

8. Are Are you you seeing seeing double double yet yet??

    a. Yes. Yes.

    b. No. No.

    c. You're not going to get me with these cheap psychological tricks. You're not going to get me with these cheap psychological tricks.

9. Are you as think as we drunk you are?

    a. No! Yes. What?

    b. I'm not nearly *half* as think as you drunk I am!

    c. Hold on. I'm drinking about it.

ESSAY QUESTION: On unlined paper, write a detailed thesis on one of the following topics. Points will be given for coherence, logic, and making an effort to stay inside the borders of the page.

    Why, if I were the designated driver, it would be fun to drop everyone off at the wrong house.

    Why I suddenly love this guy who's sitting right next to me and trying to get away every time I get saliva in his ear.

    Why I worry that one day, all the grass I stepped on as a kid will join forces and eat me.

How Drunk Are You?

How you call them "fingers" but you never see them *fing*. Y'know?

HOW TO SCORE: Give yourself one point for every time you answered "a," two points for every time you answered "b," three points for "c," etc. (E.g., you get twenty-six points for every time you answer "z.") Then take the total of your points, add the digits together, and multiply by your age. If you have taken the time to do this, you're fairly sober. The rest of us are already using this book as a drum.

TRIMMING THE FAT

I know this column doesn't usually cover major news, but I've recently come across a press release so utterly shocking that I just have to share it. In fact, you might want to sit down for this.

Are you sitting? Good. Now hold onto something.

It turns out that, according to a study at the University of Ulster (in Ireland), published in a recent news release, scientists have now proven that — get *this* — eating large portions of food makes you fat.

Whoa. Remember where you were when you first read this.[4]

I bet most of you are slapping your forehead and going, "Oh my goodness! This changes *everything*! Why didn't they figure this out sooner?"

---

4. You were sitting.

Trimming the Fat

OK, so it's not really shocking, especially to those of us who, when we sat down a couple of paragraphs earlier, made a loud exhaling noise and adjusted our pants. But what's really shocking is that they're only just now coming up with this study. Didn't we already *know* this? How else would scientists explain the existence of cholent belts?

For those of you who don't know, cholent belts are (and you may want to sit down for this again) special belts that can be adjusted based on how fat the wearer is at any particular moment.

Basically, the way it works is that men are in total denial about their weight. If a man buys a belt, and the first time he puts it on the pin fits in the third hole, then that man will wear the belt with the pin in the third hole for as long as he owns that belt. He will wear it that way for years, and he never has any reason to switch it, because the poor hole is always stretched out to his current waist size. But meanwhile, the belt *bentches gomel* every time he takes it off at night, until finally the whole thing just splits in half, lengthwise.

But this becomes a serious problem when it comes to cholent. Men love cholent, especially at a kiddush. Hands down, the best way to eat cholent is standing up and holding your bowl. So sometimes, your shul will have a kiddush, and of course you'll eat the cholent, because you've been smelling it for almost three hours, and there's no way you're going to go home without having some. And then you go over to a kiddush of one of your friends, and he has cholent as well, which you of course have to sample, because you've just walked all the way across town for this. And then you go home, and even though you're content to sit around and digest for a little while, your wife wants to eat lunch *right now*

WHAT IS THIS — SOME KIND OF JOKE?

because she's *starving*, because it turns out she didn't eat a thing at either kiddush. ("WHY?!" I don't know.) And she's going to be insulted if you don't eat her cholent after you've already proven that you will eat everyone *else's* cholent. So you have to eat that too, for *shalom bayis*. And by the time you're done, you feel like someone has to roll you back out to the living room. Hence the adjustable cholent belt.

The point of a cholent belt is that it doesn't have holes. Instead, it has a million little grooves, and the wearer has no idea which groove he wears it in, so he can wear it in a different groove every day. It's basically a belt that fights denial by not letting the guy know that he's gaining weight until the belt doesn't make it all the way around him anymore. But my point is that, what with the existence of such a miracle of modern technology, I'm pretty sure we all figured that science already knew that eating more makes you gain weight, right?

Typical scientists. They don't believe in anything until they prove it themselves. Sure, we've been guessing that there was a link for years, but they didn't want to say anything until they'd verified it scientifically.

To understand how this all works, think of your body as a car. If you put in fuel, it goes. If you don't put in fuel and try to go, it will start to shut down pretty quickly and give you a "low fuel" warning light. An example of a "low fuel" warning light is when you go shopping on a fast day, when you have no strength to do so, and your body subconsciously puts one of everything in the entire store into your cart. But on the other hand, if you put fuel in the car three times a day and then don't drive anywhere, there will eventually be no more room in the tank, and you'll have to put some of that fuel in emergency storage cans in the back seat.

Trimming the Fat

To conduct the study, the scientists kept a group of forty-three people in controlled conditions for four days, and fed half of them large portions of food, and the other half standard-sized portions. By the end of the study, they found that the standard-portion group had eaten the large-portion group.[5]

Not really. What they found was that *everyone* gained some weight, because they were all kept in a closed area where they could do nothing but eat, but the large-portion group had gained 1–2 pounds more than the standard-portion group. On the other hand, we can probably assume that the amount they ate more than the other group, over four days, came out to *more* than 1–2 pounds, and the food was free. So it was definitely worth it. Also, this was Ireland, so I'm guessing there were a lot of potatoes involved.

Professor Barbara Livingstone, who ran the study, said that in the past few decades, there has been more and more overeating, due in part to inventions that allow us do less running around and burn less energy. And what do we do with the time that we save? We eat.

"Another possible reason for overeating," Professor Livingstone said, "was that consumers tend to eat what they are served, even if it's an inappropriate amount for their energy needs."

Personally, I think this is your mother's fault. When you were a kid, your mother made you eat everything on your plate, right? Even though she was the one who put it there. And even though, as kids, our bodies were still in tune enough to tell us exactly how much we needed to eat, and as soon as we had enough energy, we

---

5. And then Pharaoh woke up.

WHAT IS THIS — SOME KIND OF JOKE?

ran into the living room to play. But then our mothers yelled at us to come back and finish what was on our plates.

Why? So we could have *more* energy?

But then who ate the food that was left on our plates? Our parents. They originally took as much food as they needed to give them energy, and now they're eating *more* than they need to. It's a good thing you can't gain weight from things you eat off someone else's plate.

And how about eating things that you wouldn't normally eat, just because you have to get rid of them for Pesach? We never remember this in the store. Shoprite had a "Can-Can Sale" in January, wherein they sold boxes of noodles (don't ask me why) for fifty cents each. I piled my cart with them before I remembered that Pesach is in March. So now I have a ton of noodles. I'm going to be so sick of noodles by the time Pesach comes around, I'm not going to be able to look at them for a *week*. I'm eating noodles with cheese, noodle kugel, noodle soup, and even, in an effort to maybe lose some weight, noodle salad. Because apparently, noodles become a vegetable when you add mayonnaise.

It's a good thing we have to run around cleaning.

Hey, why are you sitting down?

BEE HAPPY, BEE HEALTHY[6]

We're lucky to be living in an age where there are many exciting advances in the world of medicine, mainly in the form of fixes that cure some symptoms by giving you so many others that you forget which ones were the original symptoms. One such exciting advance, for example, is the new healthcare reform.

OK, so it's not really exciting, even though, judging by how much time people spend talking about it, you'd think it *was*. I don't really follow current events, for the most part. Most of the current events that I follow are more along the lines of Iranian scientists sending turtles into space. So for a while, I didn't even know what "healthcare reform" was exactly, but I was hoping they'd reform the part where I keep getting Cobra bills in the mail for totally random

---

6. Source: Honey Nut Cheerios.

WHAT IS THIS — SOME KIND OF JOKE?

numbers, and I have to call the health insurance company so I could be transferred to several different continents, all pretending to be Iowa, and then finally be informed that the only person who might have an answer to my question will only speak to my former employer, who I'm sure wants nothing more than to spend all day on the phone trying to fix the health insurance of someone who no longer works for him.

A lot of people are vocally against healthcare reform, though, and I was wondering why, because simpler statements are definitely something I can get behind.

But when the bill finally passed, I looked into it to figure out exactly what it was, and I have to tell you — I can't say anything negative about it. Literally; I *have* to tell you that. The government has their hands in so many things nowadays that I have no doubt that, as I type these words, they're monitoring me through the fillings in my teeth. (I have so many fillings, I'm surprised I don't pick up police bands.)

Basically, if I understand it correctly, which I don't, the purpose of the plan is that everyone should have health insurance, including young people who never go to the doctor anyway. That way, the young people will basically be paying for the older people, and the health insurance companies can finally start making some money for a change. Then, when these younger people get older, the insurance companies will get money from *their* children, which they are more likely to have, thanks to health insurance. It's sort of like the social security system, which, if you listen in on conversations of people who read the news, is currently in crisis.

The issue that prompted this reform, I think, was that, on the one hand, young people don't want to get health insurance so they can pay a thousand dollars a month for a bad plan that doesn't cover anything except the cost of sending them incorrect statements. Considering how often they go to the doctor, it would be much cheaper to pay him when they see him. In fact, I say this to my wife every time we get any kind of medical bill, because I *do* have health insurance, even though I consider myself a young person (except in that one article I wrote where I didn't). I pay for health insurance despite the fact that I haven't been to a doctor at least since I got married, unless you count the dentist, which most people do not. My wife does go to the doctor occasionally, as do my kids, who I'm pretty sure are on some kind of Disease Timeshare Program with everyone in their school.[7]

I hate paying for it, though. In fact, back when I was getting health insurance through the yeshivah that I teach in, there was one year that the yeshivah kept paying for my health insurance and forgetting to deduct it from my paychecks. So when I finally got through to them about the mistake, they made up for it by double-billing me for the entire year after that. And if there's one thing more painful than paying for health insurance you're probably not going to need, it's paying for *last year's* health insurance that you *know* you didn't need.

So I totally understand why young people don't want to pay for health insurance. Nevertheless, my wife and I are convinced that the second we stop paying our premiums, we're all going to develop some horrible unexplained condition, such as fin rot. And then of course we won't be able to get insurance, because it will be a pre-existing condition.

That was the other problem with the system. Because the only

---

7. It's like a hamster. Every weekend a different kid gets to bring it home.

WHAT IS THIS — SOME KIND OF JOKE?

people who had health insurance were me plus a bunch of people who used the doctor too much to be profitable, the insurance companies didn't want to accept any new customers who needed to actually use the health insurance. (That's like a furniture store that's only willing to accept money from people who don't want to walk out with furniture.) But even though that's not really a nice thing for the insurance companies to do, you can't really blame them. Imagine someone wants to buy car insurance, so he drives down to the insurance office, and crashes right through the wall. Then he gets out of his car, glass and overturned desks everywhere, and sits down. Would *you* sell him car insurance? Or would you tell him he has a pre-existing condition?

So the government passed this healthcare bill, and everyone's major problem, as far as I can tell, is that sure, there was a problem with the system, but that doesn't mean the *government* has to get involved.

But look at it from the government's perspective: It's like when two kids are fighting over a truck, and the mother takes it away and puts it on top of the *sefarim shrank*. So now neither of the kids is happy, because they don't have the truck anymore, and the mother is not happy, because now the kids are fighting over *another* truck. They don't really want to *play* with trucks, they just want to fight over them. I'm not sure where I was going with this.

So now I guess we might as well make the best of it. I say that since we all have health insurance, we should try out new kinds of therapy, such as bee sting therapy, which I read about in a recent Reuters news article. (This is the kind of news article I read.) Bee sting therapy is an ancient Chinese method of curing symptoms of rheumatism and arthritis. The ancient Chinese were a very advanced society and were always coming up with methods of healing people, and mixing sauces with meat and vegetables, and holding auctions, and cleaning their Shabbos suits without using water. They also invented walls. Before that, people had to take turns holding their roofs up manually. This led to a lot of sore muscles, and hence, bee sting therapy.

Basically, the way it works is that doctors place hundreds of live, angry bees on key pressure points on the patient's body, using tweezers (or, if they're incredibly dexterous, a pair of chop sticks), and then jump back and wait for the bees to sting. Talk about side effects.

Surprisingly, the patients say that it feels good. Apparently, the whole discomfort of bee stings comes from all the shrieking and swatting. And in fact, the doctors say that more than 90 percent of patients have recovered or felt some improvement in their condition. (The rest have left a patient-shaped hole in the wall.) It's getting so that there are entire bee clinics devoted to this therapy. I'm guessing this is because when they tried doing it at the actual hospitals, the other patients complained. Especially the ones with flowers.

So I think we should start trying all these new therapies. And in fact, to show our support for the new healthcare system, we should lobby to give everyone in Congress free bee sting therapy. Not me, though. I'm going to continue paying my health insurance bill, like I've always done, as a *segulah* against getting sick.

THIS YEAR'S IG NOBEL PRIZE WINNERS ARE WEARING TWO PAIRS OF SOCKS

I would have to say that, as a spectator sport, the Nobel Prize ceremony is a real snooze fest. I can barely even make it through the list of winners. Take this one:

"The 2008 Prize for Physics went to Yoichiro Nambu of the United States for the discovery of the mechanism of spontaneous broken symmetry in subatomic physics, and Makoto Kobayahi and Toshihide Maskawa of Japan for the discovery of the origin of the broken symmetry which predicts the existence of at least three families of quarks in zzzzzzzzzzzzzzzzzzzzzzzzzzzzzzzzzzzzzzzzzzzzz zzzzzzzzzzzzzzzzzzzzzzzzzzzzzzzzzzzzzz

Sorry, I blacked out for a minute there. What were we talking about?

Oh yeah! Quarks!

I mean, quarks are important and all. After all, everything is

This Year's Ig Nobel Prize Winners Are Wearing Two Pairs of Socks

made up of molecules, right? And molecules are made up of atoms, atoms are made up of protons and neutrons, and protons and neutrons are made up of quarks. So you can just imagine how much time these people spend straining their eyes and trying to stay awake, doing something that no one else wants to do. They earned every penny of that prize money. But no one wants to hear about it.

Enter the Ig Nobel Prizes. The Ig Nobel Prize ceremony is held in Boston every year, and honors research that, in the words of the Annals of Improbable Research (the organization that runs the event): "First makes people laugh, then makes them think." My articles are designed to do the same, except for the thinking part. Also, the Ig Nobel Prize winners don't actually get any real money, so that's another similarity to me and my columns.

And with that, we present some of this year's winners:

The **Prize for Physics** went to a group of scientists in New Zealand for demonstrating that, on icy sidewalks, people are less likely to slip and fall if they wear their socks on the outside of their shoes.

That definitely stands to reason. For one thing, these people will get invited out of the house less often as well.

"Are you ready to go?"

"Yeah, one minute. I have to put on my socks."

"What are you doing? Oh. Forget it, we're not going."

To prove this, they did an experiment in which they stood at the top of a hill and asked pedestrians if they'd like to put on socks over their shoes. Hilarity ensued.

They ended up with thirty volunteers who didn't back away or

WHAT IS THIS — SOME KIND OF JOKE?

call the cops, and none of those people fell, except for one guy who put on the socks but then took them off because he felt ridiculous, and he promptly fell over. Eventually, the scientists had to call it a day, because the volunteers kept walking off with the socks.

It's weird, though. When we were growing up, whenever we ran around without shoes and we fell, our mothers would say, "See? It's because you're wearing socks!" I wonder what would have happened if we'd run around with socks on *over* our shoes. Probably our mothers would have noticed that they didn't always match.

Meanwhile, the **Prize for Management** went to Alessandro Pluchino, Andrea Rapisarda, and Cesare Garofalo of Italy, who demonstrated mathematically that organizations would be more efficient if they promoted people at random.

This explains so much about your boss, doesn't it?

Their conclusion is based on the Peter Principle, which says, "In a hierarchy, every employee tends to rise to their level of incompetence." Basically, most people are bound to be promoted at some point, so long as they work competently. But eventually, they get promoted to a position where they're no longer competent, and they stay in that position for the rest of their career. In other words, most people spend a huge percentage of their careers attempting to do something they're bad at.

The principle was proposed in the 1960s by Dr. Laurence Peter, who was a scientist for most of his career.

"In time," Peter says, "every post tends to be occupied by an employee who is incompetent to carry out his duties." Maybe this is what happened to Congress.

Using this principle, Alessandro and his associates say that if every well-thought-out decision you're going to make, when it comes to promotions, is eventually going to turn out badly, then, mathematically, you'd be better off promoting people at random. Perhaps even off the street.[8]

The **Prize for Public Health**, meanwhile, went to Manuel Barbeito, Charles Matthews, and Larry Taylor of Maryland. Basically, the three of them worked in a containment lab with someone, who, one day, decided to grow a beard. When his colleagues objected, he told them that there was no evidence that the beard posed any kind of hazard. So Barbeito, Matthews, and Taylor spent seventy-three days growing beards of their own, sprayed themselves with harmless bacteria, and demonstrated that it's harder to wash the microbes out of beards than off plain skin. (This is why a lot of scientists choose to go bald.) Then they put a fake beard on a mannequin, sprayed *that* with harmless bacteria, put it in a cage with a bunch of chicks and guinea pigs, and noted that some of the animals got sick. By that time, they'd forgotten what they were working on in the containment lab in the first place. Eventually their colleague shaved, just to get them to stop.

The **Prize for Medicine** went to two doctors in the Netherlands for discovering a revolutionary treatment for asthma: roller coasters.

It's definitely more fun than inhalers.

How did they come up with this idea? Were they at an amusement park when suddenly someone had an asthma attack, and they said, "Don't use your inhaler; let's go on the roller coaster

---

8. But not the ones wearing socks over their shoes.

WHAT IS THIS — SOME KIND OF JOKE?

instead!" And then, after a short forty-five-minute wait followed by sixty seconds of screaming, lo and behold, the person was feeling better?

No. I read the study, and it actually says *"repeated* roller coaster rides." So I think the first time it didn't quite work, and they were like, "Don't worry! Let's try a few more times!" And then, three short hours later, the person was better. Nauseated, but better.

Personally, I think it was just an excuse to go on repeated roller coaster rides under the guise of research. I could see it. I would certainly *go* on a roller coaster for a column.

"You know, only *one* of you has asthma. You don't have to *all* go on."

So you should definitely try to convince your doctor to put in a roller coaster.

"Really, Doc! It's good for asthma! And raising blood pressure!"

"I see. Are you wearing shoes?"

"Yes! They're under my socks."

"Oh yeah, I guess you are! I can see them through the holes!"

Finally, the **Prize for Engineering** went to a group of scientists from the United Kingdom and Mexico for developing a method of collecting the fluids ejected from whales' blowholes.

"What do they need it for?"

You don't want to know.

Actually, you *do* want to know. Whales are endangered, so scientists don't want them to get sick. I'm not sure what the scientists are going to do if the whales *are* sick — perhaps try to figure out how to get them on a roller coaster. The thing is, the most

This Year's Ig Nobel Prize Winners Are Wearing Two Pairs of Socks

humane method of studying the whales is through their "blow," which is a nice, humane way of saying "snot." But unfortunately, collecting the blow presents some obvious challenges.

So the British and Mexican scientists thought long and hard about how to collect the blow, and they came up with an idea: pay the Mexicans to do it.

OK, that's not nice. The idea they came up with was to fly a remote-controlled helicopter over the whales as they surface. When the whales blow, it gets all over the chopper, which then flies back to the scientists, who cannot believe they get paid to play with helicopters and look at whales. The scientists then reach out and grab the chopper with a good pair of socks over their hands. All in all, this is a much better method of collecting the blow than the way the scientists were getting to it *before*. It's also very non-invasive. In fact, I think doctors should use a similar method for examining their patients.

That way, no one has to get off the roller coaster.

A SHOT OF SODA

It's 7/11, and I'm sure you all know what that means: it's 7-Eleven day!

How profound. And I wrote a column making fun of July 4th.

7-Eleven is a convenience store, in that if you suddenly need, say, Tylenol, at eleven o'clock at night, you can just go on over there, and then the next night you can go again, because everything they sell there is very tiny.

Except the drinks. 7-Eleven is mainly known for their really big cups of soda. And we're not talking *stam* big. We're talking about where it looks like they basically took a soda bottle and emptied it into a cup. As a kid, it's really exciting to get those sodas, because at home, the best you can do is fill your 8-ounce cups to the very top so you're afraid to move it, and then you have to slurp the first four ounces with your nose in the cup, and then go get a paper

A Shot of Soda

towel. And even as an adult, the cups are nice, because a cup of soda that big can really keep you awake and moving. Even if there's no caffeine in it.

They also have a big frozen cup of soda called a "Slurpee" that is not the same as you putting a bottle of soda in the freezer and then taking it out, all excited, and then having the whole family sit around the Shabbos table waiting for it to decide to drip out through that tiny hole at the top of the bottle.

Instead, 7-Eleven has a machine that swirls the soda as it freezes, so it's basically the same consistency as the brown snow at the side of the road, and then you get a straw with a spoon at the end, so you can either scoop it into your mouth, or use it like a normal straw and make a noise that sounds like an elephant with an ear infection.

But my point is that if you go to a 7-Eleven any year on July 11th, they will give you a free Slurpee in honor of the date! But don't get too excited, because it's only 7.11 ounces. Thanks to Mayor Bloomberg's new soda ban.

In case you didn't hear, Mayor Bloomberg has recently proposed a ban on cups of soda larger than 16 ounces. Basically, we're all really fat, and someone sat down and decided that the reason was: soda. You know the ingredient in candy that makes it fattening? Soda is basically that ingredient.

The ban only affects restaurants, though. 7-Eleven can still sell big cups, because they're known for their big cups of soda. Whereas if your restaurant is known mainly for its big cups of soda, then maybe the restaurant business isn't really for you.

I don't know why restaurants can't serve a lot of soda, though.

WHAT IS THIS — SOME KIND OF JOKE?

I always thought they *should*, considering they bring you the glass about a half hour before they bring the rest of the food. (You ordered everything at once, and soda takes less time to prepare.) The waiter always gives it to you with half the paper still on the straw, like, "Don't worry, I didn't touch the half that goes in your mouth. I only touched the part that's in the soda." They're not bringing my meal with half the *wrapper* still on, to show me that the chef had nothing to do with it, right? Or is it only the *waiter* that doesn't wash his hands?

So what happens is that you find yourself drinking the entire soda before the food even gets there, because you don't want the 75 percent of it that's ice to water down the 25 percent of it that's soda. So bigger cups might actually last until the food gets there.

So I don't really know the point of the ban. I hope the mayor realizes that even these 16-ounce cups are really only 4 ounces of soda and 12 ounces of ice. What does he have against ice? Maybe it's a crackdown on charging three bucks for a cup of ice cubes. What are they, the hospital?

But meanwhile, 7-Eleven is still allowed to sell big bags of ice in their freezer. That's legal.

A lot of people are against the proposal, though. Apparently, they feel that soda is healthy. After all, the main ingredient is corn syrup, and what exactly is wrong with corn? Also, because of the bubbles, soda actually makes you feel full faster, and chances are you'll eat less. Of course, this is only a benefit if the thing you're eating is actually more fattening than the soda. Also, the soda in restaurants doesn't have a whole ton of fizz in the first place. It's mostly ice.

But the real reason that people are upset is that our founding

A Shot of Soda

fathers fought long and hard for the freedom to drink soda out of big cups (this is stated explicitly in the Declaration of Independence), and also that people should be allowed to make their own bad choices. Which they've been doing. The mayor, they feel, should work on things like fixing healthcare, so all the people who drink too much soda can afford to get sick.

The Coca Cola Company has issues with this too, obviously. Their feeling, finances aside (yeah, right), is that banning isn't the answer — the answer is giving people healthy alternatives, which is what they've been doing, with their eight different indistinguishable kinds of diet coke. They also make a can of coke that they advertise as having the same taste as regular coke, but with fewer calories, and which, as it turns out, is just a smaller can.

But the mayor's response to this is that he's not saying you can't drink more than 16 ounces — you can drink as much soda as you want. But you shouldn't drink it just because it's there. "If you want," he says, "you can order two 16-ounce cups." Like that's the same. Buying two cups costs twice as much money, whereas supersizing the one you have is about five cents more. But his logic is that part of what makes us so fat is that we're lazy, and if we have to order a second cup to get more soda, most of us wouldn't bother. This way, we can make our laziness work *for* us. Not that it wants to.

Now the truth is that we definitely *are* lazy, and the proof is that a lot of these restaurants offered free unlimited refills anyway, but people were still buying bigger cups. So there you go.

Personally, though, I think that this new regulation will probably make people even fatter, thanks to the Peltzman Effect. The Peltzman Effect says that whenever there's a measure enacted to keep the public safe, people rely on that and do dangerous things

WHAT IS THIS — SOME KIND OF JOKE?

they otherwise would not. In other words, if there were no shoulder bars, fewer people would go on upside-down roller coasters. He came up with this observation in 1975 to explain why there were more car accidents after the seat belt law was enacted than there were before. Basically, people figured they were safer since they were wearing seat belts, and they took more risks. But what they didn't realize was that you can wear all eight seat belts stretched across the car and wrapped around you at once, but that won't stop you from actually bumping into the other cars.

So in other words, if there's a law that says that people should have smaller drinks and therefore gain less weight, people will figure that they can order the bigger burger with pastrami and chili and onion rings on it, all between two pieces of fried chicken instead of buns. Because, "Hey, my drink is smaller!"

That's also what 7-Eleven figures, I think. Because it turns out that they've *always* given tiny cups on July 11th; it has nothing to do with the law. They want to get you into the store, but they don't want you to fill up. They're hoping that once you're there, you'll buy other things, because, "It's OK, all I have is a tiny Slurpee that doesn't quite last until I get to the car."

But my point, I guess, is that if you live out of state, this is not a good summer to come to New York, if you're thirsty. Maybe wait until the fizz settles.

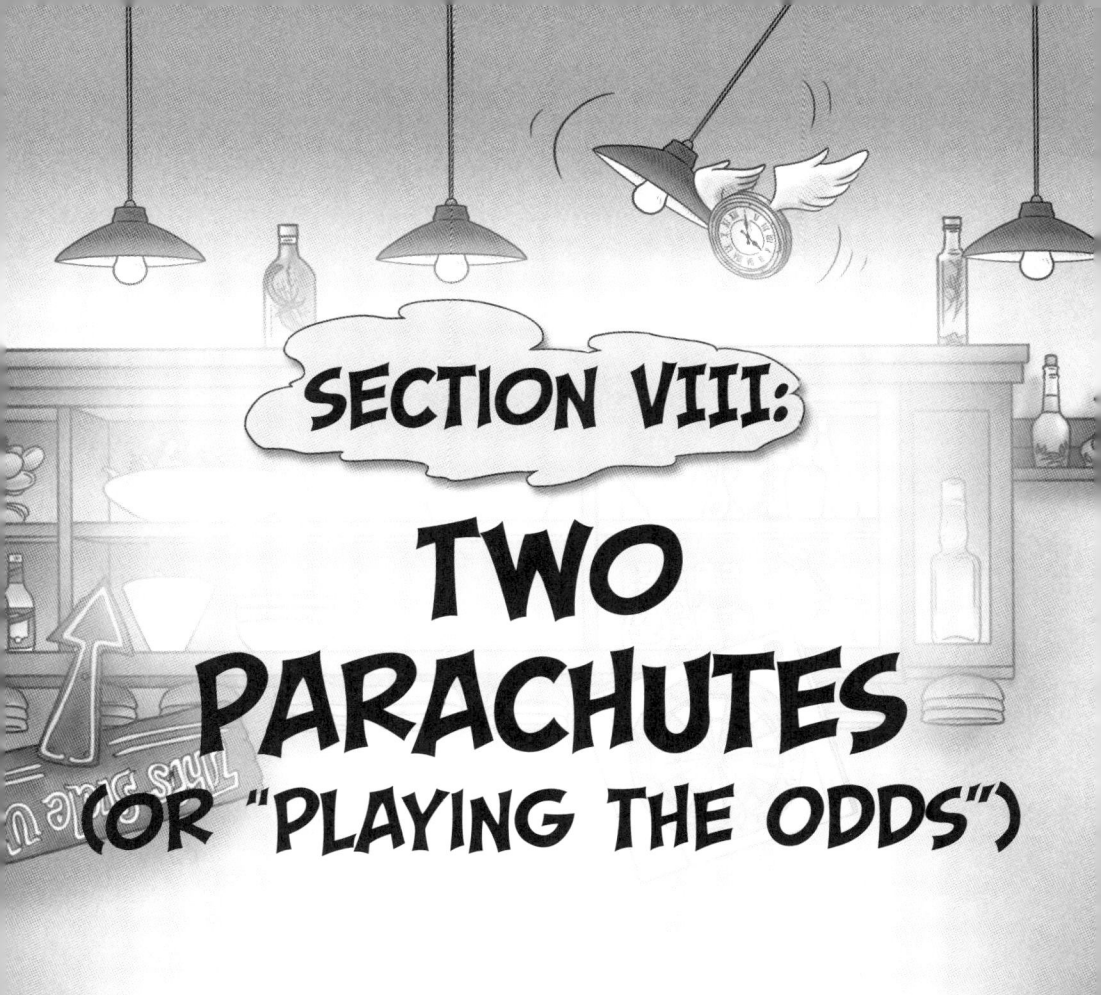

SECTION VIII:
TWO PARACHUTES
(OR "PLAYING THE ODDS")

There are a lot of jokes that begin this way: three characters, two parachutes. Why are there only two parachutes? Also, after the joke is over, what happens to the pilot?

I guess the assumption is there *were* three parachutes, but the pilot jumped before he said anything.

And so we have another joke that involves people dying. But what's with all these planes not having enough parachutes? Is that like how no boat has enough life jackets, because they don't think things will actually go down?

This whole parachute shortage thing is actually very believable nowadays, because we're allowed to carry less and less luggage onto planes. They accommodate planes to fit more and more people, but they don't actually make the planes bigger, so the luggage gets squeezed out. For all we know, this was one of those biplanes that have one seat in the front for the passenger and one in the back for the pilot, and they tried to get three people of three very different ethnicities to share the one seat.

Because why are there only three people on a plane? Is this a private jet? Why are three people who don't know each other taking a private jet together? Where are they going? Or is this just a really really really empty commercial jet, like maybe on a Christian holiday, so the only people flying are a chassid, an Arab, and a person of Asian descent?

And then the chassid said, "If we have room to stand around arguing about this, why isn't there room for another parachute? We had room for this kid's knapsack!"

Also, parachutes aren't life jackets. When a plane starts going down, people don't just grab parachutes and jump. *Yeah, let's open the door. That'll help.* I have never once seen that on the news. Usually parachutes are for when the passengers want to go down and the plane is not.

"Um, that was my stop."

"Yeah, I'm not taking you to the door. This isn't a door-to-door service. There are enemy soldiers down there! You'll have to go *yourself* the rest of the way. Don't forget your knapsack."

Anyway, this section is about luck and *hashgachah pratis*, and playing the odds. Like maybe you'll end up on a plane with enough parachutes!

YOU WIN SOME, YOU LOSE SOME

I recently started working out at the gym. (And by "started," I mean that I've gone three times, two of which were strictly for the purposes of this article.) I've been meaning to work out for a while now, because I really need to fit into my suit.

Not that I have a *simchah* coming up. In fact, if I *had* a *simchah* coming up, I would just go out and *buy* a suit. But I know that as soon as I buy one, one of my siblings is going to get engaged, and by the time they get married I'm not going to fit into that suit anymore. We should all have such problems.

So for now, I have to squeeze into my suits every week. I bought these suits a little more than three years ago, and I remember exactly when that was, because I wrote a column about it.[1] At the

---

1. That article appears in my second book, *A Clever Title Goes Here*.

WHAT IS THIS — SOME KIND OF JOKE?

time, I was very proud of myself for buying two suits, because I figured that it would take twice as long for them to wear through. But I've since realized that buying two suits at the same time just means I'm going to grow *out* of them at the same time. It's not that I'm fat, per se, but I am definitely bigger around the middle than I was when I got married, because it turns out I'm a very good cook.[2]

So you figure that if I'm not going to buy a new suit, I should at least make a real effort to fit into the ones I *have*. That's what I tell myself every Friday as I suck in my gut, but by the time Sunday comes, I'm back in my weekday pants, and I no longer care.

And then my wife and I won something at a Chinese auction. This is an annual fundraiser, which apparently originated in ancient China, wherein you enter your name in a whole bunch of raffles, and the more money you give, the more chances you have of not winning anything anyway. At least that's how *we* do it. Schmutters, in general, never win anything. The very night that we won a prize at the Chinese auction, my parents and siblings were in Kmart, where they entered a raffle for some jewelry. In total, there were twenty tickets given out, and my family had nine of them. But they didn't win. I'm pretty sure that if there had been only *ten* tickets given out, they *still* wouldn't have won. We should all have such problems.

So most years, my wife signs up for all of the drawings involving *sheitels*, and then we go through the book, picking objects at random:

"A car? What are we going to do with a third car? Our oldest is seven!"

---

2. My wife's OK as well.

You Win Some, You Lose Some

"What's the difference? It's not like we're going to win."

On top of that, the book said that if we paid $150, we could get $300 worth of tickets. But there wasn't $300 worth of stuff that interested us. So toward the end, we were very desperate to just finish up already, and we were going back and forth through the book looking for something to do with the last ten dollars, and my wife said, "How about the year-long gym membership?" and I said, "Are you crazy? I don't have time to work out!" because that's what you say when you're too *lazy* to work out, and my wife said, "I'll tell you what. You can worry about that *after* we win the gym membership."

And guess what? We won the gym membership. The one prize that I didn't even want. So now I officially have my wife's permission to worry about it.[3]

They say that once you start working out, you learn a lot about yourself and your limits. The first time I went to the gym, for example, I learned that my limits were that I didn't know how to work any of the machines. And anything that I *did* know how to use, such as the treadmills, had a whole bunch of confusing buttons, and most of them, when pushed, did not seem to do anything. Well, except for the one marked "Speed-*plus.*"

My wife suggested that I sign up for the "One-Time Free Fitness Training Session," in which you meet with a personal trainer, and he teaches you how to use the equipment, and which equipment you would use to work off your particular gut.

So I met with the trainer, whose name, which I am not making up, is *Brad*. I could not have planned that better. I think legally, if

---

3. See? You try to do a good thing, and this is what happens. I hope they're happy.

WHAT IS THIS — SOME KIND OF JOKE?

you're a fitness trainer, your name has to be *Brad*. They don't let you be a trainer if your name is *Walter*.

Brad started our session by taking me into his office, which consisted of a desk, two chairs, and the biggest bottle of dietary supplements I had ever seen in my life. Then he told me that I should forget about losing weight, because a lot of the exercises he was going to give me would help build my muscle tone, and muscles weigh more than fat does.

"Then why would I want to build muscle tone?" I said. "I don't *want* to do exercises that build muscle tone, because then how am I going to figure out how much *fat* I'm losing? Do I have to go home after every workout and try on Shabbos pants?"

But I didn't say this out loud, because Brad had a lot of muscle tone.

Then he asked me what I'd eaten for supper that night. And the night before. And the night before. I was glad he didn't ask me what I ate for supper on Friday night.

"Let's see... I had a cup of wine, then some bread, a piece of fish, a bowl of soup, some noodles, chicken, rice, meat, potatoes, green beans, and a salad...and a piece of cake. Oh, and I started at nine thirty."

(You'd think I'd actually eat less on Friday nights because my suit is so tight, but you forget that when I *make* the food, I'm wearing my weekday pants.)

So Brad told me about this new diet that I'd never heard of before. It's based on the theory that if your body gets hungry, it starts wondering where your next meal is coming from, and then the next time you eat, it starts storing fat, in case you forget to eat again. Basically, no offense, but your body is not too bright. It's kind of like a loyal dog that follows your head around. If you didn't

You Win Some, You Lose Some

have a head, it would probably just wander off. So the idea, Brad said, is to not let your body go hungry *at all*. And the way to do this is to have a snack between every meal.

"That's awesome!" I said. "I already *do* that!"

"What do you have?" he asked.

"Whatever I want!" I said. "Chips, chocolate, chocolate chips, sour stix..."

So he said, "No, not junk food. I meant *healthy* snacks, like yogurt or granola bars."

"But that's lunch!" I said. But not out loud. *If that's what I'm eating for snack, what on earth will I eat for lunch?*

Anyway, this whole theory surprised me, because I'd been pretty sure that Brad's entire diet consisted of dietary supplements.

"Do you ever miss junk food?" I asked him.

"I didn't give it up," he said. "Once in a while, I let myself have something. Why, just the other week I had a bagel!"

Whoa.

"That's junk food?" I asked. "When I eat a bagel, I reward myself with chocolate!"

"So are you going to change your diet?" he finally asked. Like I was going to pay him for training sessions so he could pester me every week about what I was eating.

"Sure," I said, because I really wanted to get to the part where he showed me how to work the machines. So do you, I'll bet. Now you know how *I* felt. We'll continue this next time.

Until then, keep snacking!

NO WEIGHTS!

We now present part two of our article on physical fitness, because if you want to have physical fitness, you can't expect it all to come in one week.

It takes at least *two* weeks.

For those of you just joining us,[4] last week I wrote about how my wife and I accidentally joined a gym. And by "accidentally," I mean that we won a year-long membership in the yeshivah's Chinese auction, even though the main reason we bought a ticket for the gym membership in the first place was that we were sure we wouldn't win. So now I go to the gym from time to time. I don't really *want* to, but I figure, "Why not? It's for *tzedakah*."

---

[4]. I'm aware of how weird this sounds in a book, but some people just open up to the middle and start reading. I have no idea how novels handle those people.

No Weights!

Also, along with our membership, I signed up for one free personal training session, so I could learn how to use the machines, which seem to go out of their way to complicate activities such as walking. I met with the personal trainer, who, for the first half hour, seemed primarily concerned with changing what I eat. My feeling was that the whole reason I was there in the first place was to find out how to work *off* what I eat. That's like if I would bring my car to the mechanic, and I'd ask, "How do I stop this part from breaking again?" and he said, "Well, you could stop driving the car."

But then why even *have* the car?

Actually, that's not so accurate. It's more like if the mechanic said, "You can drive the car, but only to these seven places."

The main gist of his suggestion, though, was that I should have a snack between every meal, so that my body would never be hungry, and therefore never try to store fat for "later." I'm not sure whether this is a proven diet, or whether Brad was just using me as a guinea pig, but I do think it's very sound advice, at least on paper (or in a book). If you look around, you will notice that most people who eat all the time are extremely thin, while most people who watch what they eat are not.

Also, for the sake of my articles, I have taken to calling the trainer "Brad," because even though that is his actual name, it is probably the name I would have used anyway if I'd had to come up with a fake one. Brad is a muscular guy who carries a clipboard and freely uses words like "bench."

"How much do you bench?" he asked me.

"Every time I eat!"

Brad also uses words like "sets" and "reps." ("Reps," I later found

WHAT IS THIS — SOME KIND OF JOKE?

out, means to do something again and again, as in, "Fifteen reps in one day? I'm going to stop answering my front door!") So he'd say something like, "This is how many reps you should bench on this set." Or maybe he said, "This is how many benches you should set on this rep." I could check later, because he wrote it down on the clipboard.

But he was very helpful. He took me to each machine and showed me how to use it, and also told me how many sets and reps I should be doing, and on what setting. I don't know how he judged what setting I should use; I think he was going by my facial expressions. Like he would put the machine on "4," and I would do all the reps without any major injuries, and he'd say, "Nope! You need it on '11'!" But if I was turning various shades of purple and my face had an expression like I was trying to manually grow a full beard in one day, and I was still grunting, "2!...3!..." he would say, "Yeah, that seems about right!" And he'd write it on my chart for all eternity.

Anyway, as it turns out, I don't bench very much. Brad walked me over to the weights and told me I should bench the bar with no weights on it *at all*. Just an empty bar.

Sure, I guess the bar had *some* weight to it (forty-five pounds, I found out later, when I lugged it over to the scale), but I can't help but think that people are going to keep coming up to me and going, "You know, you're supposed to put weights on that." Brad assured me this was nothing to be embarrassed about, but I bet he went home that night and laughed about it with all of his personal trainer friends (all of whom, I assume, are named "Brad").

"I got another guy to lift the bar with no weights! *No weights!*

No Weights!

Tomorrow I'm going to see if I can get someone to do step exercises on the scale!"

He also had me do a lot of exercises that seemed to accomplish the same thing. At least it seemed that way to me, because when I started doing them, the same muscles hurt. For example, he had me sit at a machine where I held onto a bar and pushed outward, thereby pulling a string that lifted a bunch of weights that turned the lights on and off. OK, so it didn't do that, but it did seem like a roundabout way of getting these weights picked up. Especially since it seemed to be the exact same exercise as the one where I lay on my back and lifted the weights directly.

In total, Brad had me do about twelve different exercises. The only time he let me stop was when I was drinking water. I tell you, I never drank so much water in a one-hour stretch in my *life*. I almost drowned.

While I was drinking, I noticed a sign that said the following:

Stop exercising immediately if you feel:
Lightheaded
Confused
Nauseous
Excessively fatigued

"Hey!" I said. "I'm at least *four* of those!"

But I will say this about Brad: He was a big believer in using the machines only when absolutely necessary. For example, at some point he took me over to do some crunches on the mats that were lying on the floor in the corner. (I was very disappointed, because I thought those were for naps.) He also had me do step exercises, sixty times with each leg, on a platform mounted to the back of a bench, that was higher than any step I would have to use in real

WHAT IS THIS — SOME KIND OF JOKE?

life. If an architect would put sixty of these into a building, he would be fired. If you want to get some idea of what I was doing, stand with your arms down at your sides, and see how many times you can step up onto your kitchen counter.

"You know," I said. "There's a stair climber right over there."[5]

Finally, at my request, he agreed to show me how to use the elliptical. I knew how to use it, but I had no idea what to do with all those buttons.

"Which button do I press?" I asked him.

"Press whichever button you *think* you should press," he said.

So I pressed the one marked "Fat Burn."

"No!" he said. "You should just press *Quick Start*. Fat Burn doesn't do anything."

So apparently he didn't know either.

I came back the next day to try the exercises without him, and to see if I remembered which random words that he wrote on my chart referred to which exercises. And the whole process, from when I told my wife, "I'm going to work out now," until I was back to sitting around the house, took about two hours. I don't mean to make excuses, but I have no idea how I'm going to make that kind of time on a regular basis.

So I figure that sometimes, to save time, instead of, say, benching 30 reps of 45 pounds, I can bench 15 reps of 90 pounds. Or seven and a half reps of 180 pounds. Or — why not? One rep of 1,350 pounds.

Yes, I did the math. I'm not *that* confused.

---

5. Yes, I said, "Over there." I didn't actually point, because I could no longer lift my arms.

SECTION IX:
WHY THE LONG FACE?
(OR "AGING GRACEFULLY")

It's a famous joke: A horse walks into a bar. Because apparently they let just anyone in. Religion doesn't matter; species doesn't matter. And the bartender looks at him and says, "Why the long face?"

(And the llama says, "His mother just died, you idiot!")

I don't know if this joke was originally written to start a section on aging, but it's going to.

The reason it's a joke, in case I have to explain it, is that horses literally have long faces. Though if you understand the story *that* way, the bartender is asking why he has a genetic situation that all horses technically have. So the bartender either looks insensitive for bringing up a physical abnormality in a paying customer, or he's pointing out something that is true of all horses and he wants to know why horses in general have long faces.

"I don't *know* why horses have long faces. Why do humans need ten separate toes?"

The truth is that most animals without hands have long faces. They need to be able to eat without putting their entire head in their food. If you, the reader, try to drink water from a river without using your hands, you'll drown. A horse can't be shaped like that. Sometimes they have to be able to, for example, eat a bowl of oatmeal without getting their eyes in it.

So the horse is probably sitting at the bar, and the bartender is like, "Why the long face?" And the horse is like, "So I can drink without using my hands. I don't want to drown in a cup of schnapps. I have hooves. You want me to break all your glasses?"

Point is... I don't know; something about aging. I don't remember.

LOOK AT THIS CLOWN!

I would have to say that the most important thing that I learned in my day at Mitzvah Clown Training — aside from how to put on makeup — was that, no matter what happens, I should not give out medical advice.

I wasn't planning on it. My plan, if someone started kvetching to me about his problems, was to complain about my own.

"Look at me!" I would say. "My skin is pale, my nose is swollen... See how unruly my hair is? And this is a wig! And look at my shoes. This is really how big my feet are!"

Mitzvah Clown Training is not like your typical clown school. Regular clown school takes years to complete, and teaches things like how to purposely walk into walls by accident and how to deal with children who are very wary of adults who look like they fell face-first into several vats of food coloring. Whereas Mitzvah Clown

WHAT IS THIS — SOME KIND OF JOKE?

Training takes about an hour and focuses mainly on how to make upbeat conversation with old people.

"Mitzvah clowning" is the process of getting dressed up and bringing happiness to senior homes and children's hospitals. It's basically *bikur cholim* on helium. The session that I attended, which was sponsored by an organization called "Areyvut," is designed to teach entire groups of people the basics of mitzvah clowning, after which they take the entire class over to a nursing home. But not all in the same car.

The class is given by a man named Cookie, which might not be his real name. Cookie started off by saying that you don't actually have to have a specific talent to be a mitzvah clown, although it doesn't hurt. You're not performing for a very discerning audience; you're performing for an audience that is so happy to see a clown dancing around and making balloon animals that they don't care that all you know how to make is snakes and eels. (Also worms. Making a worm is a lot like making a snake, except that you don't bother blowing up the balloon.) And if you make a fool of yourself, no one knows it's you, because of all the makeup.[1]

Cookie started by teaching us some of the basics of mitzvah clowning, such as, "Don't all come barging into a nursing home dressed as clowns without an appointment. Unless you want to end up on the news."

He then talked about choosing a name. It's very important, in mitzvah clowning, that you give the patients something to call you, because it makes them feel more at ease. It's not important what

---
1. And the obviously fake name.

Look at This Clown!

your name actually is, so long as you give them one. But there are several basic guidelines to follow:

1. If you're clowning with a group of people, don't all choose the same name.
2. Don't randomly change your name in the middle of a visit. If a patient calls, "Hey, Puddles! Puddles!" and you don't respond, he's going to start to think that maybe your name isn't really Puddles.[2]
3. It's important to use an upbeat name, such as "Sunshine" or "Happy," as opposed to a depressing name, like "Mildew." Also, "Buttons" is a better name than "Zippers," "Cornflake" is better than "Raisin Bran," and "Patches" is better than "Potches."
4. When introducing yourself, you don't have to say, "I'm Potches the Clown!" You can just say, "I'm Potches!" It's pretty obvious that you're a clown.
5. But just in case, don't give out medical advice.

Then we talked about balloons. Cookie stressed that balloons are very important, because they break the ice and give you something to talk about, and they also serve as a reminder of your visit. He also showed us how to make some basic balloon shapes, such as hats (the elderly like to wear hats), dogs (small dogs, like the kind who are always being carried around in enormous handbags or getting sucked into recliners), and of course, swords. (I don't know why the elderly would need swords. Perhaps to fend off clowns.) We were also taught to have a one-liner prepared for when the balloons pop, so no one has a heart attack.

---

2. Because seriously, when were you named "Puddles"? At your *bris*?

WHAT IS THIS — SOME KIND OF JOKE?

Cookie finished off the training by giving out makeup kits. The good thing about clown makeup is that it comes off really easily. The bad thing is that it usually starts coming off before you get to where you're going. It gets on your hands, on the inside of your glasses, and, if you choose to blow up your balloons without a pump, all over your balloons. Also, the makeup melts in your hot car while you're at the senior center, and it gets all over your nose. The red one, that you left in the car.

I had never put on makeup before, but Cookie said that we should put on the lighter colors first, and then do the darker colors. So I started off by painting my entire face white. And I do mean my entire face. By the time I was done, I had white paint in my hair, my eyes, and the inside of my nose. Then I started painting my lips red, but because I'm a lefty, the right side of my mouth looked like I put the makeup on while driving. So I took a paper towel and attempted to wipe it off, but rather than coming clean off, it smeared across my chin. So I started to put more white on my chin, but it started mixing with the red. And then my whole chin was pink, and the more I tried to fix it, the more it kept mixing, and the next thing I knew, my cheeks were pink too. So I gave up trying to fix it, and decided to just make my whole face pink. Then I put a little bit of blue around my eyes, but that started mixing with the white as well. You know how you learned in science class that if you mix all the colors of the rainbow, you get white? At some point, I had all the colors on my face, and I definitely was *not* getting white.

Now I know why it takes my wife so long to get ready to leave the house.

When we were all dressed up and made up, we went over to the nursing home. And no, we didn't pile into the same car; we went in a procession of cars, sort of like a clown funeral. At some

Look at This Clown!

point someone tried to merge in front of me, but I didn't let him in, because I didn't want to lose the car I was following. The guy looked over at me, and I could tell by his facial expression that he did not think I was a responsible driver. I'm not totally sure what he could tell from *my* facial expression.

"Look at this clown!" he was probably saying to his wife. "I'm trying to merge, and this clown just cuts me off! Someone should wipe that big grin off his face!"

As it turns out, the seniors were very happy to see us. They were all full of comments.

"Nice shoes."

"What?! No, these are my shoes!"

But whenever I tell this story to anyone, they all want to know the same thing:

"Old people like clowns?" they ask. "What are they, five?"

The truth is that old people are not, in fact, five.[3] I'll tell you what old people *do* enjoy, though. They like stories. There are not a whole lot of new stories when you're living in a senior center. But now they have a new one, and they can tell it to their kids when they come to visit.

"The strangest thing happened the other day! There were clowns! There was Sunshine, and two Cookies, and one of the clowns was pink! And the pink one took off his shoes!"

"Yeah, OK. I'm going to go talk to the nurses now."

"No, really! I thought I imagined it too, but look! I have a balloon!"

---

3. Also, as noted earlier in this book, no five-year-olds like clowns.

PHYSICALLY ILL

I've been feeling kind of lousy lately, and I'll tell you why. I went to the doctor.

Now before you panic, I want to stress that I didn't go for any serious reason. I went for my annual physical exam, which I get approximately every ten years.

In truth, I don't even remember the last time I went to the doctor, except that:

1. It was definitely before I got married.

2. My mother brought me.

3. The doctor in question was a pediatrician.

So my wife has been bothering me for the past couple of years to "for goodness' sake go to the doctor already." You know how women can be — *nag nag nag*. "Go to the doctor." "Lose some weight." "Have a salad."

Physically Ill

Seriously. What do these women *want*?

I finally went for a physical because I was applying for a substitute teacher position within the public school system, and one of the requirements was that I get a form filled out by a doctor. I don't know if it's because they don't want people having a heart attack in front of a room full of kids, or if it's because they want to make sure my reflexes are up to par. I didn't actually *have* a doctor, but I wasn't about to tell them that. So I opened up my big fat health insurance book and looked around for a nice Jewish doctor.

It turns out the doctor I found is indeed very nice. The first thing he told me, right off the bat, was that I'm fat. Actually, he didn't even use the word "fat" — that's how nice he was. He used the word "obese."

This was a total shock to me. I knew I was overweight, thanks to my *eishes chayil*, but to me, "obese" is a term reserved for someone where, if you are asked to describe the person ("Sholom Bergstein? Which guy is he again?"), you either feel the need to use the term "a little on the heavy side," or you totally trip over yourself trying *not* to say that. But as I later found out, according to the body/mass index chart, I am indeed considered obese, for medical purposes. Even my wife was surprised.

Then the doctor asked me a whole bunch of questions, like he was afraid that if he didn't find anything wrong with me, I probably wouldn't come back for *another* ten years.

"Are you on any medications?" he asked.

"No," I said. It would be pretty weird if I *were* on medication, considering I hadn't been to a doctor in ten years.

Then he asked if I'd ever had any number of health issues, and

WHAT IS THIS — SOME KIND OF JOKE?

I just answered no to everything. Even for the things that I had no idea what they were.

"Do you ever have heart palpitations?" he asked me.

"No," I said. "Wait. What are heart palpitations?"

"That's when your chest hurts for a moment."

But what *kind* of "hurt"? I'm not going to say my chest has never hurt, but for all I know, it was something I ate. What's the difference between heart palpitations, heart burn, chest pains, heart ache, tummy ache, and shortness of breath? Every one of those can be defined as, "that's when your chest hurts," and yet he asked me about each one separately. I think that with all these advances in modern medicine, there should be some kind of system to define pain, like the one employed years ago by my ninth grade *chavrusa*.[4] One time, my *chavrusa* told me that he got into an argument with his little brother, and that he gave his brother a dead arm. I didn't have any older brothers (I still don't, actually), so I asked, "What's a dead arm?"

"This!" he said. And he gave me a dead arm.[5] So I'm saying that the modern medical system should have some kind of machine that can temporarily duplicate the different kinds of pain, or else they can hire my ninth grade *chavrusa* to do it.[6] And that way, when you come into the doctor's office, and he asks, "How are we feeling today?" you can show him.

My other issue is that in general, when people ask me how I

---

4. CHAVRUSA (*n.*): Study partner. Very little study was involved.

5. This is why G-d gave us *chavrusos*.

6. I don't know why I feel the need to point this out, but he's a fireman.

am, I almost always say, "Good, *baruch Hashem*." It's my natural reaction. The only person I'm ever honest with is my wife, because I find that if she thinks I'm feeling better than *she* is, she comes up with a million things for me to do. So with her, it's always a contest of who's feeling less fine. If anything is even slightly bothering me, I make sure to mention it, for the record. In fact, now I'm thinking that's why my wife wanted me to go to the doctor so badly. ("Oh my goodness! He's never feeling well!")

But my point is that when the doctor asked me all these questions, I kept telling him that I was feeling fine. I'm not going to share with him how I'm *really* feeling. I just *met* the guy.

In the end, he told me a couple of things: First of all, he told me that my calcium is a little high, and my vitamin D is a little low. He didn't tell me what that means, but he did tell me to come back in two months or ten years, whichever came first, so he could run some more tests.

He also told me that I may someday have high blood pressure.

So how does one lower his blood pressure? The most obvious way, of course, is to cut out stress. But the doctor didn't tell me to do that. In principle, if you tell someone to cut out stress, he's not going to say, "Yeah, come to think of it, I *do* yell too much." He's going to say, "Well, if everyone around me would stop doing stupid things…"

On top of that, a doctor can't very well tell people to cut out stress, because there's nothing more stressful than going to the doctor, especially if he tells you that you may have high blood pressure, and that you have to come in for more tests, but you can't come in *yet*. It's not even like I can fix things on my own:

WHAT IS THIS — SOME KIND OF JOKE?

"I'm low on vitamin D, right? What has vitamin D? Milk!"

"Wait. Milk has calcium."

In fact, the best way to stress someone out is to tell him that he has high blood pressure, and that he should cut down on stress. Because now, every time I'm stressed about something, I'm actually *doubly* stressed. I'm stressed about the original problem, and I'm also stressed about the fact that I'm stressed.

So he recommended that the best way to lower my blood pressure is to lose weight. That would actually lower the pressure on a lot of things, such as my waistband, my belts, and my office chair. So that's what I'm doing. I've already added a salad to every meal. Also, I have a free gym membership that I haven't really used since I wrote an article about it that one time. I went for a few weeks, but I found that I wasn't losing enough weight to make it worth the time I was spending. (Did you know that a pound is 3500 calories? And that's if you don't eat anything between workouts!) So I just decided to spend the money and buy a bigger suit.

My point, though, is that I used to be carefree and not think about my health, and now, everything that happens causes me to think: "Am I gaining weight? Was that a heart palpitation? How about *that* one?" So going to the doctor has definitely aged me.

I'm not saying you shouldn't go to the doctor. In general, nothing can be gained by not going, besides, you know, a few hours of actually getting other things done. You either have nothing wrong with you, in which case you're better off knowing that for sure, or you *do* have something wrong with you, in which case the sooner you know, the better. I'm just saying that in my particular case, I was better off not knowing. All this knowing is *not* good for my blood pressure.

SECTION X:
CHICKEN ON THE ROAD
(OR "TIPS FOR TRAVEL")

This section is about travel, obviously, with and without a GPS.

Why?! Well, wouldn't *you* like to know.

This is probably the most famous joke, for some reason. And I have no idea why. Why are we so obsessed with why a chicken crossed a road? Who cares? Chickens move around all the time; we care if one crosses a road? Why is this even *our* business? We're not farmers. If you're not gonna help...

And why is it THE chicken? What was so special about this chicken *before*?

Maybe the answer is more obvious than we think.

Q: Why did the chicken cross the road?

A: It wasn't a chicken, and it was delivering *shalach manos*.

I think the original answer, though, was, "To get to the other side," which, to be honest, makes the whole thing not even a joke. "To get to the other side" is like, "I just wasted your time. Thanks for wracking your brains trying to come up with an answer." Though maybe it's actually some genius punch line that I just don't get because I've never owned a chicken. I bet back when everybody owned chickens, this was *hilarious*.

Another really famous answer goes like this:

Q: "Why did the chicken cross the road?"

A: "To get the Chinese newspaper. Get it?"

"No."

"Neither do I. I get the (*insert name of newspaper that paid you to advertise for them*)."

But this version just leaves me with even *more* questions. Why does a chicken need a Chinese newspaper? I think that's a better question than, "Why did it cross the road?"

But as I said, I honestly have no idea how the chicken-on-the-road joke is as famous as it is. There is no punch line for this joke that is good enough to have spread as far as it did. And there are much better jokes than this that you've never even heard. It's not even like a pun.

Yet somehow this joke was known all over the world, even before the internet. There are cave paintings about this joke.

I could see it maybe having originally worked as a legitimate question: "Why is this chicken crossing the road? All the other chickens are on *this* side of the road. This is everyone it knows. Where's it going? Does it have a job? Is it sick of corn?"

Is this a pun with *side* or something? Like "side of chicken"? They should at least add a punch line:

Q: "Why did the chicken cross the road?"

A: "Because she had a MEATing! Get it?"

"No, because you *said* the joke. You didn't write it out. I have no idea how you spelled "meet" in your head. All I know is you *yelled* it.

Point is, this section is about travel. Why? Don't ask.

LOOK, MA! NO HANDS!

We live in exciting times. I recently read an article about a company in England that, in an effort to show people how to live green, created a prototype car that runs on coffee. They figured that if *people* can run on coffee, why not cars?

OK, so there are still some bugs to work out. For example, in order to drive one mile, the car needs to burn an equivalent of fifty-six cups of espresso. And because the tank can only be so big, you would have to stop every thirty miles to refuel. Thankfully, there are coffee shops on every street corner.

"I'd like to buy 840 cups of coffee, and hurry! I'm late for work!"

And on top of that, you also have to stop every sixty miles to change the coffee filters.

But on the other hand, the car smells *great*. Maybe that's not such a good thing, though, because you'd have to keep a constant

WHAT IS THIS — SOME KIND OF JOKE?

eye on your car, or people would keep siphoning coffee out of the tank while you're at work. And come to think of it, at four bucks a cup, you may as well ride a bike. On fifty-six cups of coffee, you can go pretty much *anywhere* on a bike. You can cross *oceans*.

Thankfully, there is some other car technology that is actually closer to being ready. A company in Germany is currently developing a car that a driver can steer with his eyes. This frees up his hands to do whatever it is he needs to do while driving, such as play with the radio. OK, so he can't do that, because he still needs his eyes to drive. But he can definitely do things he *doesn't* need his eyes for, such as scratch his feet. He can attack his feet with both hands, so long as he keeps his eyes on the road.

Anyway, they plan on putting this car into production as soon as they have all the kinks worked out. I wouldn't worry. What's the worst that can happen?

OK, so you'll have to stop rubbernecking at accidents. You also can no longer discipline your kids in the back seat, like you were able to back when cars were steered with your hands. And if you're driving on mountain roads, you don't want to look at the view.

Q: What if the driver dozes off? Or what if he blinks?

A: Actually, the car automatically stops when you close your eyes. So, for example, if you come to a red light, you have to close your eyes to stop the car, and then try to guess when the light has turned green again, based on the honking.

Q: But what if one of the *passengers* looks at the windshield? And what if everyone in the car is looking in a different direction?

A: They've fixed that problem too. In order to steer the car, the driver has to wear a modified bicycle helmet, so the car knows

Look, Ma! No Hands!

whose eyes to follow. So if you get this particular car, you'll be sure to look really cool, driving around and scratching your feet with a bike helmet on.

"What's with the bike helmet?"

"It helps me steer the car with my eyes!"

"Sure."

They're also solving a lot of the problems by creating a second mode in which you can set the car to do all the driving on its own. The car will sense obstacles and speed limit signs, and you'll be free to stare adoringly at your phone until you come to the intersection, when the car will stop and wait for you to space in and look in a particular direction.

But isn't that just typical, though? Society has a problem of people driving and texting at the same time, so instead of creating some kind of, I don't know, hands-free texting system where you just talk into the phone and the phone types up what you say and sends it to the other person's phone, which then reads the message out loud to the person, they went and made a hands-free car! Those silly Germans. What will they think of next?

Now before I get a bunch of stern letters sticking up for the Germans, I want to point out that I am not actually hurting anyone. In fact, a lot of the questions we're asking are, in fact, helping them improve their technology, so that one day, before we know it, cars will be able to drive entirely by themselves, and we'll be able to go places without even being in the car.[1]

And in fact, humor columnists throughout the ages have always

---

1. Before you decide that's ridiculous, think about your kids' carpool.

WHAT IS THIS — SOME KIND OF JOKE?

made harmless jokes about technology. Let's go back in time and take a look:

Hamodia Magazine, June 1959

Don't Take the Belt!
A Humor Column
by Morris Kenneth Schmutter

So I hear that Volvo just patented something called a "seat belt." Apparently, it keeps your pants up, but only if you're sitting in a car.

No, I'm just kidding. It's supposed to keep you in your seat while you're driving. Because otherwise you'll just wander away, apparently. Maybe we should start putting them on the seats in my classroom[2] so my students will stop getting up.

Seriously, what is this obsession with safety nowadays? When I was growing up, we just roamed around in the back seat, and when my father wanted us to be quiet, he would hit the brakes, and we would all SLAM into the back of his chair. We had no seat belts, and we all turned out just fine, except that I no longer finish all of my

Hamodia Magazine, June 1910

This Is Not a Crank
A Columne of Humour
by Myron Hyman Schmutter

So Ford just came out with a car that doesn't have a crank on the front. No crank? How are we supposed to wind it up in the morning? With a key? Not only that, but they say that this new car is supposed to go faster than a horse. They're even throwing

---

2. Morris Kenneth is a high school teacher.

Look, Ma! No Hands!

around words like "horsepower," like they're taking actual horses and putting them under the hood. I looked under the hood, and I had no idea what I was looking at, but I definitely didn't see any horses.

Apparently, the car can do all this because it runs on gasoline. Gasoline! Why don't we just run our cars on *dynamite*, while we're at it? We'll just attach a few sticks to the back of the car, and hope we don't have to make any sudden turns!

Also, when are they going to invent brakes?

Hamodia Magazine, June 1886

Where Does One Stick the Carrots?
A Comedy (*in that all are still alive at the end*)

by Melvin Clarence Schmutter

So I hear from the newsie on the corner that they're inventing a new kind of cart. I get all my news from the newsie — but not by purchasing a paper, mind you. I've discovered that if I stick around long enough, he eventually screams out the entire contents of the paper, including *Ziggy*. (That Ziggy is a delight! And what a marvelous head of hair he has!)

Anyway, it seems that the Germans are coming out with something called a "horseless carriage," or "car" for short.

Q: Horseless? So it's not going to move?

A: Apparently, it will move by itself. At least downhill.

But my question is this: Does it *have* to be horseless? My horses have become part of the family; I don't want to lay them off. Perhaps they can sit in the cab with *me*.

WHAT IS THIS — SOME KIND OF JOKE?

Q: What if the car breaks down? Do we take it to the side of the road and shoot it? Also, how is one supposed to make it go faster? There's nothing to whip!

A: Perhaps you're supposed to whip the car in front of you. Personally, though, I've never whipped my horse to make it go faster. I just give it coffee.

Q: Those crazy Germans. What will they think of next? So if the horse isn't the one pulling the cart, who's going to wear the blinders?

Hamodia Magazine, Present Day

Wait. I just had an idea.

DAY TRIPS

If you have a chance before Yom Tov, you should probably start thinking about where you want to go on Chol Hamoed, unless your idea of a fun Chol Hamoed is sitting around the sukkah for four days, going, "I don't know; what do *you* wanna do?" "I don't know; what do *you* wanna do?" and looking through the same AAA book for the 500th time, hoping you'll suddenly find places that you've never heard of before even though you haven't ordered a new tour book since 1992.

For the most part, you don't really *care* where you go, as long as it meets the following three requirements:

1. It can't be too expensive.
2. It can't be too far away.
3. You don't want the whole rest of the world to be there.

Unfortunately, every place you can think of that is not far away

WHAT IS THIS — SOME KIND OF JOKE?

or expensive, the whole rest of the world *is* going to be there. For example, you can't go to a concert and expect no one else to be there. Likewise any park that has a sukkah. You're probably better off eating yogurts and hard-boiled eggs, or taking your Chol Hamoed trips at times when the rest of the world *won't* be at these places, such as the week before Pesach.

But that's not the point. The point is that you need to think of somewhere to go. Let's start with the most obvious place:

The Zoo

This is by far the most popular place to take little kids. Basically, the way a zoo works is you pay money to look at animals who could not be any less interested that you're there. In fact, as far as my kids know, most animals look like a tiny ball of fur in a log at the back of the cage.[3]

Alternatively, if you don't want to pay money, you can take your kids to a pet store and tell them it's a zoo. It's better than most zoos, actually, because some pet stores have a little cage where they can lock you in with a dog you don't know and see if you can get it to like you. A lot of these pet stores can be found at major shopping malls, although I have yet to see anyone walking around the mall with several shopping bags and a parakeet.

Miniature Golf

You can also play mini golf. Mini golf is just like regular golf, except that they frown on people driving around the course in a golf cart. So don't even ask. Also, mini golf takes approximately

---

3. Basically, we're coming to the animals' homes to watch them sleep through a fence. It's very creepy.

Day Trips

eighteen minutes for each person playing, which is just about the average person's tolerance for golf, whereas regular golf can take the better part of a week just to find your ball. And anyway, I don't think they make golf carts big enough for the average *frum* family, plus a stroller, plus a cooler, plus a cardboard refrigerator box, and some branches.

Batting Cages

Another fun destination, if your family likes sports but doesn't like all of the walking involved, is batting cages. The way batting cages work is that you put on a helmet and climb into a cage, and at the other end of the cage is a dog you don't know.

OK, there's no dog. You basically just stand there, and a machine at the other end of the cage tries to kill you with baseballs. Or, if you like, you can bring a bat in with you and try to hit the balls back at the machine. Of course, you won't be able to do this, because the whole point of batting cages is that you're so bad at getting the ball where you want it to go that no one you know is brave enough to actually pitch to you. That's why you have to be locked in a cage. So the most efficient thing to do is to just walk up to the machine and pound it with your bat. That's how *I* do it.

But even if you're not into baseball, batting cages are worth going to, because they basically give you the fun part of baseball, which is trying to hit the ball, and take out the part where you stand out in the field for hours looking at airplanes.

Apple Picking

Another good day trip idea, especially in the fall, is apple picking. Unless you live in a region where there are no apples, such as Brooklyn.

WHAT IS THIS — SOME KIND OF JOKE?

The interesting thing about apple picking is that normally, when you go to the store, you can buy apples for like seventy-nine cents a pound. But if you go to the orchard, they charge you eight dollars so you can go all the way out into the field with no golf cart and pick your own apples. You'd think that for eight bucks, a guy would follow you out there and pick the apples *for* you, while you lay under the tree and point. Then he would bring you to the next tree in a wheelbarrow. Basically, it's like if you go to the mechanic, and he says, "I can fix this for three hundred dollars, or, if you want, you can fix it yourself with no tools in the hot sun, and you'll pay me three thousand."

"WHAT?"

"No, you're paying for the experience. It's fun!"

Maybe for eight *hundred* dollars, they'll let you plant the apple trees too.

The truth is that the orchard charges you eight dollars because they know how many apples you're eating out there. You're going out there with ten people, spending five hours, and coming back with one small bag of apples. They weren't born yesterday. I guess the real question is, if orchard apples cost eight dollars and store apples cost seventy-nine cents, then how old are those store apples?

Hiking

Yes, I'm essentially telling all my readers to go take a hike.

A hike is basically like a walk, except you have to drive to get there. You get out of the car, and you walk and walk and walk, and for a while your kids don't say anything, because they're hoping that you'll eventually reach some kind of destination, and at the end of the day you get back to the car, and they're like, "That's it? We walked all this way to get to the *car*? We were already *AT* the car!"

That's why amusement parks are so popular. If you're going to end up where you started anyway, you may as well take a train.

The truth is that if your family is up for it, there are some pretty nice places to hike. You don't have to keep stopping every twenty feet to wait for the light to change, and it's very cheap, unless it's a place that charges you to hike, which I'm pretty sure is worse than charging you to pick your own crops.

Museums

There are a lot of different kinds of museums, but most of them feature old historical objects, such as George Washington's teeth, that you pay money to look at only because they're really old. If you were sitting around with George Washington two hundred years ago, and he offered to show you his teeth, you would yell "NO!" and jump backward and spill your ale.

"That's it! I'm voting for the other guy!"

But teeth are a bad example, because there's a pretty good chance that when George Washington was alive, no one knew he had false teeth. Then he passed away, and everyone said, "OHHHHHHHHH! *That's* why it always took him so long to answer the door!"

But whatever they paid for those teeth, they got ripped off.

Anyway, have fun at these places. I'm not going to be there, of course. My plan is to direct you to these places so that I could go somewhere that the whole rest of the world is not going to be.

WHAT IS THIS — SOME KIND OF JOKE?

The whole rest of the world, if I emphasized the aspect of price correctly, is going to be crammed in a pet store somewhere.

PLAIN AND SIMPLE

I would have to say that the worst thing about getting back from a summer vacation, aside from the part where you're back from vacation, is all the people saying, "I'll bet now you need a vacation from the vacation, right? Ha ha!"[4]

But it's really all a matter of perspective.

For our summer outing this year, my wife and I drove the kids out to Lancaster County, Pennsylvania. On the surface, Lancaster looks like a big, wide-open space punctuated by the occasional cow, but there's actually a lot to do there. For example, one thing we did was walk through a gigantic corn maze. Because getting lost while *driving* wasn't enough for us.

The maze that we walked through was five acres, and was

---

4. People: repeating old jokes since the year 1.

WHAT IS THIS — SOME KIND OF JOKE?

called "The Amazing Maize Maze." Sure, that name is very, um, *corny* (sorry) but it's not a name you're bound to forget. And "The Amazing Maize Maze" is way more fun than "The Amazing Mayonnaise Maze."

We wandered around the maze until the kids got tired, at which point my wife suggested that we ask one of the park rangers for directions, which I was really against, because to me, it felt like cheating. I feel the same way when we're *driving*. My wife is like, "Let's ask that guy on the side of the road." And I go, "No! Where's the sense of accomplishment that we're going to get if we finally make it to our destination?" ("Hey, you found us!" "Not really. We asked someone for directions.")

But we definitely spent a lot of our trip lost, because as it turns out, all farms look exactly the same, and there's no one to ask directions from but the cows on the side of the road. We're driving around, squinting at maps and trying to read road signs, and the whole time the kids are in the back going, "Look, a cow! Look! Another cow!"

Before we left the house, I had tried, unsuccessfully, to borrow a GPS,[5] just in case this happened. But then my wife put it in perspective. "We're going to visit the Amish," she said. "We need a GPS?"

The other main activity in Lancaster, besides getting lost, is visiting the Amish. The Amish describe themselves as "plain people," and are easy to spot by their plain clothes and, in the case of the men, their beards and their suspenders. The name "Amish"

---

5. This was in the days before everyone had a GPS. Nowadays pretty much everyone has one, except for the people that are still lost. The *aseres hashvatim*, for example.

Plain and Simple

comes from their founder, Jacob Amish, who, three hundred years ago, visited Colonial Williamsburg and said, "You know? I really wouldn't mind living like this!" Then he had to walk back to Pennsylvania. In retrospect, he should have made this decision *after* he got off the train.

Ever since then, the Amish have been living without any of the conveniences of modern life, such as cell phones. Many of them are farmers, and nowadays, most farmers have cell phones so people can reach them while they're driving their tractors out in the fields. Of course, it's probably pretty boring out in the fields, so I'm guessing the farmers spend most of that time sending text messages. ("Oops! I just PLOWED into the side of the barn! Get it? LOL! Send an ambulance.") But the Amish don't have cell phones, except for one Amish guy that I saw while waiting for a buggy ride in a town called "Ronksi," which, I have to admit, is a fun name for a town. Ronks Ronks Ronks. It sounds like a duck clearing its throat.

    I later asked a non-Amish tour guide about it.

    TOUR GUIDE: "The Amish don't use electricity, because they don't want any wires coming into their house from the outside world."

    ME: "I saw a guy on a cell phone today."

    TOUR GUIDE: "Um... Cell phones don't have wires."

I don't know if that was the right answer, but I think it's pretty funny that with all our wireless technology, we're actually catching up to the Amish.

I later found out that it's only their *homes* that can't have wires — they can have wires to their places of business, if they need them.

WHAT IS THIS — SOME KIND OF JOKE?

This explained the telephone numbers on all the Amish brochures I picked up.[6]

I learned a lot from those brochures. For example, I learned that one of the Amish houses that we visited was built in 1805. The brochure was very proud of this. I don't know if I was supposed to be impressed that it was built in 1805, considering they build their houses exactly the same nowadays.

Another thing that was very big in all the brochures — every attraction advertised that they had one of these — was covered bridges. The Amish cannot get over their covered bridges.[7] To them, it's the greatest thing since sliced bread. Actually, I'm not entirely sure the Amish *have* sliced bread. That wasn't covered in the tour.

Another convenience of life that the Amish don't have is schools with more than one classroom. All of the schooling takes place in one-room schoolhouses, goes up to the equivalent of eighth grade, and consists of a very limited number of subjects. There's not much in the way of science, for example. There's also little point in learning history, because their history books kind of just stop three hundred years ago.

"What happened since then?"

"*Nothing. Nothing* happened since then."

So the Amish basically just learn "the three R's," which are reading, riting, and rithmetic. (Spelling is not one of the R's.) This allows them to solve practical math problems:

---

6. It also explained how they were making brochures. They didn't have a scribe and a painter somewhere, churning them out.

7. Oy.

Plain and Simple

"If Ezekiel leaves Lancaster in a buggy traveling west at three miles per hour, and Jebediah leaves Ohio traveling east at four miles per hour, and neither one has a cell phone, how many years will they spend just missing each other until they finally give up?"

Another way the Amish are different is in their manner of speech. For example, they can't use a lot of the simple expressions that we use nowadays, such as, "I think we got our wires crossed," or, "It's like we're playing *Telephone*." On the other hand, there are some expressions that mean more to them than they do to us, such as, "When father gets home from the market, he's going to have a cow."

"Why? We already have *thirty* cows!"

Another expression that the Amish can use is, "You've got to wake up pretty early in the morning to fool me." This is because the Amish wake up pretty early in the morning in the first place, because they have a lot of chores to do, and they have to get them all done before the sun goes back down. So they wake up at the crack of dawn, which is what time you wake up when you don't have an alarm clock, and they plow the horses and feed the cows and milk the chickens. Or something like that. It's four thirty in the morning, for goodness' sake.

The Amish also have it tough when it comes to parental discipline. The kids are out of school by eighth grade, so it's entirely up to the parents to discipline their teenagers and get them out of bed in middle of the night and give them long-winded speeches, such as: "You kids don't know how good you have it. When I was your age, we didn't even *have*... Wait. You don't have that either.

WHAT IS THIS — SOME KIND OF JOKE?

Well, we had to walk... Well, you have to walk too. Oh, I got one! When I was your age, we didn't even *have* covered bridges."

"Whoa, really?"

"Yeah. All our bridges were *un*covered."

"Wow! What did you *do*?"

So visiting the Amish really makes you think about what we have, and how easy life is for us. Even what we call "working" doesn't involve plowing fields or anything, and we still need a vacation from it. But on the other hand, aside from all the hard work, life is pretty simple for the Amish. Not easy, but simple. It's something to make you think, until you get home and find that you have a million messages to get back to. So in conclusion, the Amish can live the way they do because they never have to come back home and check their messages.

GET LOST

A few months ago, my wife and I finally caved and decided to buy our first GPS device.[8] Unfortunately, we couldn't find the store.

OK, we didn't "cave." This was a very calculated decision. We're *always* the last people to get any kind of new technology, because we like to wait until they've fixed all of the bugs, such as the one that makes the new technology very expensive. In this case, we wanted to wait until the technology had improved to the point that it was no longer steering people into walls. We kept hearing all these stories about people, on the advice of their GPS, driving onto train tracks, through walls, onto construction sites, etc. As a humor writer, an invention like this is a gift from *Shamayim*. But as far as

---
8. Our trip to the Amish country played a pretty big role in that decision.

WHAT IS THIS — SOME KIND OF JOKE?

my actual life, we decided that we wouldn't buy a GPS until there were fewer stories like that.

I'm not saying there are no GPS mishaps anymore. There was a recent story in Long Island about two cars that collided at an intersection because one driver's GPS told him to turn left, and apparently it didn't care that there was a red light.

But that wasn't the GPS's fault; that was the *driver*. Apparently he's one of those people who drives by looking at his GPS the whole time, because it basically shows your car on the road, and what else do you need to see? Besides, you know, street lights. And the other cars.

And in fact, it's because of drivers like that that there has never been another invention that more people who don't own them are proud not to own. Not one person who doesn't have a GPS is upset that he doesn't have one. They never say, "Actually, we can't afford it right now." No. They proudly announce, "We don't have a *GPS*! What, you *have* one?"

Like, "I can drive and read a map at the same time, thank you very much."

Sure, overreliance on technology is never good, but no one says, "An oven? We were *thinking* about getting an oven, but then I figured, 'What's the big deal? You squat in the backyard, you roast your chicken — for that you need an oven?' My *wife's* not so happy."

But in case you're one of those people, I should explain: A GPS, which stands for *Satellite Navigation System*, is basically the equivalent of someone sitting next to you as you drive and holding a map and going, "Whoa, you just missed a turn back there!" in case for some reason you don't have your wife in the car.

OK, not exactly. Usually, my GPS is pretty good about corners,

Get Lost

although once in a while it loses its satellite connection, and takes longer to find it again than it does for me to get lost, apparently. And I'm not even aware that it's forgotten where I am, because it's pretty quiet about it. At least if the person next to you has a lapse like that, you notice right away, because all of a sudden he's folding and refolding the map and telling you he thinks you've driven off the edge.

And if our GPS conks out, *then* what do we do? We don't even know what *town* we're in! We do keep some maps in the car, but not a lot, and they're all for very specific places. Like we have one that tells us how to get around Six Flags. But then we get into an intersection, past the point where it's socially acceptable to turn, and all of a sudden the GPS wakes up again: "Make a right here! No, wait!"

Also, sometimes you actually turn it off while you're driving because it's being annoying and telling you things you already know. Like for instance, we're out on the highway, and we know that we're going to be on this particular highway for the next three hours, but our GPS is making a point of telling us, as we pass each exit, that we should stay left. But if we turn it off and then turn it back on later, it wakes up and thinks that we're still wherever we were when we turned it off. It's like if your passenger falls asleep even though he's supposed to be reading the map, and then he wakes up, and he's like, "Where *are* we? *This* isn't Connecticut!"

In fact, as I write this article, I have turned on my GPS for research purposes, and even though, as far as I know, I'm at my desk at home, my GPS is thoroughly convinced that we're out on a highway somewhere.

Yes, I keep my GPS in the house. This is because if you have a GPS, you have to take it out of the car every time you get out,

WHAT IS THIS — SOME KIND OF JOKE?

or else someone is going to break into your car and steal it. Like some criminal is walking down the street, going, "Where *am* I? *This* isn't Connecticut! Ooh, a GPS!"

I'd like to think that by now, everyone who wants a GPS already has one. That was the whole point of my waiting to buy one. So why would they want *mine*? What's the point of having *two*? You already *know* where you are!

But I do feel that if I have to carry it into, say, a dentist's office, then it should at least have some games I can play while I wait. Like maybe that game we all had growing up, where you're in a racecar on a road with three lanes, all of which are going the other way, and you're trying to squeeze between all the cars coming at you and hoping you can make it to the next exit. Except there *are* no exits. It's kind of like Route 17 in New York.

So I don't use it every time I'm in the car. But this conforms with a recent study in England, which was reported in a Reuters news article titled, "Men More Likely to Overrule SatNavs[9] Than Women."

No kidding. If we overrule *women*, there are repercussions. So I'm guessing that what the headline *means* to say is, "Men More Likely *Than Women* to Overrule SatNavs."

According to the article, researchers found that 83 percent of male drivers have admitted to ignoring their GPS commands and taking "a *better* route." This is as opposed to women, who, according to the article, disobey their GPS *less than 75 percent of the time*.

---

9. "SatNav" is a portmanteau word that stands for "Global Positioning System."

Get Lost

Whoa.

OK, so they're pretty high numbers either way, but that can be accounted for. First of all, the survey was taken in England, and as it turns out, most of the reported GPS accidents so far have happened in England. For example, there is a road that SatNavs keep telling drivers to use, despite the fact that the road gradually narrows so that one end is not actually wide enough for cars to pass through. They keep getting wedged between the buildings. It's gotten to the point where there are signs in certain places in England to *ignore* SatNav commands.

Why is England more prone to these things? I don't know. Maybe when you drive on the left, it confuses the GPS, which then resolves to do anything it can to make you get off the road before three lanes of cars start coming at you.

Also, I know a lot of Americans use the British voice on our GPS, even though we don't quite know what half the words mean. ("What's a *roundabout*? Is that like *trousers*?") So it occurs to me that the British are driving around with American accents on *their* SatNavs, and of course they don't respect American accents enough to listen.

The article cites these statistics as if they mean something negative about men, but they don't. If you know where you're going, you SHOULD override the GPS. A GPS should *aid* your abilities, not *replace* them. I think the question the survey failed to ask is how many people have ignored their GPS *and then gotten lost*.

Anyway, I have to go. My GPS is telling me to turn off here.

SECTION XI:
ORANGE YOU GLAD I DIDN'T SAY "BANANA"?
(OR "PROTECTING YOUR HOME")

What kind of screening conversation do you have before you let someone into YOUR home?

The orange thing is, of course, a "knock-knock" joke. The way a knock-knock joke works is that one person says, "Knock-knock," and the other person says, "Who's there?" and the guest just says a first name, like that's usually enough, right?

"Nah, it's OK. We're really close."

But apparently you're not as close as he thinks, because then the *ba'al habayis* says, "Banana? Banana who?"

Like how many people do you know named *Banana*?

"I don't know. At least three of them just knocked."

If we're not close, why not just say your last name? If someone actually tried that on me, I wouldn't let him in.

Sometimes it's actually the *ba'al habayis* who drags it on, though:

"Knock-knock."

"Who's there?"

"Mordechai Schmutter."

"Mordechai Schmutter who?"

"That's...that's my whole name."

I mean you want to ask who it is to be safe. But the guy is making up names on the other side of the door.

"Who's there?"

"Atch."

"Atch? That's not even a real name. It sounded like you said *Atch*."

"I did."

"Atch who?"

"Gesundheit."

"Gesundheit? I thought you said *Atch*!"

See, this is why I have a peephole.

I mean, I get the banana situation:

"Knock-knock."

"Who's there?"

"Banana."

"Banana who?"

"...I don't have a last name. I'm just *Banana*."

Though how does an actual banana knock on the door without getting mushy? I guess that's why he has to actually say, "Knock-knock."

It sure is great when your joke involves the listener, though, isn't it?

"I want to tell you a joke, but you have to work for it. And it won't even be funny."

I don't even go for this joke. When people say, "Knock-knock," I just yell, "Come in!"

I see who you are. You're standing right here.

Point is, my home is my castle. It's old, it's drafty, and it only has one throne room. The following section is about keeping your home together and protecting it from outside elements, such as cold air, water damage, and, in extreme cases, *chametz*.

But fruits with peels are OK.

QUESTIONS AND ANSWERS

This week, in honor of Yom Tov, I am presenting my very first Pesach-advice column. I feel compelled to do this in question-and-answer format, but I'm not sure *why*.

Q: What is a good time to start cleaning for Pesach?

A: YOU'RE ASKING THIS *NOW*?

Q: Yeah, I thought...

A: Go clean!

Q: Fine. *Don't* answer my question.

A: As far as the rest of you, there are varying opinions as to when one should start cleaning, based on the size of your house, how many people are helping, whether or not you have a day job, and how many little kids are following you around, eating pretzels. But most of us end up starting the day after Purim.

WHAT IS THIS — SOME KIND OF JOKE?

Q: Is there any news this year in the world of cleaning?

A: Yes. A museum was recently opened in Britain, called "The Museum of Vacuum Cleaners." So we figure that going there will provide inspiration for your family, as far as cleaning for Pesach.

"If you don't help with the cleaning," you can say to your kids, by way of inspiration, "we're going to take you to the Museum of Vacuum Cleaners."

Q: According to my custom, I don't sell real *chametz*. But when I clean my kitchen a week before Pesach, I suddenly find hundreds of boxes of cookies and crackers and noodles that I'd bought and then buried in the back of the closet, and then forgot that I'd bought them, so I bought some more, and now I have no idea what to do with them. So my question is this: do you want some of my noodles?

A: We find that the best thing to do is to go through all of your cabinets several weeks before Pesach, and to take out everything that is real *chametz*, and then put it all into one cabinet.

Q: And this will help?

A: Not really. You're not going to finish the foods at the back of *that* cabinet either.

Q: How about all these cookies? If I gain weight *before* Pesach, what hope do I have on Pesach itself?

A: Cookies are easy to get rid of. Just leave an open package on your kitchen table every night before you go to sleep. When you wake up, the package will be empty, and your kids will feel like they got away with something.

Q: Are there any specific things I should look out for while I'm cleaning?

Questions and Answers

A: Cheerios. Even if you don't eat Cheerios, you will still find them all over your house. Cheerios were invented by anti-Semites who totally don't care about Pesach. They said, "Hey! Let's make a product that cannot possibly be any more *chametzdik*, and we'll make it really tiny and the perfect shape to hit the ground rolling, and we'll market it to toddlers!"

Q: What should I do about my children?

A: The best thing to do is to get them to help you clean, and to make sure they understand what you're doing. Take a lesson from *my* life: One year, the night before Pesach, we were down to our very last box of Cheerios, and I decided to leave it on the table when I went out to Minchah so my kids could make it "mysteriously disappear" like they did with all the cookies. And when I got home, I noticed that half the box was gone.

Great job, right?

But then the next morning, right before I went out to burn the *chametz*, my wife happened to open up my two-year-old son's riding toy, and she found the other half of the box. Apparently, our son was worried about all of his foods disappearing, so he decided to stash some away, just in case.

Q: My friend told me that she was cleaning her house the other day and she found a hundred dollars. Am I cleaning the wrong house?

A: Don't worry, you'll find plenty of things also. Most likely you will find little plastic pieces that you have no idea which toys they go with, or an embarrassing amount of chocolate wrappers, or the floor of your kids' room.

Q: Is there any specific place that I should not forget to clean?

WHAT IS THIS — SOME KIND OF JOKE?

A: Under the couch cushions. You'd be surprised at what you can find down there. There was a woman in Spokane who bought a used couch for $27 last year, and she noticed, as soon as she brought it home, that there was a weird noise coming from somewhere in the house. After days of searching for the source of the noise, she got her husband to flip over the couch, and they found that there was a cat living under the cushions. So you definitely want to check underneath your couch cushions, or your kids will be in for a real surprise when they try to hide the *afikoman*.

Q: I'm making Pesach for the very first time. Which kitchen utensils should I buy?

A: Before you buy anything, you should bear in mind that you can live without certain things for the first few years, such as loaf pans. What are you making loaves of, on Pesach? That said, you should probably make a menu first, and then buy the tools that you need to prepare those foods. And whatever you do, don't forget to buy several peelers, and some containers to put things in *after* you make them. If you can't find any that are big enough, I would suggest those sealed plastic containers that people use to store clothing in the attic. And if you're hosting the Seder, for goodness' sake don't forget a corkscrew.

Q: How do I keep my kids from stealing my *afikoman*?

A: I would say you could offer them a prize *not* to steal it, but I'm assuming the reason you're asking in the first place is that you don't want to buy them a prize. But even if they steal it, you can always take spare matzah from one of the boxes and eat that instead.

Questions and Answers

Q: I am a third grade boy, and my friends and I take great pride in coming into school and announcing what time our Seders were over. Do you have any advice for making the Seder take even *longer*?

A: There are a few tactics you can use:
1. Ask your father some really good questions that you've looked up beforehand, but don't tell him which *sefarim* you found them in.
2. Hide all the boxes of spare matzah.
3. Hide the corkscrew.

Q: Every year, we get into an argument about whether it is our *minhag* to stand for *Lefikoch*, or to sit for it, or to lean for it, and we never remember what we did the previous year. Do you think it's something in the wine? Also, I have no clue how much of anything I bought last year, because I threw out all the receipts during Pesach cleaning.

A: What a lot of people do is they sit down after Pesach every year, and they write themselves a letter:

Dear Future Me;

This year we had a really exciting Pesach. Our Seder went until four in the morning, because first we couldn't find the corkscrew, then we had a half-hour argument about whether we stand for Lefikoch, and then one of the kids hid all the spare matzah before we even washed. We bought enough matzah to have one matzah per person per meal, but we have tons of extras because we couldn't actually find the boxes for the first couple of days. We also bought a can of potato starch, because my parents always have it in the house, so I think it's our minhag. But we

WHAT IS THIS — SOME KIND OF JOKE?

didn't use it for anything, because I'm pretty sure that it's not even a food. Where is it the rest of the year? And what is that crunching sound coming from under the couch cushions?

Eh; I don't care. I'll get to it next Pesach. Future Me can deal with it.

EXTREME WEATHER

My wife is thinking of sending me out to patch up a crack on our roof.

"Wait a minute," you're saying. "Didn't I already *read* this article?"

Well, you didn't. Apparently this is just something that happens a lot in our family. The main difference this time is that it's a slightly different roof, and we don't know for sure how bad the crack is, and I'm heavier now than I was back then. So if this is my last article for a while, you'll know why.

OK, so I shouldn't make jokes about falling through my roof. But I also don't want to say for certain that it *won't* happen, because I've found that one of the biggest risks I take as a humor columnist is when I say that something will never happen. Like a few months

WHAT IS THIS — SOME KIND OF JOKE?

ago, I wrote an article about baby products,[1] and I made fun of something called a "hearth cushion," which is a cushion that you put around the little step in front of your fireplace so that your kids don't hurt their head. My argument was that parents who let their kids play near a fireplace aren't the type of parents who are likely to go out and buy a hearth cushion. But then, before that article even saw print, my son was playing a game wherein you put a blanket over your head and trip over your toys, and he hit his head on the step in front of our fireplace.[2]

And that's not the only time this happened. Last week I wrote a column about small talk, and I wrote that even though a lot of people say you should talk about the weather because it's a neutral topic that can't possibly lead to *lashon hara* ("Some weather we're having!" "Yeah, the weatherman was *way* off!"), weather is very boring. I also said that the only time it's OK to talk about weather is if it's *extreme* weather, such as — yes — the weather we had right after I finished writing that column.

Now I want to start off by saying that I in no way intend to make light of the damages done by *real* extreme weather, such as hurricanes.[3] But at least with hurricanes, you have some idea that they're coming. The media announces it weeks beforehand, and everyone marks his calendar and runs out to the supermarket to buy tuna fish. (Experts advise never to go into a hurricane without an adequate supply of tuna fish.) But here in New Jersey, we don't get a lot of hurricanes, and we don't get major announcements

---

1. This article appears in my fourth book, *Cholent Mix*.
2. This article also appears in *Cholent Mix*.
3. Not yet, anyway.

Extreme Weather

either. Basically, the radio says something like, "There's going to maybe be a *shtickel* rain on Shabbos. Also it might be windy." So my first indication that it was extreme weather was when I found myself chasing my hat down the street.

This is how it works. You're walking to shul, and you have one hand over your head, holding your hat on, because what makes this hat your rain hat is the fact that it's now about three sizes too small. Your other hand is in your pocket, because it's important that you keep that hand dry. Your kids, meanwhile, are not holding your hands, because you find that when they do, you're way too close to them when they purposely jump into puddles. But then it's time to cross the street, so you take your hand out of your pocket and hold one kid's hand, and you take your other hand off your head and hold the other kid's hand, and you take a step out into the street, and — WHOOSH! There it goes.

Also, I know that rain on Shabbos is a *brachah*, but when you're trying to find your raincoat in shul after *davening*, it's no picnic.

Basically, when shul is over, everyone, at once, goes into the wet, drippy coatroom to find his raincoat, and the only real difference between any two coats is the buttons. I usually find my coat relatively quickly, because mine is the one that is currently closer to grey than black, and one of my buttons is cracked. You'd think I'd buy a new raincoat, but it's deficiencies like these that help me find the coat in the first place.

This week after Minchah, however, I couldn't find it. I kept going back and forth through the coat racks, getting closer and closer to *shkiah*, with each passing moment raising the chances that some poor fool had walked off with my coat. And in the meantime, all the people behind me are spouting annoying clichés at each

WHAT IS THIS — SOME KIND OF JOKE?

other, like, "Make sure to pick a good one!" So I finally gave up and borrowed a coat from a neighbor who was staying in shul for *seudah shlishis*.

Most of Shabbos afternoon, however, was spent watching our recycling fly around to the front of our house and down the block. We also lost two of our garbage cans, including the first one we'd ever bought.

Our very first week in the house, we'd bought a garbage can — the kind with wheels — and we unwisely left it out with the garbage. And that very first week, the wheels disappeared. So now we have a can that can't stand up on its own, but when we leave it out at the curb to be picked up, the sanitation people won't take it because they think it's *supposed* to be there. We've pretty much given up trying to get rid of it, especially since every subsequent can we've bought has either been stolen or blown away. So most of the time, we fill it with garbage and prop it up against a telephone pole.

Anyway, that can finally blew away, as did another one that we'd bought not two weeks ago. And we found two other cans in front of our house, one of which looked like it was run over by a truck. So it looked like we pretty much broke even.

My wife keeps saying that we should paint our house number onto our cans, because it isn't the first time this has happened.

Like whoever finds our can is going to attach sufficient postage and mail it back.

I ended up finding my old can a few blocks down (I knew which way to go, because I had chased my hat in that very same direction), and I knew the can was mine, just like with the raincoat, because it's now closer to grey than to black, and its wheels are

Extreme Weather

cracked off. I also found another can, not far from it, that looks reasonably similar to our new one.

And then there's the matter of our roof. We found little bits and pieces of a roof on our lawn, and after a few minutes of panic, we said, "Whew, these aren't from our roof. They're from other people's roofs. Ha ha." And then we went inside and found that there was a major puddle in the ceiling of our kitchen. So my wife is thinking of sending me out there, because of my extensive roofing experience.[4]

My basic point, though, is that I don't want to say that I *won't* fall through the roof, because then, knowing my luck, I probably will. But if I say that I *will* fall through the roof, I probably won't. On the other hand, once I said *that*, in an article, then I probably will anyway.

So I have an idea: maybe I shouldn't go up onto the roof in the first place.

OK, I'll admit it; I'm just stalling. We all know I'm gonna go up there.

---

4. My extensive roofing experience, as detailed in the book, *A Clever Title Goes Here*, is hugging the roof and trying to figure out how I'm going to get down.

TOO MUCH ENERGY

In the old days, there was no such thing as home energy audits. Instead, we had fathers. Our fathers would say things like, "Turn off the lights when you leave the room!" and, "Close the door; you're letting all the cold air in!" Then they'd ask if we thought they were made of money.

But getting an energy audit is the thing to do nowadays. Especially in a leaky house like mine. We even have cold air coming through the electrical outlets. It's like the power company is sending us cold air. Personally, I think it's a ploy to make us use more gas.

Over the years, my wife and I have tried several things to make our home more energy efficient. We put several tons of old clothes in the attic to keep the heat in. We put sheets of plastic over our windows during the winter, most of which have subsequently blown away. We even replaced the humongous, 1960s-era, 300-pound air

Too Much Energy

conditioner that was stuck in the wall of the dining room, which used a lot of power but made up for it in noise. It hung right over my head, and whenever we had people over for Shabbos meals during the summer, I couldn't hear one word they were saying. I would see their lips moving, and I would go, "What?" and then I would see their lips moving again, so I would nod politely or say something I hoped was a safe answer, but probably was not in any way related to what they were saying. None of these people ever invited us back to *their* houses.

So when we heard that there were government programs that would send people to audit our house and do some of the work for free, we jumped at the idea, because we happen to know that our home does not have any insulation. We know this because when we opened up the wall of the dining room to replace the air conditioner, we peered inside and noticed that the entire house is insulated by what appears to be a huge, single-ply sheet of aluminum foil. And we figured that a project like this was something we could never afford ourselves, because it basically involves building an entire second house out of insulation and somehow inserting it into the walls of our current house, which is made of, as far as I can tell, spackle.

So we had some guys come over, and they looked at our house, and they counted how many windows we had. They also spent a lot of time crawling around the water heater, and they conducted a test wherein they closed all of our windows and set up an exhaust fan in our doorway that basically sucked all the air out of the house, so they could tell if there was a leak. Basically, if your house implodes like a soda can, you don't have a leak.

Then they sat down and looked at our heating bills, and they said they'd present our case to find out how much work we'd qualify for.

WHAT IS THIS — SOME KIND OF JOKE?

"But we're going to qualify for insulation, right?" we asked.

They hoped so. In fact, they didn't put many other recommendations on our list, because they were hoping for insulation. And then they left.

That's how it goes. The auditing guys don't actually do the work; they just suck out all the air, point out what's wrong with the house, and then they leave. They're kind of like a mother-in-law.

A few weeks later, another pair of guys came in to do all the work. These guys were *extremely* energy efficient, by which I mean "lazy." Almost everything they did actually made our house worse. For example, they installed weather stripping on our front door, but they put it on a little too close to the inside of the house, so that the door latch no longer caught in the hole, and the door would sometimes blow open by itself. The only way it would stay closed was if we locked the top lock. So now, thanks to the weather stripping, there was actually *extra* air blowing in around the door — so much, that I had to deal with it by thumb-tacking a blanket over the door every night. (*After* Ma'ariv — I didn't make *that* mistake twice.)

Another thing they did was break the pull-down stairs to the attic. I think the logic was that if we never opened up the attic, we would save on our energy bills. We didn't even know they broke it until the next time I tried pulling down the stairs, and a huge metal spring jumped out at me. So we had no access to our attic, and a month later our son was born, and guess where all his clothes were?

I could not tell you how happy we were that the government was paying to break things that we could have broken ourselves, for free.

Too Much Energy

But we didn't qualify for insulation. It turns out that the government doesn't care how badly you need insulation, they just care how much you've been paying for heat. The more you've been paying, the more work you qualify for. And because we always keep our house at a temperature where we don't actually have to remember to put the milk back in the fridge, we never paid enough to qualify for such a big job.

"So can we crank up the heat this winter and apply again?" we wanted to know.

"No," they said. "Not for another five years."

"But we don't have insulation!" I said. "I checked when I was putting in the air conditioner!"

So they gave us a big plastic cover to put over the air conditioner during the winter.

Thanks.

A few months later, we heard about another energy program, so we applied, because we were still hoping to get insulation. So they came over, counted the windows, crawled around the water heater, sucked more air out of the house, and asked us what that weird plastic box was in our dining room. And then they did the math and said they would definitely be able to get us insulation. And a couple of months later, sure enough, we got a letter informing us that because we'd had the other company do some work, we wouldn't qualify for ANY work with this company.

And then I received a call from a friend of mine, Yossie, who, as it turns out, is studying to become an energy auditor. He told me that for his final exam, he needed to audit an actual house with an instructor looking over his shoulder and then give a list of

WHAT IS THIS — SOME KIND OF JOKE?

recommendations, which the homeowner would then be free to toss. So he asked if he could use my house.

I said, "Sure, why not?"

Then he asked me if I'd ever had an energy audit.

Yossie ended up scheduling the test for four days before Pesach. I offered to show him the results of our previous audits, because my idea was that he would come into the house, sniff the air, touch the wall and taste his finger, and go, "This house doesn't have any insulation!" and totally bowl the instructor over.

But what I didn't think about, before they came over, was that since they were going to test the appliances and exhaust systems, it was not great that the entire kitchen was covered, top to bottom, in thick silver foil (*l'kavod* Pesach).

I also hadn't considered what the non-Jewish instructor would think. He walked in and was totally blown away. It looked like we were preparing to put the whole kitchen in the oven.

"Whoa," he said, trying to be polite. "It looks like a diner from the 1950s!"

"Yeah," I said. "This is what the *last* energy auditor suggested we do."

In the end, Yossie did catch some things that the other guys missed, and he gave us a list of recommendations, which we've subsequently tossed. Because now we've had three audits, and so far, according to our bills, we haven't saved on heating at *all*. Maybe a few more audits ought to do it.

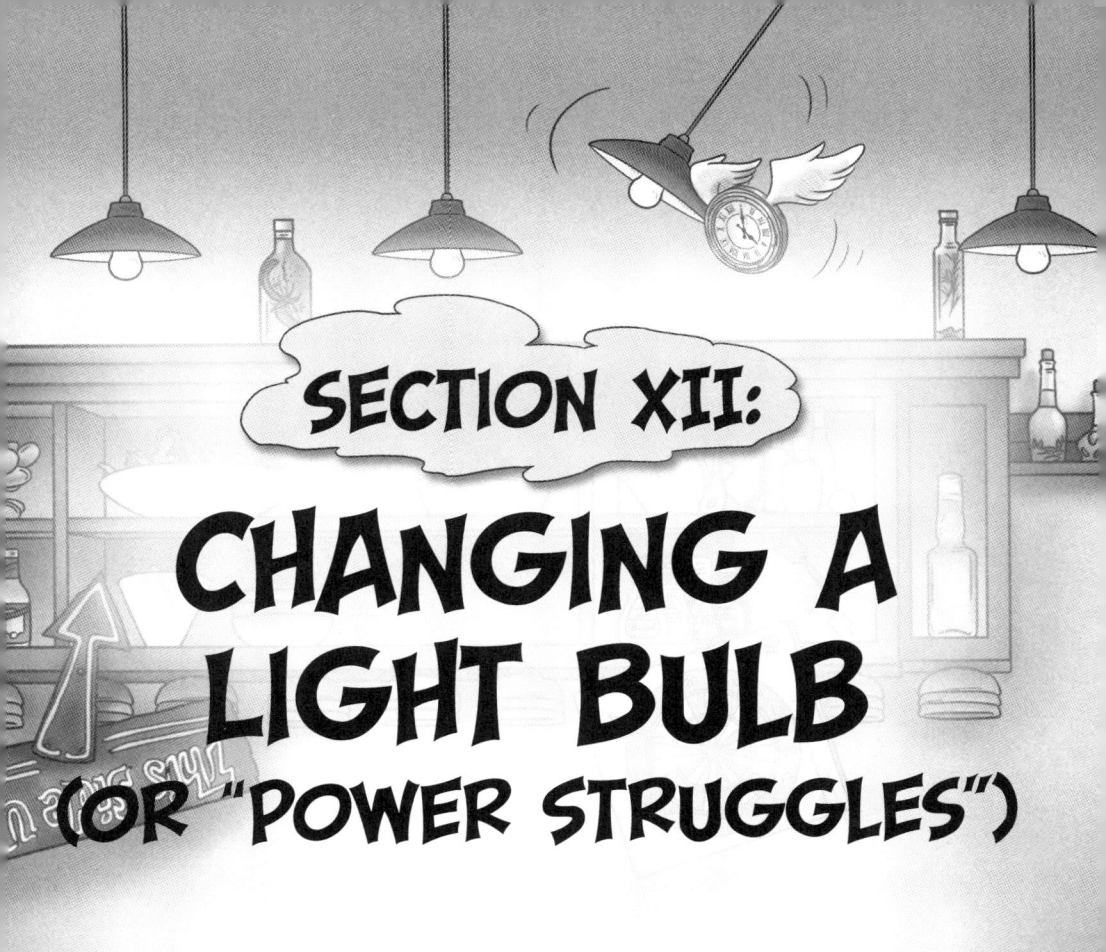

SECTION XII:
CHANGING A LIGHT BULB
(OR "POWER STRUGGLES")

There are literally hundreds of light bulb jokes out there, and none of them are very bright. They're all low-wattage, energy-saver kind of bulbs. I also have no idea what they used to make these kinds of jokes about before light bulbs were invented.

"How many philosophers does it take to put more logs on the fire?"

Or,

"How many *Chashmona'im* does it take to refill a lamp?"

"Not so many, but it takes them eight days."

Outside the realm of jokes, this kind of question is usually asked by someone who's frustrated that they're waiting for you to do something that should be pretty quick, but rather than finishing up, you're standing around in a whole crowd and talking about it.

"Oh my goodness! How many people does it take to do one simple task?"

And you yell, "Six! Five to hold the ladder..."

In my house, it actually takes several people to change a light bulb: One kid to get the new bulb, one father to climb up to do it, one person to hold the swivel chair I'm standing on because I'm too lazy to figure out where my kids hid the stepstool, one person for me to hand the old bulb to so I don't drop it on the floor (because the swivel chair person won't stop turning me), another kid to go down and see what's taking the first kid so long to find a bulb ("How many kids does it take to find a light bulb?!"), and one wife to go to the store and buy more light bulbs so I could finally get down from the chair.

But at least we have lights. In the old days, they had to travel eight days to get more oil.

WHAT TO DO DURING A POWER FAILURE

1. To be honest, not many people really *have* a *minhag* of what to do during a power failure. Seriously, what did your great-grandfather do when *his* power went out?

2. The first thing to do, when the power goes out, is to determine if it was something you did. Because if the entire state blacked out because of something you did, you're going to have to barricade yourself into your house, because everyone is going to come after you with torches.[1]

3. To determine if it's just you, every article I've read recommends that you go down to the basement, which is the darkest room in your house, and check your fuse box, which you have no idea how to understand when there's

---

1. The torches might not be for you.

WHAT IS THIS — SOME KIND OF JOKE?

light, so you can determine if this is just your house or if it's the whole neighborhood. I usually just look outside and see if the neighbors have power. It's a lot easier.

4. One way to tell if your neighbors don't have power is if they also come out of their houses. Then you nod at each other like you're in some secret club, and you're all having some shared trauma that's bringing you closer together, in that you can't turn on the lights.

5. But really, it's more like the old days, when everyone knew each other because there was nothing else to do when the sun went down but stand outside and nod at each other.

6. The truth is that there are several reasons for power outages that *aren't* your fault. There could have been bad weather, although chances are you would know about that. It could be that someone at the power station accidentally flipped the switch off before he went home and didn't realize it. Or it could be that everyone is using too much power at once. We tend to think of electricity as infinite, mostly because we have no idea how it works. We assume that there are a bunch of hamsters running on wheels or something. But if we're all using computers and air conditioners and charging our phones at the same time, the hamsters will poop out. And then we'll have to wait for the electric company to buy enough *new* hamsters, which sometimes takes several days.

7. The first thing you should do, once the power is out, is grope around in the dark for the flashlight that you used to keep who-knows-where until someone moved it to make shadow puppets.

What to Do during a Power Failure

8. One idea is to put glow-in-the-dark stickers on your flashlights. That said, put them on your kids too.[2]

9. If the blackout happens during the day, don't panic. There's a pretty good chance you can still see.

10. One article that I read, once the lights came back on, said, "Putting a few items in a small shoe box and storing it in an easily accessible location will help you spring into action during a power outage."

11. *Spring into action?* How much action are you expecting during a power outage? Be prepared for a lot of *in*action, is what *I* say. What's your rush? You're going to be the only one jumping around, tying your fridge closed and lighting candles and battening down the hatches for when the neighbors come pounding on your door.[3]

12. If you do have a shoe box, you should probably keep the phone number of the electric company in it, so you can call them and ask them to flip the switch back on or start hamster shopping or whatever. If you don't, the number is handily printed on their bills, which they helpfully send you every month, and which are in a filing cabinet in the basement.

13. My wife has a tradition, during every power outage — that she has to go around lighting candles in every room. This is some ancient tradition, dating back to when her ancestors had blackouts in ancient Europe, and houses had, at most,

---

2. And on shin-high furniture.

3. If you have a lot of hatches, you're going to need a lot of supplies. You're also going to need to look up what "battening" means. Without power.

WHAT IS THIS — SOME KIND OF JOKE?

one room. Some of the candles she lights are *yahrtzeit* candles.

14. My opinion is that there's no point in lighting a *yahrtzeit* candle for a blackout. It's never gonna be dark for twenty-four hours. You light a candle for a few hours, you go to sleep, and the next morning you have daylight. If you light a *yahrtzeit* candle, then by the time night comes again, it's burned out.

15. Another ancient tradition that my wife brought into the marriage (we follow her *minhagim* on this) is that she doesn't let me open the fridge or the freezer. I can die of thirst, as long as we don't jeopardize our $10 worth of leftovers. This blatantly goes against *my* old *minhag*, which is that as soon as the power goes out, I try to finish all the ice cream.

16. But seriously, don't open the fridge. A well-stocked fridge, if not opened, will keep the food cold for about 4–6 hours, and the freezer will keep food cold for about two days. And by "well-stocked," we mean full of things that should have been thrown out ages ago. Keep them around, in case of a blackout. If your fridge is so full that you can't close it, that's perfect. Except for the fact that you can't close it.

17. Make sure you have canned foods, in case your wife doesn't let you open the fridge. Also, a can opener that's not electric.

18. If you *have* to go into the fridge, know what you want before you go in. You know how you decide what to make for supper by standing in front of the open fridge for a few minutes and spacing out in the general direction of whatever's inside? Yeah, don't do that.

What to Do during a Power Failure

19. One great idea, if the blackout is long enough that you have to rescue everything in your fridge, is to make an emergency barbecue. And no, I have no idea how long it takes to grill a brisket.

20. Don't shower during a blackout. I know that the water is not the thing that's blacked out, but it's possible that the power needed to clean the water *is* blacked out. Don't use it up.

21. Find something to do, rather than sit around on the couch and wondering how long it's going to be until you have to eat the pillows. For example, as we speak, I'm occupying myself by writing this article by candlelight. And my wife is occupying herself by asking me why I'm using a quill. *"Just because the power's out?"*

22. Learning is an option as well. You can pretend you're learning in the old days. Get a candle (there should be one in every room by now), squint over your Gemara, and slowly realize why, in those days, they found it easier to just memorize things.

23. Another thing to do is to try to get extra sleep. I don't go to sleep during blackouts, because I know that as soon as I get into bed, everything in the house will suddenly come back on. And I do mean *everything*. Because one of the first things people do during blackouts is go from room to room turning on switches: "This one doesn't work. Maybe *that* one will work. Maybe *that* one will work." *What, do you think this light switch is on a circuit from a different block?* And then all of a sudden, the power comes on and the entire house roars — air conditioners, computers, fans,

alarms, radios — everything comes blaring at once. It's like the world's biggest alarm clock, and you're *inside* it.

24. But seriously, make sure to turn on everything in the house, so when the power comes back on, you'll know, no matter where you are. Even if you're not home. Though if the power went off because too many things were on, turning *more* things on might not be the best idea.

25. So you know, the electric company will not give you a discount on your bill, even if the power was out for several days. If anything, they need *more* money for those days, because of all the repairs they were doing. In fact, you should probably help them out by donating extra money. Or, if you don't have extra money because you used it up buying the store's entire supply of bottled water so your family could bathe for Shabbos, just get a box and mail them a few hamsters. I'm sure they'll appreciate it.

SANDY WEATHER

(NOTE: The following were my observations during Hurricane Sandy and the blackout that followed. This is just my own account, in Passaic, New Jersey. I understand, as I learned once the power came back on, that there were people in much worse situations than just not having power for eight days, and I thank Hashem that I had to write this column on a clipboard in the dark, rather than in water up to my neck. Our thoughts and prayers go out to the people who are not as fortunate.)

DAY 1 — MONDAY, OCTOBER 29
2 p.m. (approximately — I don't know; my clock is out)

My power's just gone out. That's pretty impressive. According to the weathermen who have to stand outside on the beach in slickers and report on the wind with waves crashing around them before we go "back to the warm studio" to the guy making random gestures at a green screen, the storm's not even supposed to hit us until eight o'clock.

I've decided to chronicle my thoughts, because there's no telling what else this storm will bring. We could have a weatherman come crashing through our window. And also because there's not much else to do in the dark besides write. I definitely can't *read*.

Oh. Turns out it's not that dark yet. My eyes just had to get used to it.

This morning, before the power went out, I got an e-mail from *Hamodia* saying, "We noticed that five weeks ago, you sent an article for next week (the November 7th issue) about blackouts.[4] You must have *ruach hakodesh*, because apparently, a lot of people are probably going to lose power this week." "No," I said. "No *ruach hakodesh*. Hashem knows that I have to write this column in advance, and every inconvenience that happens to the people around me happens to *me* six weeks before them, so I can write about it." Then my power went out.

My kids are taking turns asking, every five minutes, when the lights are coming back on.

My wife takes out a corded phone that she keeps for such situations. This is why we never updated our line. "Where's the TALK button?" my kids want to know. "You just pick it up," my wife explains. "Wow!" they say. "That's so cool! Where's the END button?"

What's *not* cool is having to leap for the phone every time it rings. But at least, thanks to the cord, we know approximately

---

4. They were referring to the previous chapter in this book, "What to Do during a Power Failure."

Sandy Weather

where to find it. Which is great, because we're going entirely by sound.

I didn't really have time to buy food before the storm. We'd just come from my sister-in-law's *chasunah* in Boston on Sunday and didn't have time to stock up. Actually, we're officially supposed to make *sheva brachos* this Thursday. I hope that either our power comes back on by then, or her travel plans are canceled. Or she brings the food.

But are we going to starve in the meantime? Nah. We have plenty of cans of tuna fish.

DAY 2 — TUESDAY, OCTOBER 30

I am so sick of tuna fish. Got to get out to the store.

Seriously. It's like you stock up on tuna fish, but what are you supposed to do about mayonnaise? We have these Costco-sized jars of mayonnaise that say, "Refrigerate after opening." My wife won't let me open the fridge. So should we just eat the whole jar of mayonnaise? A jar of mayonnaise can feed an army, and a can of tuna can feed one and a half people IF they also eat bread with it.

My kids' yeshivah is out of power too. I know, because we tried to call to see if there was school, and the machine didn't come on telling us whether there was or not. I assume there's not.

I don't blame them for not having school, though. I teach in the *mesivta*,[5] and when the lights go out for two seconds, everyone yells, "WhooOOOoo!" I don't want to think about what will happen in a *yeshivah ketanah* if there are no lights ALL DAY. I don't even

---

5. Really.

WHAT IS THIS — SOME KIND OF JOKE?

want to think about the noises my students make after lights out in the dorm all night.

I hear that one school in Monsey said that the kids should come in, but they should bring their own flashlights. I guess the *chinuch* there is just that there's school during a blackout. Because if you put thirty flashlights in a room, no teaching is getting done *at all*. Even if the boys are all good about it, and agree to aim them all at the *rebbi*.

Somehow, the *mesivta* I teach in has lights. So no "whooing." But at least I can plug in all my devices while I teach.

What did our ancestors do? I think they ate things that didn't have to be refrigerated, like potatoes.

Driving to the store takes forever. Half the streets are blocked by trees or police tape or long lines of cars making K-turns one at a time. I feel like a rat in a maze, trying to get to the cheese at the end.

I got to the supermarket. Bought cheese. That'll take some of the pressure off the tuna. We also bought ice, which will be interesting, since my wife won't let us open the fridge to put it in.

The store is out of *yahrtzeit* candles, though. We find a few hidden in the baby food section, but other than that, we buy mostly scented candles — berries, melon, and one with a "clean linen" smell. That should come in handy, since we don't actually have any clean linen. So instead, the house will smell like clean linen that is for some reason on fire. Also, Halloween is coming up, thank G-d, so the store has plenty of candles with spiders and bats all over them.

We come home and put the ice in the freezer. The kids are very

Sandy Weather

disappointed, because what we told them was an entire carton of ice cream that they could finish is really just melted cream with chocolate chips floating in it. They eat it anyway.

I'm reading my kids a story every night to keep them from making messes in the dark and jumping around with the candles lit. *The Mystery of the Missing Bar Mitzvah Gift.* It's a fun book, but the bar mitzvah gift goes missing in Chapter 7. We're not going anywhere.

It turns out that aroma candles provide almost no light. You light it, and the entire middle starts sinking with the flame, but the outer edges don't go down at all. They just block the light. Our house is still dark, but it smells like berries and melon.

I don't know how they ever managed to do anything in the old days. By the time the kids go to bed, it's too dark.

Should we just go to bed when it gets dark, and then wake up with the sun? But that's when our kids wake up. How are we supposed to get anything done EVER if every moment we're awake is a moment our kids are awake too, AND they're home all day?

We invite the neighbors over for a game night. No one is entirely sure what their cards say. Someone wins, we think.

Someone asks if we're cooking a pie.

DAY 3 — WEDNESDAY, OCTOBER 31

"Is this the line to make a K-turn?" I ask. "No, we're buying gas." "Where? I don't even see a gas station!"[6]

---

6. Turns out that, with nothing to do, people had taken to sitting in their cars all day and waiting to buy gas.

WHAT IS THIS — SOME KIND OF JOKE?

"Don't open the fridge!" My wife keeps saying. At some point, I'll be scared to.

This thing is definitely bringing the community together. I've seen more people in the past couple of days than I've seen the entire year put together, if you don't count teaching or shul. Also, my shul is closed.

It occurs to me, after all these people wondering why I'm not cold, that my house still has heat. Apparently, my heater was built before the invention of electricity.

After enough days of the kids being home, some *rebbeim* and parents have graciously agreed to have individual classes of boys take their homes apart for an hour and a half so the parents can get some sanity. The girls' building, meanwhile, has power, but not school.

We're very thankful for the boys getting out of the house, because while I've been messing around with my clipboard, my wife has been playing board games with the kids for three days straight. I feel for her. At least two of my sons feel that when it's their turn to roll the die, they have to stand up, walk to the opposite wall, and throw it across the house. We have, by this point, lost every die we own. The good news is that I've been finding them barefoot in the dark.

It finally occurs to us that if the fridge is dead, why not just leave all that food out on the porch? If this goes on for long enough, we can bring the freezer food out there too.[7]

My sister-in-law calls to tell us that they couldn't change their travel plans, and yes, we're still making them a *sheva brachos*

---

7. Option #2 is leaving it at the home of people who don't have heat.

Sandy Weather

tomorrow night. That gives us twenty-four hours to prepare. It's not like we would have had anywhere to store the food if we'd have made it earlier anyway. Can we stick four pans of made chicken out on the porch? Wait. How are we making chicken?

Our shul is still dark, and even the emergency exit lights have burned out. It looks like we're going to have to make the *sheva brachos* by candlelight, and serve mostly canned goods. ("What did you get?" "Chick peas. What did *you* get?" "I don't know. It's not *good*." "Um, is this the men's table or the women's table?")

Knocked on a neighbor's door to find out if they want to come to *sheva brachos*. They're not home. It turns out they went to a wedding. I later find out that they went primarily because they miss ice cubes.

DAY 4 — THURSDAY, NOVEMBER 1

NOVEMBER 1. Halloween candles are cheaper today. Stock up for Shabbos.

The gas lines are so long that people are driving to Connecticut for gas. I don't get that. Instead of spending two hours waiting, they're spending an hour driving each way to spend ten minutes waiting.[8] The way I see it, they're still ten minutes over. Maybe more, because not everyone's GPS is working.

Should we buy a generator? Drive to several stores looking for one like everyone else so we can wait in line for more gas for the car and also *stand* in a separate line for gas for the generator, plus the constant worry that the generator is going to be stolen? Nah. Who would steal a generator? It's loud. The entire block will hear

---
8. And then getting back with half a tank.

WHAT IS THIS — SOME KIND OF JOKE?

you moving it past their houses. And if you turn it off, the entire neighborhood will know too.

We found a place to have the *sheva brachos*. It turns out one of the guests has light. Now we just have to figure out a menu.

"What are you serving?" everyone asks. "I don't know," my wife says. "It depends what's left at the store."

Nothing is left at the store, except some frozen solid chicken cutlets with all the bones still in them. I guess I know what I'm doing today. In the dark.

People are coming forward with kindness and ingenuity. I have food going in three people's ovens. And two people are making dessert, so I don't have to figure out what kinds of cake I can make on a stove.

It's not easy to cook when you can't see and still make sure it will look nice enough plated in a house where you *can*. I can't even tell by smell. All I smell is berries.

Most people at the *sheva brachos* are just happy to have heat and light. Anyone who already *had* heat and light said they didn't want to come because of the gas lines. And the rest of the guests are friends of ours that the *chassan* and *kallah* don't know but who we invited anyway because they made dessert.

People keep saying, "Why are we so helpless? What did our forefathers do?" I'll tell you what our forefathers did. First of all, our forefathers had fireplaces set up for cooking. They didn't have ranges that stopped giving off light the minute you put a pot on them, or fireplaces with outlets in them, like I have in mine.[9]

---

9. Also, in the old days there wasn't a sudden run on *yahrtzeit* candles.

Sandy Weather

Also, our ancestors had hundreds of years to figure out how to live like that. We had hundreds of years to *forget* how to live like that, and then three days to figure it out again.

I'm in the dark. About what's going on in the rest of the world, I mean. I got my news from *Hamodia* this week. Can you imagine?

Our neighbors bought a generator, because apparently they didn't have *enough* things to wait in line for, and then turned it on for the night. It sounds like they left their lawnmower running amok on their lawn and then went to bed.

DAY 5 — FRIDAY, NOVEMBER 2

The neighbors turned off the generator. "We were embarrassed by the noise," they explain. They're going away for Shabbos.

Found a sign at one of the working shuls that says that a local business, The Sukkah Outlet, is letting people work at their office. Thank goodness for people still buying *sukkos* after the season. Are they cheaper? There is plenty of room to sit over there, because they also sell folding chairs. I bring along my wife's laptop, and, for goodness' sake, a shaver.

So I'm plugged in at the Outlet. Someone just came in so he could pay his electric bill online. "It's already past the end of the month," he says. "What are they going to do?" everyone asks him. "Turn off your power *more*?"

What did they do in the old days?! Well, for one, they didn't have this problem of being locked out of their refrigerators. They also knew how to maximize daylight time. We've been finding things to do to stay up in the dark and then waking up regular time, dealing with the kids, putting them to bed, and then finding that it's dark again. I don't even want to think about what's going to happen

WHAT IS THIS — SOME KIND OF JOKE?

when we change the clock. *What* clock? We only have one clock that works.

People ask if we're going away for Shabbos. We could, but we'd have to buy gas. And the lines are such that I don't know if we have enough gas to make it to the front of the line. I'm pretty sure I saw people in line pushing their cars to the gas station, one car length at a time.

It's really not a big deal to stay home. I can make food on the grill for Friday night, we're invited out for Shabbos lunch, and after cooking for forty people in less than twenty-four hours, cooking for Shabbos is really not a big deal.

My wife just called the *eruv* hotline. The *eruv's* up, *baruch Hashem*. But the power still isn't. Maybe we should have the *eruv* guys fix our power.

Shabbos is coming, and we've set up *yahrtzeit* candles all over the house. People are walking in and going, "Whoa. Who died?"

Everyone who doesn't have heat is praying that it stays warm. We, who are keeping our food on the porch, are praying that it stays cold. It seems we've been praying harder. Now I *feel* bad.

DAY 6 — SHABBOS, NOVEMBER 3

It turned out that our lunch host is a great cook, but the quality of the food wasn't even important to us. The main thing was that we could see it. Friday night we had black barbecue meat on black plastic *sheva brachos* plates in the dark. "Are you finished eating?" "I don't know."

A neighbor with no heat and no light asks if his family can sleep on our couches, since we have heat but no light, which is not really

Sandy Weather

essential to sleeping anyway. It's nice that we can still help people out, even if it's a very specific window of need.

We don't actually have any clean linen.

Called the power company after Shabbos. They say that if we want to know when power is coming on in our area, we should visit their website. Thanks.

My wife points out that at least we don't have a kid in diapers right now, because then we'd be changing him by candlelight. "Is he clean? I can't see. Move him closer to the fire."

We're officially supposed to change our clocks tonight, if we have any. We decide not to, because the last thing we want is for it to get dark earlier.

DAY 7 — SUNDAY, NOVEMBER 4

I got someone to check for me. According to the power company's website, our power came on last night at midnight. Oh. I was sleeping; I must have missed it.

Laundry is starting to become an issue. I'm down to wearing my backup Shabbos shirts. I think it's time to start looking for a river.

My son tells my wife that he doesn't have any more pants. So my wife says, "*Daven* that the power should come back on." "I *can't daven*," my son tells her. "I don't have pants."

Some neighbors offer us the use of their washing machines. I don't think they understand what they're getting into. We can't even see our laundry baskets anymore. And my three-year-old, who's scared of the dark, has wet at least two other people's beds that we know of. So we do one load, which is not really enough to make a dent. But at least my son will have pants for *davening*.

WHAT IS THIS — SOME KIND OF JOKE?

People are still asking what our ancestors did. There are times you can ask that question, but there's a limit. You can ask it when someone says, "I lost contact with my relatives; I have no phone or e-mail." So you can go, "What did our ancestors do? Send them a letter!" The post office is thrilled about this turn of events. They're *specifically* bringing mail like three times a day. "See? We don't shut down. We're still using tiny mail cars that we power with our feet!" Isn't it Sunday?

But you can't *always* ask that question. "How did our ancestors dial phones when they couldn't see the numbers?" "How did they charge their devices?" "At what point did they just barbecue everything in the freezer?"

DAY 8 — MONDAY, NOVEMBER 5
6:30 p.m. (I think. The clock is blinking: 12:00! 12:00! 12:00!)

The power's back on! Only 172 hours with no lights! Oh my goodness, this house is filthy. I thought we were scrubbing.

What on earth did I write on this clipboard? I can't read a thing.

We still have a bunch of mostly used *yahrtzeit* candles, if someone has like half a *yahrtzeit* coming up.

GRINDING HALT

Today's driving question is: what is the correct way to proceed at a four-way stop?

The correct answer is: C. While honking. That way, any driver that can't see you — what is he, *blind*? — can at least *hear* you.

Though I guess it depends on your car. My minivan, for example, has a normal horn, but I also have a smaller car — a Honda Fit — that we got a while back because it's fuel efficient, at least in the sense of not being able to hold a lot of fuel in the first place. And the thing we forgot to test before we bought it was the horn. It gives this little, wimpy unsure "meep" sound that makes you laugh the first time you hear it. When I honk, no one moves. At most, they look around for a giant bird.

But the truth is that it depends. Most four-way stops are at intersections where there's not quite enough traffic for a street

WHAT IS THIS — SOME KIND OF JOKE?

light, but enough traffic that there has to be *something*. Usually, two people come to it at the same time, and it's not a big deal. You motion for the other guy to go, and then he motions for *you* to go, and then you do that for a while. "No, you." "No, I insist." "Oh, I couldn't *possibly*." And then you both finally pull out at the same time and honk at each other.

But in general, what's SUPPOSED to happen is that whoever gets to the intersection first goes first, and if you all get there at the same time, the guy on the right has the right of way, especially if he doesn't stop.

But what if four cars get there at the same time? Everyone's on *someone's* right, right? Of course, timing-wise, the odds of this happening on a regular basis are really slim, and if it does, generally what happens is the city puts up a light.

But that's why I'm asking here: In my neighborhood, there is a busy street corner that had a traffic light. The light went out during Hurricane Sandy, and when the power came back on over a week later, the light did *not* — for more than six weeks afterward. Apparently, the only people who don't pass through that intersection are the ones with the ability to do something about it. And no one's reporting it, because by the time we get through the intersection, we're running late.

Sure, they noticed it right after the hurricane. They came by and brought three stop signs in buckets of concrete. Three. There are four corners. So for several weeks, we had three sets of cars treating it like a four-way stop, while the fourth just kept breezing through the intersection, honking at everyone who tried going, because they naturally just assumed that they would have the right of way until the power came back on.

Grinding Halt

Then, about four weeks in, we got a fourth stop sign. This was exciting for us, because we felt like progress had been made, but we also realized that this meant that it might be a while until someone would actually fix it. For all we knew, some driver stole the sign from a different street corner, and now there was an intersection somewhere with only *two*.

But my point is that in this situation, it's not, "What if two cars come to the intersection at once?" or even, "What if four cars come at once?" It's, "What if there are four *rows* of cars at the intersection?"

It's kind of like when you're at the supermarket, and another person comes by with one item, you're willing to let him go in front of you. If it's just one car, you're willing to wave the guy ahead, and then have him wave *you* ahead, and so on. But if four *rows* of cars come to an intersection, and you know that if you keep waving people ahead, you're never going to get through, and all the people behind you are wondering why you're being nice to everyone but them, then this is really a question. What do you do?

Ideally, the right of way should go to whoever is running the latest. Of course, there's no way to tell this unless everyone states his case, and anyway, your thing is clearly more important than anyone else's thing. But for example, if the other car is a police car, then *he* has the right of way, because you have to assume that *his* thing is more important than *your* thing, or else he'll pull you over.

BONUS QUESTION: What if four police cars come to the intersection at the same time?

BONUS ANSWER: The answer is that if four police cars are in a rush to go in four different directions at the same time, this is not

WHAT IS THIS — SOME KIND OF JOKE?

a neighborhood you want to be anywhere *near*, especially in your little meep car.

Anyway, like I said, there are never any cops at this intersection anyway. The thing is that I have to hit that intersection every morning when I'm taking my kids to yeshivah. I should go around it, but that would take an extra ten minutes. And it's the morning, so I'm not fully awake. I turn onto that block every morning and say, "Why is nobody moving? Oh, right."

So what I've noticed is that no one knows what to do at four-way stops. People either don't know the rules, or are willing to pretend that they don't. Because OK, there are official rules, but to be honest, those rules seem way more focused on safety than on actually getting where you're going.

I find that there are two kinds of people: There are people who blow through without caring ("Woo hoo! A vacation from red lights!") and there are people who spend several minutes waiting to get up there, and then they get nervous when it's their turn, like they have no idea what to do next. I'm always stuck behind an entire line of people with performance anxiety, and the other three roads are always people whose brakes don't work. It's not like there's a traffic camera anyway, because if the light is out, chances are the camera is out too. And you're not going to get a ticket, because the cops aren't coming anywhere near this place, probably because no one is brave enough to stand in the middle of this intersection and wave at cars.

It also doesn't help that a lot of times, if one car has the right of way, the car behind him decides to tailgate, like if he follows close enough, the cars in the other three lanes won't notice, and they'll think he's just the back part of the other guy's car.

Grinding Halt

And meanwhile, people are honking, like that's going to make the lines move faster, and everyone's waving, and meanwhile, my kids are sitting in the back of my car wondering why I'm talking to myself.

"Oh, good, they're waving at each other again. Stop waving!"

I don't know why I'm writing this article. Maybe this is me talking to myself. It's not like people are going to get out of their cars and show each other an article to let them know they're doing the wrong thing. You're just going to honk and hope that the guy breaking the rules will know that your honk is meant to be helpful and reminding of the rules, rather than rude and angry. It's hard to convey emotion with a honk. Car horns should have more than one tone, I think.

As it is, we use that one noise to convey the following messages:

"I don't want to die."

"Um, excuse me."

"Something just fell off your car."

"Does this horn still work? I guess so."

"I'm here to pick up someone in your neighborhood, but he's running late."

"Hello, fellow cab driver! I'm *also* a cab driver!"

"I'd like to get by, if the ten of you can just merge with the sidewalk for a second."

"Meep."

"What's happening up there? I can't see over the cars in front of me."

Seriously, I can't. I'm like two feet off the ground here. And I

WHAT IS THIS — SOME KIND OF JOKE?

never have the right of way, because if I took it, and another car takes it as well, my car is going to end up in one of his wheel wells. And then how am I going to inform him of this, with my *nebech* horn?

Maybe people will just think I'm the front part of his car.

SECTION XIII:
IS YOUR REFRIGERATOR RUNNING?
(OR "TECHNOLOGICALLY SPEAKING")

This is a classic prank call, where you say, "This is the power company. Is your refrigerator running?" And the person says, "Yeah," unless you happened to accidentally call someone in middle of a week-long blackout. If you did, be prepared for a piece of this guy's mind, because you just told him you were calling from the power company. But assuming he says, "Yeah, my refrigerator is running," you say, "Well... Go catch it!"

This is another one of those jokes where you're like, "What did they do *before* refrigerators were around?"

"Is your ice box running? How?!"

And the answer is that phones were not around either. It was a pretty small window of time where we had phones but no caller ID, and also refrigerators.

Maybe. I don't know my history.

And anyway, most people, if their refrigerator started *actually* running, would not be able to go catch it. They're out of shape, thanks to their refrigerator. I think that's the refrigerator's master plan. He's gearing up for his big escape.

And anyway, even if they do catch up to it, what's the plan? Are they going to tackle it?

Nowadays, you really can't do these pranks anyway because of caller ID, and if you block the caller ID, the person probably won't pick up. It'll go to voicemail, because they're screening, and you'll have to leave some kind of awkward message designed to get them to call you back but not know why they're calling you back so you can prank them when they do.

"Hi, this is the power company...

We just want to know if your refrigerator is running. Call us back."

Also, most of the numbers you'd randomly call these days are cell phones, so you're likely to get an answer like, "How should *I* know if my refrigerator's running? I'm driving!"

"Really? Then you can catch it easier. It's heading up the interstate."

The following section is about technology — primarily phones. The articles in this section are actually, for the most part, newer than most of the other articles in this book, because the thing about technology articles is that as soon as you write them they become outdated. But it might be good to read them anyway, because there are memories here, and the other thing about technology is that you don't have memories anymore. Unless you're reading about old technology, I guess.

Remember phone pranks? Good times. For about half of us.

TO CONTINUE IN ENGLISH, KEEP READING

One of the best things about modern technology, hands down, is that it gives people something to complain about. People just love to complain. And thanks to the miracles of modern technology, scientists are able to work around the clock to shove inventions out onto the market so fast and with so many bugs that people can complain more today than ever before.

Indeed, we live in an amazing age.

But what do we enjoy complaining about the most? According to a recent poll of the top twenty irritating pieces of technology, the invention that annoys us the most is a car alarm.

Sure, the idea is a good one. Car alarms, ideally, are designed so that when someone is about to steal a car, the car will make a high-pitched noise, at which point three things will happen:

WHAT IS THIS — SOME KIND OF JOKE?

1. EVERYONE will look around to see where the noise is coming from.
2. WHOEVER'S CAR IT IS will come running.
3. THE BURGLAR will run away, so as not to draw attention to himself.

Unfortunately, here's what actually happens:

1. EVERYONE rolls over in bed and tries to drown out the noise.
2. WHOEVER'S CAR IT IS doesn't know that it's his car, and he's just as annoyed as everyone else.
3. AND ALL OF THEM lie there and think, "I wish this guy would just steal the car already, so we can get some sleep."

The main issue, really, is that no one knows what his own car alarm sounds like. So I'm thinking that maybe we should be able to personalize our alarms, like ringtones, so that the burglar will be working on the car, and all of a sudden he'll hear some music, and maybe he'll walk off to answer his phone. Personally, I would make my alarm sound like an ice cream truck, so that everyone would come running over.

The second most frustrating piece of technology, according to polls, is that little egg timer that appears on your computer screen, especially when you're in a rush. Why are we timing eggs all of a sudden? It's not even like you can watch the hourglass filling and know how much time you have left. It's basically the equivalent of someone holding up a finger when you want to ask him something. They don't actually mean "one minute." They mean, "Stare at the ceiling for a while, and I'll get to you."

But at least there are buttons you can push, as opposed to printers. This was number ten on the list. Everyone knows how

To Continue in English, Keep Reading

frustrating printers can be. You have a tray that can hold one hundred pieces of paper, but if you put in more than five, it gets stuck. And sometimes, for no reason at all, it will print the same thing five hundred times, or sneak a blank page into the middle of a seventy-five-page business report, or have your computer make the "bong" sound.

"BONG!"

"What now?"

"You're running low on ink. Proceed?"

Yes, *of course* proceed! I'm Jewish! I have a brand-new cartridge sitting on the floor next to my printer, but for eighty-five dollars, I'm going to keep the old one in there until every last drop of ink is gone. Sometimes I even take out the old cartridge and shake it.

But when the printer breaks down, what do you do? It has *one* button. You press it, and nothing happens. You press it again, and still nothing happens. It's basically a "feel better" button. So you open and close all the little doors on the printer, and pull out any bits of paper that you think are jammed, but for some reason, the printer still thinks it's jammed.

"No you're not!" you shout. Like that helps.

So you turn the printer on and off, hoping it will forget that there's a problem, like your computer does. But it doesn't forget. It turns back on, and, to get you back, it first makes a sound that makes you think it's printing, but really it's not. You can't outwit the printer.

Meanwhile, number fifteen on the list of things that annoy people was the ball mouse — the kind of mouse that has the ball on top instead of underneath, where the *Ribbono Shel Olam* intended it

WHAT IS THIS — SOME KIND OF JOKE?

should be. Ball mice are not very sensitive. You *scroll scroll scroll scroll scroll*, and the cursor moves down about an inch. That's it? So you *scroll scroll scroll scroll scroll*, and then you look up, and it's moved another inch. It would be quicker to just make a hole in your monitor and push the cursor down manually.

Another thing that people are very annoyed at (coming in at number five) is an automated phone system. You call any big company, and a voice will come on the phone: "Thank you for calling. To continue in English, press 1."

So you press 1 (or possibly 2 — it doesn't make much of a difference in the long run), and you're presented with yet another menu. And none of the choices will sound exactly like the thing you want to talk about, and there'll be nine of them. So you have to remember: "OK, number 3 sounds like it might be the right one," and hold up three fingers to remind yourself. "OK, 5 sounds like it might be right also," and you hold up five on the other hand. "OK, 3 or 5, 3 or 5. But 8 sounds pretty good too."

And how about the ones that claim to have voice recognition technology?

"If this is correct, say 'yes.'"

"Yes."

"We didn't get that. Did you say 'no'?"

"NO!"

"We didn't get that either. Was that a 'yes'?"

Another thing that made the list, of course, was an alarm clock (at number fourteen). Yes, for doing exactly what they're supposed to do. I feel bad for my alarm clock. The poor guy takes so much

To Continue in English, Keep Reading

abuse. I get upset if it doesn't go off, and I get upset if it does. It's not *his* fault it's seven o'clock.

Or maybe it's *other* people's alarms that are annoying. The person wants to get up at seven, so he sets his alarm for six, and he keeps hitting "snooze" until nine. Then he gets out of bed and starts yelling at all the people who've been awake since six, waiting for his alarm to ring every nine minutes, about how he's running late.

But complaining about technology is definitely not a new concept. Our forefathers were *also* irritated by these kinds of things.

"Don't you hate it," they would say to each other, "when the rooster crows, and you throw a rock at it, and five minutes later it's crowing again?"

"Yeah. Not to mention the mess it leaves on the nightstand."

"Right! And isn't it annoying when the printer just…stops working?"

"I know! Those printers! The other day my printer was like, 'Ow! My hand is cramping up!' How am I supposed to print out 10,000 copies of *The Jewish Press* at this rate?"

But most of you don't care. You're all thinking the same thing. "Hey, how come these polltakers didn't call *me*?"

They probably tried, but you didn't pick up because, like the rest of us, you feel that one of the most annoying pieces of technology is whatever system these companies are using to figure out exactly when we're eating supper so they can call us up and bother us with these incessant polls. In fact, I'm surprised that this didn't make the top twenty.

WHAT IS THIS — SOME KIND OF JOKE?

Or maybe it did. Maybe these polltakers are biased.

"You know what annoys me? All these polls."

"Sorry, we didn't catch that. Can you please repeat the answer?"

"I said all these annoying polls!"

"Sorry, we didn't catch that."

"Fine. Car alarms."

REMEMBER THE OMER![1]

Frequent readers of this column will be happy to know that I am still *Omering* (apparently that's a verb now) with a *brachah*. Of course, frequent readers of this column will also remember that, because of how far in advance I have to write these columns, I am currently only up to Day 13. So it's really not such a big deal. But what's important is that I have a system.

There are a lot of creative ways that people use to try to remember the *Omer*.[2] For example, many people use some sort of mnemonic device, such as their refrigerator. They put a big *Omer* chart[3] on the fridge, the theory being that they're going to see it all

---

1. A little bit of background info: this column came out the week before Shavuos. That is all.

2. Here it's a noun.

3. Here it's an adjective. Hebrew words are a little confusing, grammarwise.

WHAT IS THIS — SOME KIND OF JOKE?

the time, just like all the other things hanging on their fridge that they see all the time, such as the grocery list from Pesach, the past three or four shul schedules (each one stuck to the fridge directly over the previous one), and the invitations to weddings that already happened in a totally different country. I can't tell you how many houses I've walked into around Sukkos time, where I found, on their fridge, an *Omer* chart that was crossed off until about Day 29. And anyway, the entire concept of using your refrigerator only works if you, unlike everyone over the age of forty-five, are willing to actually eat after 8 p.m. So, most likely, you are never going to look at the fridge, on the way to foraging for leftovers, and go, "Hey! *Sefirah*!"

But I do know people who do it the other way around. They remember *sefirah* on their own, so they go into the kitchen and read it off the fridge, and then they use that as an excuse to open up the fridge and look around. "Hey! Farfel!"

I think, if you're going to use the fridge to remind you, you're better off putting your reminder *inside* the fridge or freezer, taped to something you are likely to look for every night, such as the ice cream.

Another way to remember to count *sefirah* is to ask other people to remind you. That way, if you forget, you can blame them. ("This is all your fault! I was counting on you! No pun intended!"[4]) This method is extremely popular with women. And the night that their husbands usually forget to remind them is Motza'ei Shabbos.

But now, thanks to technology, there are services you can sign up for that will gladly take the blame off of your husband. For

---

4. This is something people say to draw attention to an intended pun.

Remember the Omer!

example, there's a service called "Sefirahcount," which sends text messages to your phone every night. This is really helpful if, like me, you have never quite figured out how to get text messages off your phone, and are pretty sure that it will cost you like sixty dollars a month if you do. And that's a lot of money to pay, considering you might not be able to understand the messages anyway. ("Don't 4get 2 0mer <|{:^O) 2day is the 2enty 4st, which is thr33 w33ks and n0 :~(days 2 the 0mer. LOL, B"H!") There is also another service called "*Sefirah* Dial" that will call you on your actual phone, and has a whole range of plans you can choose from. Their most expensive plan, at $150 a year, guarantees that a live person will keep calling you over and over until you pick up, and then will personally count with you.

The issue with both of these plans, of course, is that they can't reach you on Shabbos. The best they can do is call you on Motza'ei Shabbos and go, "Sorry, you missed it." And then they'll pro-rate your bill. Although I think that, for $150, they should actually walk over to your house on Friday nights.

That's actually one of the biggest forgetting nights, though — Friday night. Especially if you make early Shabbos, and the *gabbai* just announces in shul that you should remember to *Omer* after the meal. Apparently, the *gabbai* doesn't know you very well. Or maybe he does, which is why he announces it again on Shabbos morning:

"Last night we counted 42."

"Who's *we*?"

My most disappointing mistake was the year I *davened* Minchah-Ma'ariv every night and then *Omered* at home, and then,

WHAT IS THIS — SOME KIND OF JOKE?

while counting in shul on Motza'ei Shabbos, I realized that I'd been one day off for the entire week.

"Wait, why is everyone counting 31? Am I *ahead*? Did everyone else forget one night, or did I count twice?"

I think what happened was that I'd spent a whole day telling myself, "Tonight I'm going to count 25. 25. 25." And then the night came, and I said, "What's tonight? I seem to remember saying '25' already."

So this year, I've come up with a way to remember that has worked so far for almost — well, let's just say that last night was 13. But bear in mind that this won't necessarily work for everybody. My theory is that the reason we forget is that there's such a small window to remember. It's like birthdays. So many times I tell myself, "OK, in three days I have to call my mother and wish her a happy birthday!"

"OK, now two days."

"OK, tomorrow. One more day. I'm gonna call."

And then the next thing I know, my wife is saying, "Hey! Wasn't your mother's birthday last week?"

But my point is that there's a small window — you can't count too early, and you can't count too late. Even if you remember early, you can't do anything about it; you have to wait around and risk forgetting about it.

So what I do, at some point in the afternoon, as soon as I remember, is I put a small box of breath mints in my shirt pocket. That way I make annoying noises when I walk, like a cow, and when my wife goes, "What's that making noise in your pocket?" I can say, "Oh, right. *Sefirah*." And then I have a mint. (The package

Remember the Omer!

says fifty; let's see if it's true.) And even if no one stops me, I'm anyway going to check my shirt pocket every night before I throw it in the laundry.

But of course, this method won't work for everybody. The only reason it works for me is because, thanks to my wife's constant advice (it's not *nagging*, it's *constant advice*), I change my shirt every day. If I kept my mints in my *pants* pocket, for example, the only thing they would do is remind me when it's time to say *Birchas Hachamah*.

But it doesn't really matter what you do to remember. What matters is that you have some kind of reliable system, and that you don't forget. Shavuos is all about remembering. Like remembering to buy flowers, for a change. Or remembering, when you're budgeting time for cooking, that you're going to have to cook *milchig* food, clean up the kitchen, and then cook *fleishig* food, and that you're best starting all of this a couple of days before Shavuos (especially if you're attempting to roll homemade sushi, which takes longer than actually *cooking* the fish), so that you have time for a nap. Speaking of memory, I do not remember the last time I actually managed to fit in that nap. It's like Shavuos always sneaks up on me. For some reason, I never see it coming.

LOOK OUT, WORLD![5]

We, as a society, have become obsessed with technology. Seriously, we can't stop staring at it. OK, maybe not *all* technology. There's a company that recently came out with a self-making bed, yet you don't see people walking down the street and pushing the remotes for their beds. But we've all seen people staring at their phones while walking, while driving, while doing that slow, crowded circle dance at weddings, and while jogging into telephone poles.

Um, why are there still telephone poles?

Apparently, they're fighting back.

Just look at the news. There was a story in April about a black

---

5. This article, along with the two that follow, originally appeared on Webchaver.com, which is an excellent service that makes using the internet a little bit safer by using a buddy system, like in swimming, so that you don't drown.

Look Out, World!

bear that was roaming around a California neighborhood — there is actually news chopper footage of this — and all of a sudden a guy comes along, staring at his phone, and almost walks into it. Talk about a Kodiak moment. Luckily, he saw it at the last moment, and ran off into his house to — I don't know — change his pants. There are also stories of people falling off piers, into open manholes, and there was a woman at a mall in Pennsylvania last January who fell into the coin fountain. And this woman actually *worked* at the mall. It's not like the fountain came out of nowhere.

But we look at these stories, and we laugh and say: "I'm glad I'm not *that* stupid."

You're not? Let me ask you a question: Have you ever made a live person wait "just a minute" while you did something on your phone? Have you ever *not* made them wait, and just continued what you were doing while they thought they had your attention? You might have a problem too.

And if you don't think that ignoring your wife while looking at your phone is the same as walking into the broad side of a bear, then you haven't been married very long. Most likely, you

Sorry about that. I just tripped over the curb.

The truth is that multitasking is nothing new. Before we were spending our driving time staring at our phones, for example, we were eating, finding something good on the radio, shaving, clipping our toenails, trying to find something our kids dropped under the back seat, and passing back open drinks.

Not only that, but we've always done other things while we were on the phone as well. Just a few short years ago, back when we all used desktop computers, we would only half pay attention to the

WHAT IS THIS — SOME KIND OF JOKE?

people we were on the phone with, who would think they had our full attention until we suddenly mumbled, "Uch, where are all the jacks?"

"Um, are you playing solitaire?"

"No! I'm...playing jacks."

But back then, phones themselves were not that interesting. Nowadays we've flipped it — we don't pay attention to the things in front of us and we *do* pay attention to our phones.

You have good reasons, of course. It's not like you're texting your BFFs to LOL about the NSA. You're accomplishing more with two thumbs than anyone since the guy who invented hitchhiking. (Sadly, no one knows what became of that guy. So now there's just you.) Not only that, but most of the time, you started what you were doing before your wife came over to talk or your kid told you to watch what he was about to do. But the *farshtinkener* phone moves so slowly and the autocorrect keeps misunderstanding your Jewish words ("*Nasal* tov? *Really*?"), and you just want to finish this one thing first — you know, get it out of the way so you can concentrate fully on the person in front of — Hey, where'd she go?

It's gotten so bad, *baruch Hashem*, that people are finally trying to do something about it. For example, some cities are trying to put a fine on texting while walking. (The good news is that you can probably pay the fine with your phone, while walking.) But most of the other solutions, instead of trying to fix the *cause*, are just trying to prevent the *effects*. For example, Google is working on a car that can drive by itself, so we can be free to, um, *Google* things. Also, some towns have been padding their mailboxes so people don't get hurt walking into them, which begs the question: why do we still have mailboxes?

Look Out, World!

There is also an app called "Walk 'n Type," in which, while you type, the phone takes a video of whatever's behind it, which you then see as the background on your screen. That's great for when you're walking down the street, so you can see garbage cans and the end of the sidewalk and the people around you from the knees down. But it's not good if your situation is that you're talking to somebody and you want him to think that you're paying attention. To get him into the shot in your background, you have to pick up the phone and hold it smack between your face and his. That's not going to make things better.

"No, don't worry. I can see you now."

A big issue with phones is that the people around you can't actually see what you're doing. You can be doing the most constructive things, but to everyone else, you're playing with your phone. *Again.* For example, sometimes, when I finish the *Shemoneh Esrei* in shul, I learn using an app on my phone, so I don't have to navigate the shul to get a *sefer* and do that thing where you time your steps so you can squeeze past people just as they're at the far part of their *shukel*, like a massive game of Frogger. Which I am not playing on my phone. I'm learning. *Gemara.* I have a *tzuras hadaf* the size of a postage stamp here, and it's two inches from my nose. But to everyone else, it looks like I'm playing with my phone. Not that it fazes them. It's kind of the *minhag hamakom*.

But it could be that *everyone's* learning. We'll never know. We're not a *talking* shul.

"Shh, we can't talk now. I'm on the phone."

My point is that maybe we should have some kind of app where, instead of taking a background video of your surroundings, it takes

WHAT IS THIS — SOME KIND OF JOKE?

a video of *you*, and shows you what you look like to other people. If nothing else, it will get us to pick that thing out of our teeth that's been driving them crazy all day.

IF IT'S ON THE INTERNET, IT MUST BE TRUE

If everyone told you to jump off a bridge, would you do it?

What if he didn't even *know* you?

I'm referring, in particular, to the community-driven Q & A websites, such as "Askville," "Answerbag," and, of course, "Yahoo! Answers." The way these sites work is that if someone has something he wants to know, he just types it into the site, followed by a question mark, even if it's not technically in the form of a question. If it's a really *nagging* question, he might follow it with four or five question marks. And then magically, answers start appearing.

It's very convenient, and is a great way to get out all the things that you need to ask, such as:

"HOW DO I TURN OFF MY CAPS LOCK BUTTON?"

WHAT IS THIS — SOME KIND OF JOKE?

"Are there any islands left that haven't been discovered?"

"How do I get my credit card out of the disk drive?"

"Why are there school? Is a point to it?" and

"I was bitten by a turtle when I was little. Should I still drink orange juice?"

These are all real questions. I'm sorry.

Personally, I don't use these sites. Considering how convenient the internet already makes things, Yahoo! Answers seems to be for people who already find the internet too inconvenient. Google itself is great — you don't even have to know how to spell. It just asks, "Did you mean *this*?"

"Um, yeah."

But with Yahoo! Answers, you don't even have to know how to Google. Basically, it's for people who only know how to look things up in the form of a question they can ask human beings. These are the same people who can't use a dictionary, because they don't know how to just look up the word "obtuse"; they have to look up, "What does obtuse mean?" and the W section of the dictionary doesn't seem long enough.

OK, so maybe *your* questions are good ones. Maybe they're things you can't really Google, like specific personal advice questions. Like, "How come whenever *I* forget something, it's my fault, and whenever my *wife* forgets something, it's my fault for not reminding her?" I don't think you can Google that. But that doesn't mean you should blindly follow the suggestions you get.

"Of course I can trust them," people say. "It's Yahoo. This isn't some fly-by-night company."

And it's not. But:

If It's on the Internet, It Must Be True

A. Yahoo doesn't write the answers. It's kind of like saying, "Of course it's safe to take the subway. The MTA is a pretty big company."

B. You can't believe everything you read. Not even everything you read in a newspaper is accurate, and those are people who get *paid* to write things and have a professional reputation to protect. So even if something is a guess, it's at least a guess that they hope is true.

But the people answering your questions have no motivation to give you the correct answer. It's not like this is a charity thing that they do in their spare time; that they're so finished helping everyone around them that they're looking for people on the internet they can help too. You know how easy it is to write things on the internet?

Let's put it this way: Why are you asking a question on these sites? For the anonymity, of course. You can ask whatever you want, and you don't have to be embarrassed, or worry about your kids' *shidduchim*.[6] But by that same logic, everyone else can answer whatever *he* wants, and he doesn't have to be embarrassed if he's wrong. The fear of embarrassment is what keeps us researching our answers in real life, or, when we don't know, saying, "I don't know. I'll ask my wife."

It's not even like Google, where you can look at the results and say, "Well, these people took the time to build an entire site devoted to this subject, so they must have some idea of what they're talking about." These people stumbled across your question at three in the morning, and they have an opinion that their loved ones don't

---

6. Or your wife knowing you're asking about her.

WHAT IS THIS — SOME KIND OF JOKE?

want to hear anymore. For them to go to Yahoo! Answers when they don't even have a question ("how can I doctor a photo so that all my kids are looking at the camera?") that means that they basically used up everything else they can possibly look at on the internet, and your question is what's left. Or else they're on the site to ask a question, and they noticed yours and decided to answer. In which case, the people who are giving the answers are the same ones who were misspelling all those other questions.

Would you trust the opinion of someone you don't know? Probably. We ask directions from people on the street that we don't know, and whatever the guy says, we believe him. We don't even try to get a second opinion, unless we weren't listening and are embarrassed to say so. But the guy doesn't know us from Adam,[7] and what he *does* know is that the quicker he spurts out an answer, the quicker we take him off the spot. And even if he's wrong, you're never going to see him again anyway. Especially if he gets you hopelessly lost.[8]

OK, but Yahoo has a "best answer," right? That's the one to focus on.

Except that it's not. A lot of times the users don't vote for the most *helpful* answer, they vote for the most *entertaining* answer. For example, in the case of the CAPS LOCK question ("HOW DO I TURN OFF MY CAPS LOCK BUTTON?") the best answer chosen was "IT'S FOREVER IRREVERSIBLE! THE SAME THING

---

[7]. This is just an expression. I'm sure if they actually saw Adam, they would know it. The fig leaf would give it away.

[8]. By this point, I've probably steered hundreds of people into the ocean.

If It's on the Internet, It Must Be True

HAPPENED TO ME!" Alternatively, it's voted in by the person who asked the question: "Am I right, or is my boss right?"

"Well, I'll vote for the guy who says that *I'm* right. Right?"

But you know how sometimes the best answer to someone's question is not the answer he wants to hear? If you get to vote for your favorite answer, you'll never hear what you don't want to hear. You'll just hear what you wanted to do in the first place.

But you know all this. You have no intention of taking whatever answer comes over the internet as the word of Hashem. All you're looking for is someone who will listen to your question.

Shouldn't you have those people in *real* life?

WALK-INS WELCOME?

We've all been there. We're in line at the pizza shop, waiting for the person behind the counter to stop taking phone orders so that we, who actually dragged ourselves in and are standing right there, can order already.

"Why are you speaking to *him* first? I took the time to come down here!"

And the answer is that yes, you took the time to come down here. You're not about to go all the way back home just because of *this*.

"Well, where's the food?" your wife is going to ask.

"Um, the guy was on the phone."

So when the choice is waiting a couple of minutes or facing a hungry wife who expected you to be home earlier, you're going to opt for waiting in line.

Walk-ins Welcome?

Also, restaurants have found that the person on the phone is more likely to know what he wants, whereas half the people in line in front of you don't even bother looking at the menu until they get to the front of the line. Nor have they figured out how many people are actually in their party. And then they stare blankly at the menu and ask about things that aren't on it.

It almost doesn't pay to show up anywhere anymore.

We complain about this with stores and businesses, but we do it at home too. The phone rings, say, during dinnertime, and we leap over the table to go look for it, no matter what else we have going on. We don't even know who's calling yet. I guess we're assuming it's the president, and he wants to give us money. But even once we see the caller ID and realize it's not important, we pick up the phone anyway, because once we ran around the house looking for the phone, we might as well say hello.

But what about the people around us, who are left waiting in silence? Should they just sit there and eavesdrop? It's not really fun to eavesdrop when you can only hear one side of the conversation.

"No!... Well, that's what *I* said... No way! And you just let him?... That's the funniest thing ever!"

"*What* is?"

"Shh. I'm on the phone."

And what are they *supposed* to do? Say "excuse me"? If someone is on the phone and you say excuse me, they generally will not stop yapping. They've already forgotten they were talking to you. They're going to assume you meant the *other* kind of excuse me, and they'll get out of your way, mostly to avoid all your

WHAT IS THIS — SOME KIND OF JOKE?

impatient stares and the noise you're making saying "excuse me." *Just go past already!*

"Excuse me" is too subtle. It's much easier, if you want to interrupt, to just call them. It's the ringing sound that gets people's attention, I think. If you made an annoying ringing sound in person at the beginnings of conversations, I bet they'd give you some attention as well. But it might not be the attention you want.

So, for example, if you're standing in line at the restaurant, it might be way more efficient to just call in an order, so that by the time you get to the front of the line and past all the people asking if they can get onion rings without the onions, your food will be ready. That's not making society better, but a guy has to *eat*.

I recently read about a restaurant in California that gives diners a 5 percent discount if they leave their phones at the counter. I don't think the restaurant is kosher. But it might be worth it to go anyway, just to get in a conversation.

"Yes, we're ready to order. We'll both have the soda."

On the other hand, there are some people who do give priority to the person in front of them. My wife has a friend who calls us, and when we pick up the phone, we have to wait a minute while she finishes up a conversation with someone in the background before she even says "hello." On the one hand, that's great, and exactly what I'm talking about. But on the other hand, she called *us*.

But the thing is that we *know* that our phones are driving a wedge. According to recent studies, 13 percent of cell phone owners pretend to be using their phones in order to avoid interacting

Walk-ins Welcome?

with people. It could be more than that, but researchers couldn't approach a lot of people, because they were on the phone.

So basically, we have people who are just walking down the street talking to themselves, instead of the people around them. This is a great development for people like me, who actually DO talk to themselves, and now we don't look as strange. The only difference is that I've never ignored the person next to me because I had to finish what I was saying to myself.[9]

There's nothing like phones. Not only to keep in touch with people who aren't with us (*lo aleinu*?), but also to push away the people who *are*. But the good news is that once we've pushed them away, we can talk to them on the phone.

---

9. "Shh! Can't you see I'm talking to myself?"

OVERCHARGED[10]

Oh, I love that I now have a phone that is smart,
It has several apps I can buy a la carte,
And has so many uses, I know them by heart,
I can show you a list, or just make you a chart.
Like how I can look up when my plane will depart,
Or send my cousin Don a *chassidishe vort*,
Or compare how much certain things cost at Kmart,
And decide if I should load them into my cart.
(Which is not hard to push, because — here is the twist,
It's a *fake* cart that doesn't completely exist.

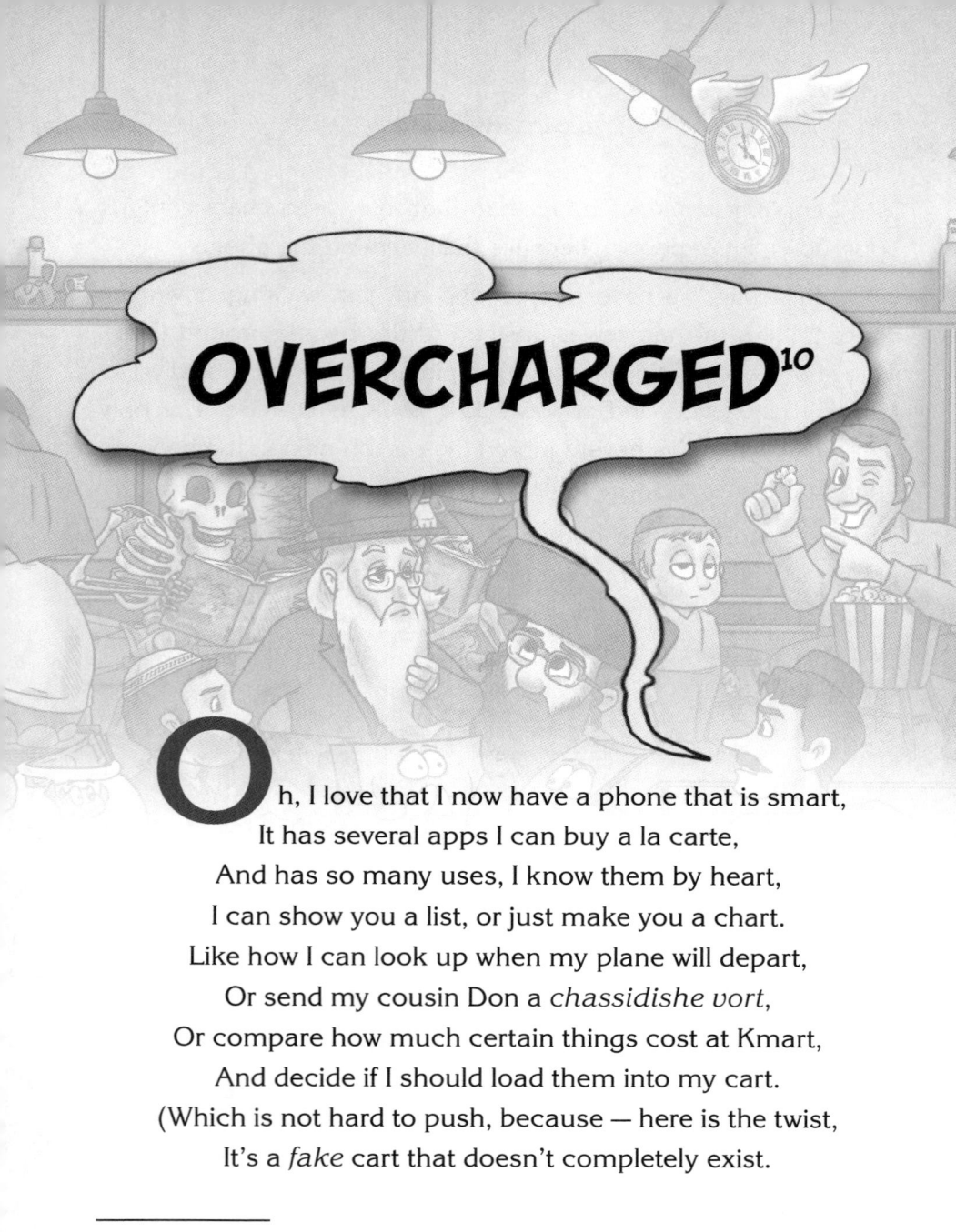

10. This article, which has never appeared anywhere, was originally written for a *Hamodia* insert about smart phones, but was eventually scrapped when they decided to go in a different direction — namely, single-panel comic strips. They figured that anyone who uses smart phones enough for it to be a problem isn't going to have the patience to read whole articles about it.

Overcharged

It has no infant seat and no one crooked wheel,
Though the money I'm charged is a thing that is real.)

I can take fuzzy pictures without any zoom,
And can know my location, right down to this room.
It can recognize voices and know what I say,
And send that information to the NSA!
And it has lots of games for when I'm feeling *blah*,
Or to occupy kids when I need them to shah!

And the best part of this phone that does a whole lot,
Is it's done with no wires!

Except when it's not.

'Cuz the thing with this tool, though it makes my life swifter,
Is that if I don't watch it, the battery's *niftar*.

I would say that it's not a big deal it expired,
It lived a full life — many years — and it's tired.
But that's not the case, and we can't ask, "How come?"
As the phone might be smart, but the battery's dumb.

'Cuz for years I had phones with reception from Mars,
And I'd walk around town in attempts to get bars.
Their main feature was phone calls they barely could make,
And they only had one lousy card game and "Snake."
And it cost a bundle to make calls at peak,
But if you charged them *once*, then they lasted a *week*.

WHAT IS THIS — SOME KIND OF JOKE?

In the old days, our phones could last days without ends,
Just as long as you didn't have too many friends.
(But how many friends do you really have, though?
Well, if you believe Facebook, you don't even *know*.)

But nowadays, we have a ton of great apps,
And we use them a lot; and our phones, they need naps.
It's like shopping with husbands — you walk around town,
And keep handing them things 'til they want to lie down.
If you make your phone handle too much of your stuff,
And put it through a lot, then it needs a nice *shluff*.
It's not like your day it is trying to hinder,
It just needs a break from yourself and your *kinder*.

But if you're like me, then your hair's going gray,
As that battery pretty much dictates your day.
"Is it almost on red? Do I have enough green?
Or is it just hovering somewhere between?"
And you sometimes just check so you know where it's at,
'Til you start getting texts from some guy named "Low Bat."

It comes up and it says how much power's remaining,
So you can save the rest for a day that is raining.
And it tells you, with timing that's almost Germanic,
"We're at 20 percent. You may now start to panic."
And then all of your insides, they go all volcanic,
And you run around like you're on the Titanic.
You start finishing business and making amends,
And you find yourself saying to all of your friends,
"Look, my power is low, and I need it to last.

Overcharged

So I need one-word sentences. Go! And talk fast."
When that battery's red, it gets into your head,
And you feel like your whole world just hangs by a thread.
"What will I do if I don't have my phone?
It will just be my thoughts and myself, all alone!
And how will they reach me? And what of my wife?
She will think I got up and moved on with my life!"

"We're at 15 percent!" says "Low Bat" guy. "Dismiss?
Did you hear me? I'm dying! Don't leave me like this!"

"Yes, the battery's *low*! Do you think I don't *know*?
Thanks for posting alerts and disrupting my flow!"

But it keeps on reminding you, lest you forget it.

"Do you not think I know? Come on, give me some credit!"

Though the truth is it honestly thinks you forgot,
As it's right in the name — your phone's *smart* and you're *not*.
And it views you as someone who's somewhere beneath,
'Cuz you use it to see if there's food in your teeth.

So sometimes you really just think that it's lying,
Or maybe that phones really do enjoy dying.
As it just does not stop saying, "Hey! Look at me!"
It's like some guy who's proud that he's drowning at sea.

When my car's low on gas, does it put up a load
Of bright text on my windshield when I'm on the road?

WHAT IS THIS — SOME KIND OF JOKE?

No, it trusts me to know, and say, "Oh, it is low,
Let us go get some mo' and forgo lots of dough."

But my phone, which does not even have enough juice,
To let me make calls or take pics of a moose,
Yet it has enough to announce twelve times an hour,
With an ear-splitting sound, that it has no more power?

And it doesn't let up, and it makes me a wreck,
And if I had my druthers, I'd say, "Wait a sec!
Something about this whole practice seems shifty.
I bought a new cord, and it cost thirteen fifty.
It's supposed to be good, and it didn't come cheap,
And I figured I'd charge it whenever I sleep.
So I plugged in last night, and it charged until morning,
And it lasts a half hour, then gives me a warning?
The box says 'seven hours'! How can it be low?"

Yes, it says "seven hours." But not in a *row*.
They write times on the package, but people confuse it.
Those only apply if you don't really use it.

But you *can* save the life of your old battery,
With transfusions, some tubes, and a tiny I.V.
Wherever you are, just plug into a wall,
Or plug into each outlet you pass in the hall,
But for only a sec, and move on to the next,
With your eyes on the screen so you don't miss a text.

You can still use the phone while plugged into the wall,

Overcharged

But make sure that you huddle, and don't sit too tall,
And you don't want to sit in a *comfortable* seat,
As the outlet's down low, and the cord is three feet.
You're just stuck in one place, like you're wearing a shackle,
Or it's Sukkos, and you're in a small tabernacle.
You're just tied to a wall, like a dog on a rope.
"Are you ready to leave?" And you have to say nope!
Or, "We'll leave in five minutes — I'll charge in short spurts,
So my phone can continue to send me alerts."

Though if you have a laptop, your phone can survive,
If you plug the cord into the USB drive.
Though your laptop is also *itself* not plugged in,
So let them fight it out, and let one device win.

And in the car you can plug into the lighter,
(Assuming it's *your* car, or you're a good fighter.)
But do not think about it — you'll feel like a fool,
As you're charging your phone off your five-dollar fuel.

When you go out for Shabbos, and get to your room,
The first thing that you do is feel around in the gloom,
And you pull out the beds and get down and you crawl,
Just to look for an outlet to charge in the wall.
And your hosts understand, because this is well known,
That when they put you up, they put up with your phone.
If Avraham Avinu would have guests today,
He'd insist that we charge so we don't turn away,
With outlets we can find when we're down on all fours,
So we could plug things in in his tent with four doors.

WHAT IS THIS — SOME KIND OF JOKE?

(And yes, I digress, and I really must stress,
That we get back on track, 'cuz this poem's a mess.)

But the thing with my phone is it came in quite handy,
That whole week that followed that Hurricane Sandy,
When our power went out as that storm made its mark,
About half of our town was just left in the dark.

Sure, at first it seemed like our lives weren't dented,
As that's why devices like these were invented.
To text in the dark like in the days of old,
And to huddle around it, in case we were cold.
Find our way through the house by the light of the screen,
And to make sure that all of our faces were clean.
And to write tiny notes on what looks like a pad,
And to calculate when all our food would go bad.
And to empty the fridge and to eat all that scrap,
And to enter it all on our dieting app.
And to check on the weather — is it gonna rain?
As that makes it dark *early*, and that is a pain.

The device really shines when your whole house is dark,
But in that case there's nowhere to give it more spark.
So we spent the whole week finding houses with light,
Where to plug in our phones so they'd charge overnight.

"Do you have any power?" we asked everyone.
I don't know how our ancestors got their stuff done.

Overcharged

Some said, "Yes, we have power that you can consume,
But we're putting up neighbors in every spare room."

"Don't worry," we said. "We can stay home and freeze,
But just take in our phones. Oh, and plug them in, please."

We could sit in the car with the motor turned on,
And charge our phones for hours 'til the gas was gone.
But if you recall from that fall, gas was scarce,
Sure, we could buy more, but those lines, they were fierce.
They just stretched on for miles, like some crazy prank,
Where just waiting in line, you would use up a tank!

And a lot of us plugged in at a local shul,
Where someone asked the rabbi, who said it was cool.
We could come help ourselves if we brought our own cord,
And then charge up our phones while we spoke to the L-rd.
So we took our sweet time and we *davened* a while;
We all sat near the walls — no one sat in the aisle.
We plugged strips into strips, all over the shelves,
And I'm pretty sure some were plugged into themselves.

But you know what *did* work, after Hurricane Sandy,
When I couldn't make calls, and I couldn't crush candy?
Our analog phone of a really old style,
With a long, twisty cord and a rotary dial.
We keep it for blackouts, and it works just fine.
(Though we do hate phone numbers with more than one 9.)

WHAT IS THIS — SOME KIND OF JOKE?

That one phone with no apps (I don't mean to disparage),
That one of us may have brought into the marriage,
Was the one that still worked while everything newer,
May as well have been tossed down right into the sewer.

But in moments they worked, what we saw about them,
Was each moment of life was a gift from Hashem,
We did not want to waste. So we'd quickly conclude,
And get off right away to go figure out food.

Maybe we should treat all our phones and our tech,
Like plugging them in is a pain in the neck.

There's a more recent saying: "I need to recharge,"
It means that we need to go *shluff*, by and large.
And yawning is one way to show, by extent,
That our body is holding at 20 percent.

But when we "recharge," there's no wires in our chest,
We just turn off our volume, and give it a rest.

SECTION XIV:
WHERE DOES A FISH KEEP ITS MONEY?
(OR "COLD CASH")

Q: Where does a fish keep its money?

A: At the bank. Of the ocean.

Really? He can't even access it there. Do you know what a bank *is*? I never see fish flopping up onto the beach, looking around for their money. *Whales* once in a while, but that's about it.

That would explain all the coins under the sand, though. I thought it was from buried fathers.

But then how does a fish carry its money? I'm not seeing any hands. Does it carry it in its mouth? It's not like fish have pockets. I actually have three goldfish, and there's no way they can hold onto anything. If I accidentally give them too much food, they just eat all of it, like tiny swimming yeshivah *bachurim*, and then they just have a long string trailing behind them the rest of the day.

The fish are never like, "Let's take some of this food and put it away for later."

I don't know. Maybe later it will be soggy.

And fish don't really climb up onto the beaches. You know which animals *do* climb onto the beaches? Dead hermit crabs. So it should be, "Where do dead hermit crabs keep their money?" And the answer is they're hermits. They don't really have any money.

Fish don't have money either. Horses have money, because they go to bars, apparently. Ducks do too, but they just put everything on their bill. Though I guess they have to pay those bills eventually.

Q: Where do ducks keep their money?
A: At the banks. Duh.

Point is, if you're ever going to the bank of the sea, bring a metal detector. And something you can use to move the hermit crabs out of the way.

MANY HAPPY RETURNS

It's time once again for our annual tax advice column — the only such column in the world that actually prides itself on not knowing what it's talking about. Many of these so-called "helpful" columns talk down to you like they're somehow better than you, just because they have some idea of how things work. But the thing about this column is that when I find things out, I'm just as surprised as you are.

In addition, this column comes with the following GUARANTEE: If you follow the advice below, and are not 100 percent satisfied for some reason, such as that you have been thrown in jail, and you write a letter telling me this, then I will make a concerted effort not to repeat that particular piece of advice in subsequent tax advice columns.

Today, we're going to start off by presenting some EXCITING TAX NEWS: It turns out that this year, for the first time in who-

WHAT IS THIS — SOME KIND OF JOKE?

knows-how-long, the national tax deadline actually falls out *after* Pesach. So instead of trying to figure out how, in the middle of all that Pesach cleaning, you're going to have time to sit down and do your taxes, you're going to be able to sit down, unencumbered by anything else, and wonder what on *earth* you did with all your receipts. Did you throw them out during Pesach cleaning? Why? Receipts aren't *chametz*! What were you thinking?

This brings us to the most commonly asked tax question: If we make a mistake, and the IRS sends someone to audit us, will he just let us go with a warning if we explain that it wasn't malicious, but that we just have no idea what we're doing?

Probably, right?

I wouldn't worry about it. The IRS is a fun-loving unit! They'd *have* to be! How much fun would *you* be if your job required you, on a *good* day, to squint at millions of tax forms containing little numbers scrawled by a country of which 45 percent is illiterate, and the other 65 percent is bad at math, and trying to figure out whether a particular squiggle that you've been staring at is an 8, or just a 3 punctuated with a dab of whatever the taxpayer was eating when he crammed the forms into the envelope? So if it turns out that the numbers are wrong, and you actually have to come down and talk to one of these people, I'm sure you're going to be very open to hearing them say, "Oh, I didn't realize. I'm sorry."

No. The IRS assumes that you have both read and understood the entire 10,000-page tax code, which contains at least fifty pages right at the beginning that were written in the 1700s and detail the situations in which you can deduct the cost of your *man-sheitel*.[1]

---

1. Colonial men spent a lot of time at the *sheitelmacher*, gabbing about the British.

Many Happy Returns

Thankfully, though, the IRS is willing to help you prepare your return. I know this because I recently came across a list of their "Top Ten Tax Tips."[2] I don't know who voted to make these the Top Ten, but it seems like a lot of them were written for beings who just recently got to this planet, and for some reason need to file a return. For example, one tip is: be on the lookout for W-2s and 1099s coming from your employer.

Oh, *that's* what they were? I tried to cash them!

Another one of the "most popular" tips is that if you have any questions, you can call the IRS at any time. For example, if you found a twenty-dollar bill on the street, and you want to know if you have to report it as income, you can just call the hotline, and they will tell you "yes," and also that the call is being recorded.

But if you want to know anything real or useful about filing your taxes, you're going to have to look elsewhere. I looked elsewhere, and here's what I found out. Not that this was what I was looking for:

1. If someone steals property, he has to report its fair market value in his income for that year. That's kind of an "arrested if you do; arrested if you don't" situation, isn't it? I would almost say that you shouldn't bother stealing property in the first place.

2. If your doctor tells you to get some exercise, and you consequently put in a pool, you may be able to deduct it as a medical expense. So, on your next visit to the doctor, you can try to get him to say those words:

---

2. Alliteration is one of the ways the IRS is fun.

WHAT IS THIS — SOME KIND OF JOKE?

"So would you say I can use some exercise?"

"Well, *everyone* can use exercise."

"Yes, but would you say that *I* can use some exercise? Speak into the recorder."

Also, a lot of tax experts (not me, obviously) point out that many small business owners frequently miss out on some deductions. For example, if you sell *aravos* on Hoshana Rabbah, you can deduct the cost of the rubber bands. (The same goes if you sell chickens for *kapparos*.) Similarly, you can deduct the big sign on which you have spelled the word "*Hoshanos*" wrong in magic marker. But if you have a garage sale, you cannot deduct the cost of the actual garage. As far as the government is concerned, you could just as well have had a yard sale.

Personally, I suspect that I don't take as many deductions as I can. I'm a humor writer, so a lot of the things that I write about, I should be able to take off as a business expense. Here are some things I've written about lately that I would probably deduct, if I wasn't such a chicken: a bathroom fixture that came wrapped in a *lot* of bubble wrap; two shirts that my wife bought to wear to my cousin's wedding; my son's *bris*; my sister-in-law's *sheva brachos*; four hundred pounds of potting soil; $300 worth of Chinese auction tickets; an Amish vacation; three flyswatters (*milchig, fleishig, pareve*); and, as I mention this in about 10 percent of my columns, my kids' tuition.

Whatever. So I'm a chicken. It should be a **kapparah**.

Another thing that people don't always remember to deduct for is depreciation. Depreciation is a scary word that basically makes it sound like everything in your house is just sitting there, constantly

Many Happy Returns

losing value, and there's nothing you can do about it except claim it on your taxes. And if you have kids, your stuff depreciates even faster.

Also, experts recommend that you save all your bills, statements, and receipts. But they don't say how long to save them, so the general assumption is that you have to keep them forever. If you get a phone bill in 1972, you'd better still be holding onto that phone bill when you die, so that your kids can fight over it.

"*You* take it."

"I don't want it; *you* take it. I have all the credit card bills."

Not only that, but you also have to save the envelope, and the little piece of junk mail that came in the envelope *with* the phone bill. None of us knows enough about taxes to be absolutely certain that no one is going to come after us about a piece of junk mail that came with a phone bill that we already paid forty years ago.

I got to thinking about this when I was doing some filing recently (most of my Pesach cleaning this year involved filing little pieces of paper), and I came across some of my wife's bank statements from the 1990s. I don't understand why we still have to hang onto those. None of those numbers is still true. In fact, we don't have that money at *all* anymore. But we still have the statements. Sometimes we take them out at night and look at them.

"Remember when we used to have money?"

"Yeah. What happened?"

"Depreciation."

I DON'T WORK HERE

I started thinking about my clothing recently when my wife sent me to the store. "We have a wedding coming up,"[3] she said. "You need a white shirt."

She said this because, for some reason, none of the shirts that I own are completely white. A lot of them started *off* white,[4] but now the fronts of those shirts are more of a *brownish* white. And I don't know why. I don't even eat that much brown food on Shabbos, except, you know, cholent. And kishke. Oh, and farfel. Kugel. Sometimes rice. Also liver. And meat. Oh, I almost forgot cola. And most of the cakes that I like involve chocolate. Come to think of it, maybe I should just start wearing *brown* shirts to my Shabbos meals. Or a bib.

---

3. We *always* have a wedding coming up. My youngest sibling is about four years older than my oldest child. And don't get me started on cousins.

4. Or off-white.

I Don't Work Here

But I don't really like going shopping alone, because ever since I was a teenager, people have been coming up to me in stores and assuming that I worked there.

"Do you know where I can find the cuff links?"

"I have no idea."

"What do you mean? Don't you work here?"

The first few times this happened, I didn't realize that they thought I worked there. I thought they were just making conversation. So I answered honestly.

"Excuse me, where do you keep the peanut butter?"

"Usually in the pantry. I find that when I keep it in the fridge, it tears the bread apart. Why, where do you keep *your* peanut butter?"

"I don't *have* peanut butter."

"Oh, you should get some. I think this store carries it."

I still don't always realize when they think I work there.

CUSTOMER: "I'd like to return these pants, but there's no one in that department."

ME: "I know! Don't you just *hate* when that happens?"

CUSTOMER: "What are you, a comedian?"

ME: "Umm..."

CUSTOMER: "I hate this store!"

ME: "Yeah, me too! Everyone thinks I work here!"

CUSTOMER: "You don't work here?"

ME: "No! But to be fair, half the employees don't work here."

Once in a while, if I'm not in a rush, I'll actually try to help people

WHAT IS THIS — SOME KIND OF JOKE?

find what they're looking for, especially if they ask nicely. I'll walk around the whole store, up and down all the aisles, and they'll follow me dutifully, like I know what I'm doing, and then, when I do find their item (this happens about 50 percent of the time), they'll suddenly take it too far.

"Do you have this in any other colors?" they'll ask. "How about in the back?"

"Sorry," I'll say. "They don't let me into the back." Then they ask to speak to my manager.

Like I'm going to get my wife involved.

I don't know what it is about me that screams "store employee." It's not like I'm wearing a red shirt and tan pants to Target. It's not like I'm waking up and saying, "We're going to Home Depot today! I'm going to wear my big orange apron!" I'm guessing it's that I fit the basic age profile, I look like I don't want to be there, and you could tell by looking at me that most of the foods that I eat end in "-oodle." But most likely it's that I almost always go shopping in button-down shirts and dark pants.

But at least I don't wear a tie. If I did, people would probably think I were the manager. Ties are funny that way.

"You're wearing something that cuts off the blood flow to your head! You must be in charge!"

I don't even *like* ties. I only ever wear a tie in situations where I would otherwise be the only person in the room not wearing a tie. I would like to find the person who invented ties and wring his neck. Actually, I would love to have seen the looks on people's faces when he first went around trying to explain to people why they should wear ties.

I Don't Work Here

"If you wear one of these, people will know you're the manager!"

"Can't I just wear a tag that says 'manager'?"

"Well... Oh, I got one! If you wear it to meals, your shirts won't get dirty!"

But the truth is that I can't really blame these people for thinking that I work there, because in a lot of these stores it's really hard to find salespeople. Sure, in some stores, the salespeople hover over you like hawks. They follow you around and they stand an uncomfortable distance behind you, and they ask you every sixty seconds if there's anything they can help you with. Even if you're just browsing, they will not let up. "Would you like me to help you browse? Here, browse these items!" What I usually do in that situation is I grab something off a shelf at random and say, "There it is! Thanks! You can go away now!" And then I wait for them to walk away so I can put it back. But at least they're trying to be helpful.

But there are some stores, such as the major hardware stores, where the customers don't actually know what they're looking for — you're mainly there because something in your house stopped working, and you're hoping to find some magical clue that will help you figure out how to get it to work again. And there's never anyone around to help. Once in a while, you'll see a salesperson talking to another customer, and you'll wait patiently off to the side so he should know that you're next, but then as soon as he's done, he will dart off in the opposite direction, and by the time you round the corner, he'll be gone — probably through some secret trapdoor in the Doors Department.

It's like the attitude is, "Here we are, trying to do our jobs as salespeople, and all these customers keep coming over to us and

WHAT IS THIS — SOME KIND OF JOKE?

asking us questions. Seriously. What's with all these customers? Don't these people have *jobs*?"

Occasionally, you'll actually find an employee in a different aisle, and you'll drag him over to your aisle, and he'll say, "I don't know. I don't work in this aisle."

"You work one aisle over. It's not like it's a different country. Is it possible that you maybe once overheard someone talking about something in this aisle when you were hiding between the racks?"

But sometimes, if you're lucky, he will try to sell you something from *his* aisle.

YOU: "My dining room is really dark, and I need to buy a fixture. Something I can install myself."

SALESPERSON: "I don't know anything about fixtures. How about you buy some of these windows?"

But now I know why I can never find someone to help me: I look like I work there. The employees look down the aisle and say, "Hey, someone's already *in* this aisle! I guess I can go home for the day."

One day, I'm going to apply for a job in one of these stores. I'm going to say, "Look, half of your customers already think I work here. Why not just make it official? I already know where most of your items are!"

And maybe I can get a job in a specific department, such as "pants." That way I never have to walk up and down the other aisles, and if someone comes in for, say, a pair of slippers, I can instead try to sell him extra-long pants. Also, I can answer the phone, "This is Mordechai, in Pants."

But thankfully, when I went to the store this time, no one bothered me. I don't know if it was because I went the day after Tishah B'Av,

I Don't Work Here

and I was wearing my I-Should-Have-Done-the-Laundry-*Days*-Ago shirt, or if it was because I was pushing a wagon full of kids. But in the end, I couldn't decide between two shirts, so I brought them both home to ask my wife.

"What would you do without me?" she asked.

"Nothing," I said. "I would just pick a shirt and never look back. The only reason this is even a question is that I'm afraid of what *you'd* say."

"Oh," she said. "Why didn't you just ask someone who works there?"

WEIGHED DOWN

I think my pockets are weighing me down. Between my keys, my phone, my pens, my board markers, my breath mints, my receipts, my cash, my change, my business cards that I keep forgetting to hand out, and my shopping lists that my wife apparently writes for her health, I'm kind of surprised that my pants stay up at all. But what's really getting out of hand is the pile of cards in my back pocket. It's getting to the point where I'm sitting on a slant. Like there's a tire jack under one side of me, even though my tire's not flat.

In total, I have over twenty-five cards. First of all, I have seven credit cards. Why seven credit cards? I think it's a kabbalistic thing.

My wife knows why. She tells me that *this* card is for groceries, and *that* card is for gas, and the other one is for pharmacies, and she has a whole thing worked out where each card gives us reward points or cash back that I somehow never see.

Weighed Down

For example, we have one card from L.L. Bean that gives us points that my wife uses to order knapsacks. And I think I might need one of those knapsacks to hold all my cards. In addition to the seven credit cards, I have a license, a health insurance card, a AAA card that I should probably keep in the car, bank ATM cards for several banks, a club card for a gym that I rarely go to, a library card, a library card for the town where my parents live, and ten store cards, because every store you go to nowadays has to give you a card to carry around or else you don't get the weekly discounts that they only give members, even though technically anyone can become a member.

I keep all my cards in one pocket, so that every time I'm in a supermarket and I need to pay, I have to pull out all twenty-five cards and go through them, and then flip them over and go through them *again*, because most of them look exactly the same from the back, and all the people behind me go, "So many cards?" and I'm like, "They're not all credit cards," because I don't want to get robbed in the parking lot.

And I keep getting more cards. For instance, just the other week, I found out that I need another root canal, which my current dentist won't cover, because he's out of network. So I'm trying to find a new dentist, and apparently, I was supposed to have been sent a dental card *months* ago, when I first signed up for the plan.

Great. *Another* card. I need that like I need a root canal.

People often ask me (and by "people" I mean "people behind me at the supermarket"), "Why don't you get a wallet? *I* have a wallet, and my life is so much better!"[5]

---

[5]. Except that they're behind me in line.

WHAT IS THIS — SOME KIND OF JOKE?

Well, I actually *had* a wallet for a while, and it was worse. I had all my money and cards in ONE pocket, *plus* four layers of leather.

I'll tell you when I used to carry a wallet. I used to carry a wallet when I was a kid, and I had sixteen bucks to my name. My wallet was protecting my sixteen bucks. Also my library card, my parents' extra Shoprite card, and the fake cards that came with the wallet. When you're a kid, you always keep the fake cards so you can feel like you have credit cards, and so you can get into your parents' house without a key. It wasn't the best wallet, though. I'd won it at school and it was made out of fake leather. I had to stop using it when my money started turning black.

But boys really love wallets, because they love carrying things in their pockets. It's easier than throwing things on the floor, and it's also a great way to sneak things into the laundry. You have no idea how many times I made my mother wash my wallet. I think that's why the black started coming off.

Nowadays, I have boys of my own, and while they aren't old enough for wallets, they keep making us wash their crayons, which melt all over the dryer, and have to be scraped out by an adult leaning all the way in and not being entirely sure that the door of the dryer can support his weight. And while I'm in there, I can't help but notice that the entire inside of the dryer is covered in stickers. It looks like a nursery in there.

Also, my son, Daniel, who's in first grade, crumples up his secular studies homework and puts it in his pocket, because for whatever reason, he doesn't want to get out his folder. My wife is like, "Do you have homework?" and he goes, "Nope."

"What's that in your pocket?"

Weighed Down

"Oh. It's my homework."

So he does the homework, and my wife tells him, "Put it in your knapsack," and he puts it right back in his pocket. Then he goes upstairs, gets into pajamas, and puts his pants in the laundry.

But here's what I don't understand: Every day he goes to school with his Hebrew studies folder, his secular studies homework, and his lunches and snacks. Nothing else. On Sundays, when he doesn't have secular studies, he doesn't like bringing his knapsack at all, because it's only a half day, so he just carries his Hebrew folder and his snacks. So apparently, the knapsack is for his secular studies homework only. But then the rest of the week, he carries his secular studies homework in his pockets. So why does my wife keep buying him knapsacks?

I'll tell you why. My wife is a woman, and women like carrying their stuff in a really heavy bag hanging by a strap. In addition to a pocketbook, my wife also carries five thousand keys and trinkets on another long strap, on which she also carries little tiny versions of all the store cards that I have. She encourages me to do the same, but I'd rather have a bunch of cards, because I'm not a fan of keeping a lot of stuff on a keychain. At least cards all go in the same direction.

I like cards. But there's also such a thing as *too many* cards. My wife, on the other hand, is not a fan of shuffling through twenty-five cards every time she wants to make a purchase.

"Why do you carry around the library card from the town where your parents live?" she asks me.

I don't know. For the same reason that *she* carries around her parents' house keys, even though they live four hours away and

WHAT IS THIS — SOME KIND OF JOKE?

there's no way she's ever going to visit them on impulse and then, on top of that, get there to find that her mother, who works in the house, is not home.

I think that we're all hanging onto some kind of security blanket from earlier in our lives, and we have to carry it around everywhere — be it a library card, or a key, or a shopping list from 2007. We all want to hang onto a piece of our heritage, because it's part of what makes us who we are.

And who we are is someone who sits at a slant.

SECTION XV:
A MAN WALKED INTO A BAR. OUCH.
(OR "TRAGIC ACCIDENTS")

This is our second bar-themed section title. A lot of jokes take place in bars, for some reason. I think that maybe a lot of jokes are made *up* in bars, by people who are not, at the moment, mentally creative enough to come up with anything that isn't right in front of them.

"So three people walked into a...bar. Yeah. A bar. And then the bartender probably said something."

They're not realistic anyway. A realistic bar joke would probably go something like this:

A, B, and C walk into a bar. And A says, "You wouldn't believe the day I had today." And C says, "What? I can't hear you. B is sitting between us." And A says, "What? I can't hear you!" And B says, "I'm not going to sit between you if you both keep shouting in my ear."

People don't think of bars as very Jewish places, even though I'm pretty sure the word *bar* comes from the Hebrew word *be'er*, which is a place the *Avos* went to get drinks and find their *bashert*. Nowadays, most bars actually *serve be'er*.[1]

Point is, this joke is just as funny when you say a guy walked into a *be'er*.

"Oooooooooooooooooooooouch!"

---
1. Dad joke: bonus level.

HARMFUL IF SWALLOWED

When it comes to safety, we, as a society, generally choose to look the other way. Take the popular safety instruction song, "Five Little Monkeys." The first stanza goes like this:

*Five little monkeys jumping on the bed.
One fell off and bumped his head.
Mommy called the doctor, and the doctor said,
"No more monkeys jumping on the bed."*

Now let's forget for a moment that this mother has to call the doctor to find out that her children should not be jumping on the bed. Does someone really need to go to medical school to pick up this bit of information?

"Class, today's lesson is: 'Jumping on the Bed. Good Idea? Or *Bad* Idea?'"

WHAT IS THIS — SOME KIND OF JOKE?

Now let's look at the next stanza. It starts off with this:
Four little monkeys jumping on the bed.

Do you see what happened there? These monkeys were doing something dangerous, someone got hurt, and the only monkey that actually learned a lesson from this was the one that was injured.[1] Everyone else keeps jumping. And guess what happens?
One fell off and bumped his head.

How do you like that? Obviously, these monkeys are not rocket scientists. This is further evidenced by the next two lines:
Mommy called the doctor, and the doctor said,
"No more monkeys jumping on the bed."

So maybe it's genetic.

And then the poem goes on to talk about what happens when three monkeys jump, and then two, and then one. But what do we learn from this? Well, if you're a doctor, you learn that if you dispense medical advice for free over the phone, then people will call you five times in one night about what is essentially the same problem. That's why they started with co-pays.

But for the rest of us, we can learn that when one person gets hurt, we should all try to see what we can learn from that, so that *we* don't get hurt as well. Fortunately, there are people getting hurt all the time. The world is just *full* of jumping monkeys.

Our first story today comes from a zoo in Idaho, where visitors noticed that the pelicans were tossing a cell phone around, and then, all of a sudden, it disappeared. The zookeepers spent the next three hours trying to figure out which bird swallowed the

---
1. I assume.

Harmful If Swallowed

phone. They were thinking of just waiting for it to ring, or calling it themselves, but they couldn't figure out who owned the phone in the first place. They were beginning to think they'd have to X-ray the entire flock of pelicans, which is not a fun way to spend an afternoon. Finally, the phone was regurgitated by one of the pelicans, presumably the one who'd swallowed it.

So what can we learn from this story?

Cell Phone Safety Tip #97: Don't put your cell phone anywhere near your mouth.

Cell Phone Safety Tip #98: While we're at it, Bluetooth devices are pretty small too. Don't put those anywhere near your ears.

Cell Phone Safety Tip #99: If you are missing both a cell phone *and* the owner of the cell phone, and one of your birds *regurgitates* the cell phone but you're still missing the owner, perhaps it couldn't hurt to X-ray the entire flock of pelicans, just in case.

And yes, I know you're not a pelican. (Research shows that over 99 percent of my readers are not pelicans.) But people can swallow things too. Take the woman in Sydney, Australia, who was eating spaghetti in a restaurant, when one of her friends made her laugh so hard that she swallowed her spoon. She was rushed to the hospital, where the doctors, after laughing so hard that they almost swallowed their surgical masks, were able to get it out.

I don't know if the restaurant wanted it back.

Cutlery Safety Tip #459: Don't put spoons anywhere near your mouth. You know how society always says to eat with a spoon? Well, sometimes society is *wrong*.

WHAT IS THIS — SOME KIND OF JOKE?

Cutlery Safety Tip #460: Laughter may be the best medicine, but it's not meant to be taken with food.

Cutlery Safety Tip #461: Incidentally, you're supposed to eat spaghetti with a *fork*.

And speaking of swallowing things, our next story concerns a dog, but not one of those big dogs that looks like a person who is for some reason wearing a dog costume. It concerns one of those little tiny dogs, the kind that elderly people sometimes carry around in their massive handbags, so that they (the dogs) can sit there and bark at absolutely everything, including the other items in the handbag. We're talking about the kind of dog whose diet consists mainly of pant legs.

Anyway, a couple of months ago, an eighty-seven-year-old man at the Sunrise of Naperville Assisted Living Facility called 911 to report that his tiny annoying dog (he didn't call it that on the phone) had been swallowed up. But not by a person. The dog had gotten sucked into his *recliner*. You know how, the moment you put the seat back on a recliner, all of your change comes rolling out of your pockets?

(SIDEBAR: A good way to make some extra cash would be to set up comfy recliners in public places where people are likely to want to sit down, such as outside the dressing room of a major department store, and then to come back at the end of each month and collect the change. It's a lot cheaper than setting up a fountain.)

Anyway, the man only realized that his dog had fallen in when

Harmful If Swallowed

he closed up the chair and heard a sharp "*yip!*" coming from underneath him.

Firefighters showed up and cut the chair open (firefighters *love* cutting things open) and they were able to rescue the dog, along with about $137.50[2] and three pairs of dentures.

Recliner Safety Lesson #562: If you walk around with a tiny little dog in your pocket, always check before closing your recliner.

Recliner Safety Lesson #563: If the only way you know your dog is missing is that you hear barking coming from inside your chair, your dog is too small.

Recliner Safety Lesson #564: Remember a few months ago when I wrote about a woman who bought a couch at an estate sale and found a live cat inside? Imagine if both animals had gotten swallowed up inside the same piece of furniture. Wouldn't that be funny? Not for the animals.

And speaking of inappropriate dogs, there is the story of a man in Long Island who ran into a coffee house and left his dog in the van.

Now I know what you're thinking, and you're absolutely right. You're thinking that it is extremely wrong and dangerous to leave dogs (or kids, for that matter) inside a vehicle. But if you would have said this to the guy, he would have told you, "Don't worry. I left the engine running."

What a great idea! Guess what happened next?

That's right. The dog disappeared into one of the seats.

---

2. All in exact change.

WHAT IS THIS — SOME KIND OF JOKE?

No, I'm just kidding. This was a bigger dog — the kind that, when he walks up to you on the street, is far more interested in smelling what you have in your pockets. ("Yum! Are those breath mints?")

What actually happened was that the dog got excited ("Yum! We're getting coffee!") and shifted the van into gear, driving straight through the window of the coffee shop.

Well, that was enough to wake everyone up.

Auto Safety Lesson #1: We cannot stress this enough: Don't leave kids or pets in your car when you run into the store. Having them accidentally drive into a wall at five miles per hour is the BEST case scenario.

Auto Safety Lesson #2: This applies even if you're running in for a "minute." You know those people with tiny annoying dogs in their handbags who are always in line in front of you and take an hour and a half to pay?[3] It's *never* just a minute.

Auto Safety Lesson #3: Monkeys don't grow on trees.

---

3. They always have a coupon, though sometimes it's chewed up.

LOST AND FOUND

Today's topic is: how to find things that you or a loved one has lost.

TIP #1: It's your loved one's fault.

OK, that's not necessarily true. But all of us have something that we lose on a regular basis. ("Where on earth are the pareve scissors?") For example, my five-year-old son, Heshy, is always losing his shoes. And I don't mean his *set* of shoes. I mean one weekday shoe and one Shabbos shoe.[4]

My wife and I lose things too. We have a cordless phone in our

---

4. And my one-year-old, Gedalyah, is always losing his sippy cup. Well, actually, *we're* always losing it. We fill it with milk, he crawls around with it for a while, and then it disappears. The next morning, we take Gedalyah out of bed, and he crawls over to wherever he hid the cup, pulls it out, and starts happily drinking yesterday's milk, while the rest of us make faces and try to take it away from him.

WHAT IS THIS — SOME KIND OF JOKE?

room that almost always ends up under the beds. We never notice that it's missing until it starts ringing at six in the morning, and then we have four rings to move the beds and find the phone in the dark before it goes to voicemail.

Also, sometimes, if I go to a lot of stores in one day, I lose my car. It's hard enough to remember where I parked when I go to *one* store, but if I parked in a different place at each store, it totally throws me. "It was right in front! No, wait. That was the *other* store. Did I leave the car at the other store?"

Also, every day I come into class (I teach high school English[5]), and I have to wait for everyone to find his book. And by the time the class does that, the period is over. Then I come in the next day, eager to continue the lesson, and I have to wait, again, while everyone finds his book.

So everyone loses things. But here's a more specific example: this past Motza'ei Shabbos, I lost my cell phone.

"Well, where did you lose it?"

I don't know. If I knew, it wouldn't be lost.

I'm not panicking, because it's not my main cell phone — it's my prepaid emergency backup phone. I'm not one of those people whose entire life is in his phone, and the only two numbers I've ever called from it are my house and my wife's cell phone, and I know both of those numbers by heart. So after searching everywhere in a panic, I've kind of been waiting for whoever finds it to call *me*. After all, there are only two numbers in the phone.

---

5. In case you forgot.

Lost and Found

But it's been almost a week now, and I still haven't found it. So I asked around for some tips:

TIP #2: Think about the last place you saw the item.

I remember the last time I saw the phone. My wife and I went to a presentation, and I turned the phone off right before it started. I don't even know why I brought my phone in the first place. I *knew* I would have to turn it off, and besides, I only ever use that phone to call my wife, and she was right there with me. But if I hadn't turned it off, I would just be able to call it and see if anyone picks up.

TIP #3: Check your person.

(Your person is *you*. That's just how people say it. I don't think you're expected to carry a smaller person around and go, "Hi, I'm Mordechai, and this is my person." But if you do, you should probably check him as well.)

My person doesn't have my phone. I asked him.

Tip #4: Check your pockets.

I don't know how this is different from "check your person." I guess it means you should check your pockets even if they're no longer on your person. For example, every day when I come to school,[6] I check my pants pockets for a board marker, and it's not in there. So I go into the office and take a new marker. I use it for all of my classes, and then, on the way out of school, I put the marker in my pocket — my *jacket* pocket. Then the next day I come back to school, take off my jacket, check my pants pockets for markers, and go get another one.

---

6. I'm a high school English teacher.

WHAT IS THIS — SOME KIND OF JOKE?

So I just went to the coat rack and checked my jacket for the phone, and I didn't find it. Just thirteen board markers.

TIP #5: Make sure to check the same five places sixty-eight times. Especially if it's not a likely place for the thing to be. For example, if you're looking for your car keys, make sure to keep checking the oven.

TIP #6: Call for the item. Continuously say things like, "I can't believe this! Where *is* it?" Like it's finally going to break down and go, "Here I am!"

OK, so that might not happen. But you should definitely keep muttering anyway if there's someone else in the room, so that he'll understand why you keep walking in and out and crawling in circles and opening the same three closets fifty-eight times.

TIP #7: If there's someone else in the room, he should make sure to smirk and say, "It's always in the last place you look! Ha ha! Get it? Because after you find it, you stop looking!"

Yeah. Ha ha. I wish you would get lost.

"No, you don't get it!" he'll say. "Even if it's in the first place you look, it's still the last!"

No, it's not. If it's in the first place you look, it was never missing. ("I was missing my coat, but it was in the first place I looked! Right on the coat rack!")

Does that theory always work? Sometimes I try to call its bluff. I'll stand there and go, "OK, this is the last place I'm looking!" And

Lost and Found

then I look, and it's not there. So I have to keep looking.[7] Also, sometimes it's *not* in the last place you look — you check the last place and give up, and then you find the item six months later, when you're cleaning for Pesach.

TIP #8: Calm down. Whenever I lose something, my wife ends up finding it, and whenever my wife loses something, I end up finding it. Now I know what you're thinking. You're thinking that we should stop hiding each other's stuff.

But it really has more to do with panicking. When you can't find something, you panic and start looking in ridiculous places, until you get tired, calm down, and find the item. That's why it's always in the last place you *think* to look. So the solution is to have someone else look, or to calm yourself down. If it helps, you can turn the whole thing into a game. You can walk around with a pipe and a magnifying glass and say things like "elementary!" This might not help you find what you're looking for, but you'll feel a whole lot better about it.

If all else fails, though, you can go with the most effective tip:

Tip #9: Buy a new one. As soon as you open the package, the old one will turn up. *Guaranteed*. For example, if you lose your car in a parking lot, the best way to find it is to buy a *new* car. If that doesn't work, you can use the new car to drive around the parking lot looking for the old one.

So I think I'm going to deactivate the phone and order a new one. As soon as I do this, I'll find the old phone, only by then it will be totally useless. But we'll keep it around for the kids to play

---

7. It's kind of like the phrase, "I'm not going to tell you again."

WHAT IS THIS — SOME KIND OF JOKE?

with, and from then on, it will always be on the floor, getting kicked around and in the way when we want to look for *other* things. We always lose stuff because we have so much *other* stuff to look behind because we keep buying new stuff to replace the stuff that we still have but can't find because it's behind all our useless old stuff. So maybe I'll push it off another day or two.

If you have my phone, call me. I'm at HOME, crawling under the furniture.[8]

---

8. So you know, I ended up finding my old, useless phone while cleaning for Pesach eighteen months later. I didn't even find it cleaning for *that* year's Pesach. It was deep, deep within my couch. I also found a small, annoying dog.

SECTION XVI:
ONE WAS A SALTED
(OR "CRIMINALS EVERYWHERE")

This section is about criminal activity, if you can't tell from that hilarious joke about tragedy.

I don't know if this joke even works, and not just because the double meaning of the punch line is lost when you realize that if you were trying to say "salted" it wouldn't make sense to stick in the "a," unless you also add the word "peanut" after "salted," in which case the "assaulted" meaning would make no sense. It doesn't work because when someone is told the joke for the first time, he's not even expecting the joke to end yet. You tell him, "Two peanuts got onto the subway. One was a SALTED." And he's like, "Go on... Yes..." and he expects you to continue the joke. And you're like, "No, that was the whole joke. Didn't you notice that I stressed *salted*?"

TIP: If you have to say, "No, that was the whole joke," the joke might have failed somewhere.

Why was he assaulted? Was someone racist against peanuts? Does someone have a relative who died because of peanut exposure, and now he hates all peanuts even though it's not all peanuts' fault?

"Hey, I'm not the one who did it."

Why are peanuts even getting on the subway in this age of allergies? They're on the no-fly list, but they can get in a box underground with thousands of people? They should just take a cab.

And how does assaulting a peanut get rid of the allergy problem? Now you're left with a broken peanut lying on the ground.

And why was only one peanut assaulted? Was it that Planters peanut guy with the monocle? That would explain why he's getting beat up. I'm not condoning it, but I get it.

I also think the joke would be better if we got rid of the peanuts altogether. We should say, "Two nuts got on the subway. One was salted."

OK, so the grammar is still a problem. But it raises the pun factor and takes away some of the tragedy that most of these famous jokes end with when you realize we're just talking about salty pistachios.

And do you know how many nuts there are on the subway anyway?

THE WEIRDO ON THE BUS GOES "SNIP SNIP SNIP"

For a journalist, I write a surprisingly large number of articles about unintelligent criminals. But what I've noticed is that there are so many types of unintelligent criminals nowadays that you can't even really lump them all together into the same category. So today I'm going to discuss the different types.

Yes, in the same article.

The first type of unintelligent criminal is:

1. **One who commits a crime, but on such a small scale that it's unbelievable that they even *make* scales that small.**

Take sixty-one-year-old George Nylund of Carmel, NY, who broke into his neighbors' house on a regular basis to do his laundry. He would wait until they went off to work, and then he would remove one of their screens, drag his basket down the stairs, and be out of

WHAT IS THIS — SOME KIND OF JOKE?

there by the time they got home.[1] Instead of, I don't know, going to the Laundromat. So one day he was standing on his stepladder, removing the screen, when another neighbor approached him and asked what he was doing. This was followed by a long, awkward pause, while George looked down and attempted to think of an answer.

"I'm fixing the screen," he said, finally.

He then put the screen back on and made a big show of making sure it was straight, and then he folded up his ladder and went home.

Yes, without his laundry basket.

The neighbor quickly called the homeowners, who arrived at their house to find his empty basket waiting patiently in their laundry room. I guess the moral of the story is that no good can come of a man doing laundry.

I bet that right now George is thinking he should have just scraped up a couple of quarters. But not the way the next guy did it. I'm referring to a thirty-six-year-old man in New Jersey, who was arrested when the police found a parking meter in his closet.

You know how it is — parking meters are annoying. Sometimes you're driving around, no change in your pocket, and there are meters *everywhere*. So some people try to do clever things to hide the meter, such as build a snowman over it. But this guy decided to just steal the meter and put it in his car. And then he drove

---

[1] This, to me, is very impressive. I can't even get one load done over the course of day. My wife comes home and asks me if I took the load out of the dryer, and it suddenly occurs to me that that's what that buzzing sound was every twenty minutes. So if this were me, I'd probably bring it down there and forget about it. ("Honey, do we have anything in the dryer?")

The Weirdo on the Bus Goes "Snip Snip Snip"

home with it. I don't even know how he got it out of the ground. He must have knocked it over while he was trying to parallel park. But eventually, his mother found it while she was cleaning the closet, and she called the police. (Of *course* he lived with his mother. Otherwise he would have been breaking into other people's houses to do laundry.)

Meanwhile, the police in Sweden recently arrested a ring of left-shoe thieves. These people would walk into shoe stores and steal only the left shoes of the display models. In one outing, they stole seven left shoes, totaling over $1400. The store owners were hopping mad. But that is not my point. My point is that I finally think I know what's been happening to all my left socks.

But actually, the police said that this is not uncommon. Thieves do it all the time. First, they steal a bunch of left shoes in Sweden, and then they head over to Denmark and steal all the matching right shoes. That's a lot of work to steal a pair of shoes. And it must be really tough getting through customs. What happens when the officials open the suitcase to find a whole bunch of unmatched shoes?

"What happened here?"

"Oh my goodness! I must have left all seven matching shoes back at the hotel!"

The second type of unintelligent criminal is:

2. **One who apparently takes steps to make sure he gets caught.**

Take the teenager in North Carolina who tried to rob a café by hiding a banana under his shirt and pretending it was a gun. The manager tackled him (thankfully, the banana didn't go off) and

WHAT IS THIS — SOME KIND OF JOKE?

pinned him down. And while they were waiting for the police to show up, the kid ate the banana.

Teenagers, right? They eat *everything*.

Apparently, he ate it to get rid of the evidence. That way, when the witnesses would say he was trying to rob the café with a banana, he could say, "*What* banana?"

In retrospect, he probably should have also eaten the peel. The police took the peel into custody, and charged him with destroying evidence. Because you have to charge him with *something*, right? You can't just charge him with eating a banana.

And that brings us to the third kind of unintelligent criminal:

3. **The type that does something so ridiculous that it's like the guy woke up and said, "I want to be arrested, but I don't care *why*."**

Take the man in Portland who was arrested in January for sneaking up behind people on a public bus and cutting their hair. He did this to several people on a bunch of different occasions, until one of them noticed and called the cops. Personally, I don't think it's fair that someone is cutting your hair without your permission, and the operator treats *you* like a prank caller.

The D.A. also thinks that this guy may be connected to a mysterious person last year who was sneaking up behind people on the bus and putting superglue in their hair. They think this might be the same guy.

You *think*? Maybe there are two of them out there.

And then there's the man in Canada who was arrested for licking cakes at the supermarket. Store employees noticed him in the bakery department, opening the cake boxes, touching the cakes,

The Weirdo on the Bus Goes "Snip Snip Snip"

and then licking them. So one staff member, after picking the short straw, approached him to ask just what on earth he thought he was doing, eh? And also, it's not polite to lick the cakes. So the guy said he was checking for freshness.

Yup, that's pretty much how they do it at the factory.

When the store employees told him to stop, the man threw some bread on the floor and kicked it. Well, that just took the cake. So they called the cops.

I imagine that when people get into prison, the other inmates want to know what kind of crime they committed. And you're supposed to say something like "robbery" or "resisting arrest." Or "laundering," if you're a sixty-one-year-old man from upstate NY. And you can say "robbery" even if you committed the robbery with a banana, which you then ate. The other guys don't have to know that.

But I wonder what their reaction would be if you said you were in there for "cutting hair" or "licking the cakes."

"This guy must be tough. Look how sarcastic he is."

But some crimes defy categorization. For example, you can have a person who does a really small crime AND he's begging to get caught. Like the man in Italy who walked into a convenience store, threatened the clerk with a box cutter, and stole a pack of gum.

But he had a good reason. It seems that his wife's family was over for the holidays, and he really didn't want to spend time with them. So instead of just saying he had to work late, he decided that the best course of action would be to get arrested.

And he didn't even want to commit a crime. First he went to the

WHAT IS THIS — SOME KIND OF JOKE?

police station and politely asked if they could please arrest him. But the cops said, "Go away; you haven't done anything," which is really basically a license to do something. So he went next door and stole a pack of gum. Although, if you ask us, once you have a license to commit a crime, you should probably do something a little more worthwhile, such as lick all the cakes. Or steal parking meters and stick them in the ground near your relatives' cars. ("Look at that, you're out of time! Bye now.") Then he just stood there until the police arrived, and they hauled him off to a jail cell.

"So why are you in here?"

"My wife has her family over."

"Oh, I'm so sorry! Everyone make room!"

Because there are some things that *everyone* understands.

ALL THE AMENITIES OF HOME

This summer, you should definitely take some time to go on a vacation; quick, before the kids get off from school. And since you don't take vacations very often these days, you should definitely try to get as much as you can out of this one. For example, if you go to a hotel, you should try to get some soaps and shampoos. You can also get pens, stationery, shower caps (even though you have never used one and don't understand why someone would wear a rain hat in the shower), and, if you're willing to stay in a "smoking" room even though you don't smoke, you can get matches.

Which brings us to the question: Is it really OK to take this stuff? According to recent surveys, most hotels are not only *OK* with people taking things home, they're actually *happy* that they do, because it means that:

1. The shampoo is so good that people are going, "I can't just

WHAT IS THIS — SOME KIND OF JOKE?

leave the rest of this here!" (Not that, say, Holiday Inn is making their own shampoo. There's probably someone in the back with a funnel, pouring big bottles into tiny bottles.)

But the main reason they're happy is that:

2. Whenever you use that item, you will be reminded of what a nice time you had in their hotel, and you'll say, "You know? We should really go back there! We're almost out of shampoo!"

On the other hand, what these hotels might not realize is that most people who take these things never end up using them. It's too much work to open up a new bottle of shampoo every other day, and it's too embarrassing to put it out for guests, so these people just have stores and stores of them. Yet some of these people come home with so much of this stuff that you think maybe they're sneaking into other people's rooms. And on top of all this, they're taking a really big risk, because there's nothing more embarrassing than getting stopped by airport security and having them confiscate twenty-five tiny bottles of shampoo.

Also, there's probably a line between things you can take home and things you probably shouldn't. For example, most people are pretty sure that if you use part of a bottle of shampoo, you can take the other half home. It's not like the management is going to come into the room and go, "Woo hoo! He left half the bottle! Tell Bernice that she only has to pour half as much into this one!"

But if you don't use a bottle at all, can you take it home anyway? On the one hand, the hotel is putting out the items for you to use while you're *there*, so logic says that if you don't use it, they want it back. If you go to someone's house for Shabbos, and they say you can take as much cake as you want, would you get up and dump the whole thing into your suitcase? But on the other hand,

All the Amenities of Home

why should the *hotel* benefit from your lack of hygiene? And, more important, are you specifically not showering because you want to take this shampoo home?

Yes, you definitely won that one.

Also, some people take things that are clearly not meant to be taken. The most commonly-taken item is the towel. Apparently, people really want plain white towels that have been washed five *thousand* times (or at least *folded* five thousand times), and are for some reason slightly smaller than the towels they have at home, unless all the towels they have at home came from hotels.

And that's not even the worst thing people have stolen. Apparently, rather than buying items at the store, people will pay even more money to go to a hotel *and* they will bring empty suitcases along so they can inconspicuously sneak these things out, and have the hotel inconspicuously charge their credit cards. Here are some of the items people have stolen:

- Bedsheets
- Curtains
- Paintings
- Hangers
- Mirrors
- Showerheads
- Flowers from the hallway

And those aren't even the strangest items. One hotel guest in England stole a grand piano out of the lobby. Another hotel found that someone stole the room number off one of their doors. They only noticed this later, when they saw the next guest wandering around the hall, looking for his room. ("There's no 93! It's just 91, then *this* door, and then 95!") And another hotel had a repeat

WHAT IS THIS — SOME KIND OF JOKE?

guest who, over the course of a few months, stole an entire place setting, one piece at a time. I'm not sure what he's doing at home with one really fancy place setting.

OK, so you'd think that, to prevent these thefts, the hotel management should do something, such as — I don't know — get a guard dog. That's the perfect kind of dog to have in a hotel, where every single room contains at least one person the dog is unfamiliar with. That's a great idea, right?

Wrong. Because in one hotel, the owner's *dog* was stolen.[2]

But why do people steal from hotels? Is this just the kind of thing that happens when you run a business where you have insomniac strangers roaming your premises at four in the morning and making great decisions?

"Hey, that room says 93! *Our* house is 93! What are the chances? I think we should take the whole door!"

Or else they have nothing to do in their rooms, so they spend all night lying there and thinking: "That lamp is nailed to the nightstand. But the *nightstand* isn't nailed down!"

On the other hand, some people try to rationalize. They say things like, "Oh, the hotel probably writes these things off."

What does that even mean? I'm a professional writer, and I have no idea how to write things off. If I did, I would quit writing articles and just devote my days to writing things off.

Maybe it means that they factored the thefts into the cost of the room. They said, "Look, it really costs us like seven bucks to have someone sleep here for one night; slightly more if he cranks up the

---

2. Seriously. It had *one* job.

All the Amenities of Home

A/C to much higher than he would if *he* were paying for air.[3] But what if he steals the carpet? I think we should make it $200 a night and call it even."

"Yeah, but what about people stealing towels?"

"No problem. If we make each towel smaller, we'll end up with the same amount of towels in the long run."

So where do we draw the line between things we can take and things we can't? Obviously, somewhere before "grand piano." But where? If we draw it at disposable items, does that mean we can take the light bulbs, assuming we can somehow get them home without smashing them? And if we draw the line at things that have the hotel's logo, can we take the luggage cart?

So my thought is that we can probably take any disposable items that have the hotel's phone number. My thinking is like this: Why do they put the phone number on the pens, for example? So people can call them from within the hotel? ("Yeah, can you please send up a second pen? We're playing tick-tack-toe.")

OK, so maybe you'll say that they want people to call from *outside* the hotel, and that it's more along the lines of, "If found, please call..." Like someone's going to call and say, "I'm at a rest stop in Wyoming, and I found one of your pens. Some thief must have left it here."

"Can you stay where you are? We're going to send someone out there to pick it up."

"Not so fast! Is there a reward?"

"That depends. Did you find a tiny soap there too?"

---

3. It's not like his father's going to burst into the room. ("Who touched the thermostat?")

WHAT IS THIS — SOME KIND OF JOKE?

So obviously, they want you to have their number so you can call to make reservations in the future. Because they're hoping that, if you *do* come back, maybe you'll bring their dog.

FAIR AND BALANCED[4]

H**ey! Isn't there an election coming up?** I think so. I don't often write about current events. I try to write about things that are timeless. The last time I really wrote about current events was for the presidential election of 2008, when I basically wrote that everyone should vote because it's his patriotic duty to vote even if there's really nobody to vote for. And the same thing holds true today. So I guess it *was* timeless.

So who should I vote for? To be honest, I'm the wrong person to ask. I don't have any strong political feelings. In general, if I hear a particularly convincing speech, I usually side with it. So basically, I tend to agree with whomever speaks last.

To be honest, though, I'm afraid to say anything concrete,

---

4. This column was written before the presidential election of 2011. Anything prophetic that I may have written was purely coincidental.

WHAT IS THIS — SOME KIND OF JOKE?

because no matter what I say, half my readers will get offended and come after me with shotguns. Unless they're Democrats. Last time I wrote about an election, I tried to make fun of both parties equally. For example, I made a joke about how Obama had no experience, and another about how Sarah Palin had no experience, and then I got angry letters from both sides. I can't win.

So how is this election different? Well, for starters, Obama has experience.

Has this helped him? Not really.

But what are some of the actual benefits of Obama? Well, for one thing, he killed Bin Laden. So he'd be very handy to keep around if we ever need to kill Bin Laden again.

That's it? Wasn't he supposed to do something about the economy? Maybe. To be honest, we really thought he had a plan, going in. But now he keeps saying that the economy is not his fault, and that it was bad when he got here. But to be fair, he knew this going in. He didn't get into office and go, "What? The economy is bad? How come no one told me?"

What is Obama *really* going to do, if elected? Well, we're still hoping he has a plan to fix the economy this time, and that the only reason he hasn't implemented it is that if he had done all he set out to do in the first four years, why would we vote him in for another four? So he's pacing himself.

And anyway, he keeps saying the economy is getting better, although none of us really believes him because we all live in this economy that he keeps talking about. We know that *we're* still having issues, so to us, all he's really saying is that he and some of the people he knows are not.

Fair and Balanced

Who is the Republican candidate? Governor Romney of Massachusetts, who goes by the name "Mitt" because his first name is *Willard*. His running mate is Paul Ryan. Together, they look like father and son barbers.

So what do we know about Romney? I don't know. I've been looking for some straightforward articles to teach me everything about the election, but every article I read turned out to be heavily biased one way or another, because the truth is that if you know what you're talking about enough to write an article, you probably have opinions.

For example, I read one article that spoke about how Mitt Romney said that "middle income" in this country is $250,000 a year. Now I know what you're thinking: apparently, you make less than middle income; 96 percent of the country is thinking that too.

But then, in one sentence in the middle of that article, very easy to miss, it mentioned that Obama said the same thing a couple of years ago.

How is Romney so out of touch? He has a lot of money. You can't comprehend the amount that he actually makes, in the same way that he can't comprehend the small amounts that *we* make. It's like how we would say "a million zillion dollars." However, he keeps assuring us that he had to make his way up like everyone else, by working hard, saving up, and inheriting a million zillion dollars.

Where do the candidates stand on the issues? Both of them sincerely really agree with whatever feelings you have at the moment.

So politicians just lie? I don't know if they're lying. I think it's more that they think that when they get into office, things will

WHAT IS THIS — SOME KIND OF JOKE?

be easier than they actually are. It's like a little kid saying he wants to be an astronaut when he grows up. Then he grows up, and says, "Oh." And he just gets whatever job he can, and his new focus becomes working toward vacation.

What are the candidates' differences on the issues? I don't know if there *are* any. I've spoken to a fellow writer — Turx (who, by the way, is *not* me) — and he went to the Republican convention, which they somehow decided to hold in Florida during hurricane season, as well as the Democratic convention, which as far as we know, is still going on, and he said that all the speakers at both parties sounded pretty much alike. But everyone at both conventions cheered anyway, because guess what? Almost no one going to one convention had heard the speeches at the other convention. So his thought was that maybe one way the candidates are trying to save money is by hiring all the same speechwriters.

Um, what ARE the issues? I'm not really sure. Two of the issues are:

1. How to deal with the countries that want to kill us, and
2. How to pay off the national debt.

My feeling — and this is why I'm not running for president — is that we shouldn't try to pay off the debt, because as long as we owe other countries money, they're not going to try to kill us.

How about the issue of unemployment? I know, right? How about we give the presidency to someone who *doesn't* already have a job? At least we'll be creating a couple of jobs there. Both candidates, as it stands, are people that currently have jobs. None of these conventions ever comes up with, "Oh, we found this guy on the street. But he was screaming some pretty insightful

Fair and Balanced

thoughts on the issues. His Cobra runs out in November. He needs to be president for the health insurance."

But what about Obama? Wouldn't electing someone else put him out of a job? No, ex-president is still a job. And if he gets laid off, he has plenty of unemployment extensions he can file for.

Doesn't anyone have his own opinion? It's tough. Running for president is basically like a four-year-long job interview where there are millions of people on the other side of the desk, interviewing you all at once, and whatever you say, 47 percent of them are going to get offended.

What are the candidates' platforms? Well, four years ago, if you remember, Obama ran under the slogan of "Change." Now *Romney's* Slogan is "Change," and Obama's slogan is "It wasn't my fault." Whereas if you or I would still, four years after we got a job, be blaming everything that goes wrong on the previous guy, our boss would start questioning what exactly we meant by "change."

What are the pluses of each candidate? Actually, both candidates have their problems, and there's really no good reason to vote for either one except to prevent the other one from winning. In fact, both sides seem to know this, and are focusing their campaigns squarely on why you shouldn't vote for the *other* guy.

And? Well, like I said, I tend to side with whomever I heard last. So the first guy speaks, and I say, "Yeah, the other guy is bad." And then the second guy speaks, and I say, "Wow, the *first* guy is bad. I don't even know why I believed what he was saying about the *second* guy." Then the first guy speaks again. By the time we sort through all that, it feels like neither of these *shlemiels* is suited to run a *gas station*, let alone a country.

So what do we do? Well, we have to use common sense. Common sense dictates that neither of them is really an idiot who just tripped and fell into a nomination out of pure luck. ("What? You meant *run for president*? I thought you were asking if I wanted to run in the park after lunch!") In fact, they both beat out several nominees, some of whom, I'm pretty sure, *did* trip and fall into a nomination. But my point is that they must have *some* qualifications, though there's no way *we* can figure out what they are. We only hear the bad things.

What would you suggest? Maybe we should look into balancing the ticket a little more. Candidates do that all the time in choosing their vice presidents, so they can attract the votes of people who don't agree with the president, but are going to vote for him anyway in the hopes that he'll die in the next four years.

So I say that maybe they should balance the ticket by having both presidential candidates get together and become *co*-president. They're sharing speechwriters anyway. Because after all, why do we need a vice president, really? The vice president's entire job, as far as we can tell, is trying not to embarrass the country.

I learned this approach from my mother. When I was growing up, and my sister and I were fighting over something, my mother made us share it. That way, no one was happy, unless you count the happiness that comes from the knowledge that the other person was unhappy too.

Sure, if we try this approach, nothing will get done. But nothing is *already* getting done.

SECTION XVII:

BLACK AND WHITE AND RED ALL OVER

(OR "WRITING FOR A NEWSPAPER")

What's black and white and red all over?

There are a million answers to this one, not even counting all the ones that involve some sort of animal in a kitchen appliance:

- a yeshivah guy on a date
- a zebra hiding in a strawberry patch
- a nun falling down a flight of stairs
- a penguin with too much lipstick — for a penguin
- that chicken who crossed the road just for a Chinese newspaper
- my students' essays[1]
- a deck of cards
- a chess and checkers set
- a mint candy that you dropped on the floor
- a three-pepper spice blend
- a kid after Shabbos party
- a *kittel* after wine and matzah
- a bottle of coke

and

- I don't know, but whatever it is, it's in the back of my fridge.

The most famous answer, of course, is "a newspaper," which demands a fundamental misunderstanding of the word "red," and assumes that the question is spoken, so the listener can't tell whether you said "red" or "read," and assumes you said "red" because you also said "black and white." Though it doesn't work if

---

1. I teach high school English.

you write the question out, like *I* did. And you can't write, "What's black and white and *read* all over?" without giving away the answer AND confusing people as to how to read (Reed? Red?) the word "read." So ironically, the one version of this joke that involves the newspaper can't ever actually appear in a newspaper.

Anyway, these are the kinds of things I have to deal with, writing a weekly humor column.

ANOTHER BOOK? BY MORDECHAI SCHMUTTER?

BY: MORDECHAI SCHMUTTER

I have very exciting news for you.[1] But first, a story.

The other week I got a call from a friend of mine. He told me that he'd just had his fourth daughter, and that he's totally out of girls' names, the poor guy. "What do I name her?" he asked me. "My wife and I can't decide."

So I told him that he should have thought of that *before* he gave his twin daughters double names. "You used up four names in one day," I told him. "And that was *after* you gave your oldest daughter a double name too. And then you went and named your son *Simcha*, which, if you were strapped, you could have used as a girls' name as well."

---

[1]. Admittedly, this news was a little *more* exciting back when I first wrote this article, shortly before the publication of my third book.

WHAT IS THIS — SOME KIND OF JOKE?

See, people never ask me these questions until it's too late. And now he had only two days to come up with a girls' name. Or, knowing him, *two* girls' names.

So he said, "*You've* written articles about names, right?"

And I had. I wrote one a year ago when I was naming my youngest son, and I also wrote an article asking readers to help name one of my books, which ended up being called *A Clever Title Goes Here.*

"What do you want me to do?" I asked. "Write a column asking people to come up with girls' names?"

"Maybe," he said. "What's your lead time?"

"Four to six weeks."

So no, that's not what this column is about.

I did try to help him brainstorm, though. My idea was to use a name from one of the nearby *parshiyos*. Over the course of the conversation, I came up with *Bilhah, Osnas, Hagar, Eishes Potifar,* and *Busmass,* who was one of Eisav's wives.

"Actually," I said, "don't name her *Busmass. Busmass* sounds like someone with a thick accent and a really deep voice who can lift a car over her head."

"You're not really being helpful," he informed me.

"What did you expect?" I said. "Ooh! *Osnas Busmass!*"

I'm not good at coming up with names. When it was time to name my book, I had to turn to my readers, only to have one of them point out that I'd already come up with a perfectly good name, but I just hadn't realized it. It's like when you're walking

Another Book? By Mordechai Schmutter?

around with a napkin stuck to the bottom of your shoe and don't notice until someone points it out.

"Hey, you have a napkin stuck to the bottom of your shoe."

"Oh, thank goodness! I actually *needed* a napkin!"

But when I came up with it, it had never occurred to me to use that as the title. Everyone has a talent, and coming up with names is not mine. Look at my kids — none of them have original names. They're all named *after* people. People come over to me all the time to tell me that they like my articles, but not once has someone come over and said, "I like your titles." And I'm OK with that. It's not like anyone is *complaining* about the titles either.

"Really? You called your article on names, '*Naming Names*'? However did you think of *that*?"

No, my titles kind of go unnoticed, even when they're really bad. But I still need to *have* titles, so you know where to start reading. And in fact, it wasn't until a while after I started writing articles that I realized that even though the title appears *before* the article, I'm supposed to come up with it *after* I write the article, once I know what's actually going to be *in* the article. So my strategy is usually to take the one joke that wasn't quite good enough to make it into the article and use that as my title.

But that doesn't quite cut it with a book. A book title has to jump off the store shelf at the reader, preferably making him shriek and drop all his other books, and it has to still make sense sitting on his bookshelf years later, jumping out at his houseguests. It's like naming a child, sort of, in that you want to come up with something that suits the baby *now*, but also won't make the kid

WHAT IS THIS — SOME KIND OF JOKE?

resent you when he gets older. And you have to come up with it on a deadline.

On the other hand, naming a book is nothing like naming your kids. For example, you can't just name it *after* somebody. You can't just call your book *Chaim*.

"Why *Chaim*?"

"It's after my grandfather."

That said, I am pleased to present my second-ever **Official Book-Naming Contest**. *Im yirtzeh Hashem* this coming June[2] (or possibly May), I am coming out with a third book, which will pretty much collect a lot of my columns from 2008 (about fifty columns or so), as well as feature some new material that I have yet to think of. Basically, it will be a lot like *A Clever Title Goes Here*, except with different columns, and, hopefully, an actually clever title.

That's where *you* come in. There has to be someone out there who is good at coming up with titles but can't write an article to save his life, and I'm hoping that YOU are that person. If you can think of a title, please send it in, preferably sometime before the end of January (I have a 4–6 month lead time), and the publishers and I will consider it for publication. This should come as good news if you, like many of my readers, wrote to me after my previous book hit the stores, asking if it was too late to suggest a title.

(To be fair, the title implied that it *wasn't*.)

Official Contest Rules: NO PURCHASE NECESSARY. But it *is* appreciated. To enter, send title(s) to MSchmutter@gmail.com. GRAND PRIZE: Grand Prize winner

---

2. And by "this coming June," I mean June 2011.

Another Book? By Mordechai Schmutter?

will receive one (1) signed copy of my new book, FREE. You will also receive mention in an upcoming article, as well as in the book itself. Even if your name sounds made up. Our credibility was already shot a long time ago. FIRST PRIZE: There *is* no first prize. The first prize is the grand prize. We're only going to pick one title. But some titles might be mentioned in a later article, along with the participant's initials (unless the participant has embarrassing initials, like MUD or YAK) and his home city (unless the person has an embarrassing home city, like Brooklyn). SECOND PRIZE: Look, there's no second prize either. It's not like we're ranking the titles in order from best to worst. We're picking the one that we're using, and that's it. PRIVACY POLICY: If you don't want us to run your initials and home city (because you just *know* that everyone is going to figure out exactly who you are, because you're the only person in the entire Boro Park, for example, with the initials MK), you can either let us know, or just send the titles in under a fake name. GUIDELINES: 1. Participants can send in as many title ideas as they want. 2. They can even send in titles from 2008 articles that they can remember offhand and that they think would work as a title for the entire book. 3. If we use your title, you can't come over to us after you write a book of your own and ask for it back. 4. But if we don't use it, you can use it for future projects. Make sure you keep a copy of the title, though, because we're not going to mail it back. 5. If we don't use your title, don't call us up repeatedly to ask why not. 6. Really, we mean it. We can only pick one title. It in no way means that we think yours isn't good. 7. If you're really going to get offended if we don't use your title, then look at the contest this way instead: Rather than sending in ideas for a title, you're sending in a guess as to what title we're going to come up with, on our own, possibly based on outside stimuli, such as your guess. If you get it right, you win! 8. If you're playing it *that* way, any guesses received after we announce the title are disqualified. 9. Please don't try to name our book *Chaim* or *Shlomo* or *Osnas Busmass*. 10. The titles you sent in for the last book will still be considered, so you don't have to send them again. 11. If you send them again, we might consider them twice, because our memory is like a rusty bear trap, but it won't increase your chances of winning. It's not like we're picking it out of a hat. 12. If you have any name ideas for my friend's daughter, don't bother sending them in. There is no prize, and like I said, she was born a month ago. 13. If you made it through this, you don't need glasses.[3]

---

3. P.S. This contest applies to future books as well. I keep coming up with books, most of which are collections of articles, and I'm always looking for titles. If I use yours, I'll send you a free book.

HOW TO PUBLISH A BOOK IN TWELVE MONTHS OR LESS, JEWISH TIME

It's not easy to get a book published. People think that all you have to do is write it up, send it to a publisher, and then open your front door and move quickly to the side so the royalty checks don't hurt you when they come flying in. But there's actually a whole process.

First of all, you have to come up with a title. Most people assume that when you write a book, you write the title first, because that's the part they see first. By that logic, the second thing you write would be the price. These are the type of people who come up to you and say, "I have a great idea for a book. It's called *Title*." And then they stand back and wait for you to be impressed.

"What's it about?" you ask.

"I'm not up to that," they say. "First I have to write the table of contents."

How to Publish a Book in Twelve Months or Less, Jewish Time

I'm not like that. Even with my articles, I generally write the title last, once I've written the article and then read it over to see what it's about. (It doesn't always turn out to be about what I thought it would be when I started writing.) And coming up with a title is even harder when there *is* no topic, as is the case with my books. My new book[4] is basically a collection of columns that I wrote in 2008, and the only thing these columns have in common is that they're all written in the same basic font.

But there has to be a title. Publishers are very picky about that. Titles are very important, because they tell the reader where to start reading. You might think that this is unnecessary, except in extreme cases, such as when the piece is written upside down. But if there's no title, people assume the first page is missing.

There are also other criteria for a title. One is that it has to make the book jump off the bookstore shelves at this time of year[5] and catch the attention of a potential buyer who has to split focus between reading from a list of school supplies and keeping an eye on his kids, none of whom are interested in the school supplies, and who are off at the other end of the store trying on all the yarmulkes at once. I can't just open the dictionary and use the first three words that I see. Like I can't just call the book, *Zebra Broccoli Banana*.

So back in January, I turned to my readers for help. I wrote an article saying that I had a new book coming out in May or June (Jewish time, apparently — I'm aware that it is now late August[6])

---

4. The one referred to in the previous chapter.

5. Late August.

6. See?

and that I needed a title, and that whoever gave me the one I'd eventually use would get a free book. I'd done this once before, with my previous book, *A Clever Title Goes Here*, and it was either successful or unsuccessful, depending on how you understand the title. There were some people who complained about it — mostly people who sent in *other* titles — but I couldn't use every title that was sent in.

This time, I got more than five hundred responses, which means that people really want that free book. But if I didn't use your title, that doesn't mean it wasn't funny. Some people, for example, sent in titles that were good, but would maybe be better for a different book. T.S. suggested I call the book *Drowning in the River Schmutter*, which is actually pretty clever, because if you remember from a column that I wrote in 2007, "Schmutter" is the name of a river in Germany that looks less like a river and more like someone left his garden hose running when he went on vacation. But unfortunately, most people *don't* remember that column, nor is the column in the actual book. (The column appeared in *A Clever Title Goes Here*. Where was he when I was looking for a title for *that* one?) E.L. said I should call the book *Lighter Life*, which, to be honest, sounds like a magazine for people who smoke. And A.E. suggested I call the book *2008 in Review*, which sounds like a tax file I have in my basement.[7]

Other people sent in titles that would probably get me sued: *Humor for the Soul, Jewish Humor for Dummies, A Title Made in Heaven,* and even *Jokes from When Zaidy Was Young*, which, on top of this, doesn't say anything good about the jokes. Also,

---

7. That I'm afraid of throwing out.

How to Publish a Book in Twelve Months or Less, Jewish Time

one person suggested that I call it *No Purchase Necessary*, which is a really sound business idea. So apparently I forgot to mention, back in January, that I wanted the title to JUMP off the shelves, not BE STOLEN off the shelves, and that I needed a title that would maximize sales and minimize lawsuits, because ultimately, I'm in this to make money.

(BTW, no one is in Jewish publishing to make money. But a little would be nice.)

A lot of the titles also had common themes. For example, there were a whole bunch about chickens and roads, such as *Chicken Crossing, The Chicken's Day Off,* and *Why Did Mordechai Schmutter Cross the Road?* I don't know how that chicken thing, which was old when *Zaidy* was young, came to represent all jokes. Maybe all the other famous jokes are offensive to somebody. This joke is probably offensive to chickens, but if they came in to complain, people would ask, "Why did you come in?" and they'd walk out in a huff. So as far as we know, no complaints.

But anyway, after a lot of back and forth, the title we ultimately settled on was *This Side Up.*

(*Awkward pause.*)

No, it makes sense; hear me out. Humor is all about pointing out how the world seems to be upside down. It's not the humor *itself* that's upside down, it's our perception of the world. Humor is the only thing that's right side up.

Plus, it meant we could do that thing where you write "This Side Up," and have an arrow pointing down. This is one of the three main tropes of humor, the other two being chickens crossing the road and situations where there's some sort of misunderstanding.

WHAT IS THIS — SOME KIND OF JOKE?

The title was sent in jointly by Ari Mandel and Dovid Greenstein, who are going to receive a free copy of the book, which they can fight over at their leisure.

But then I suggested to the publisher — possibly as a joke, I don't remember — that what if the arrow pointing down was actually the truth? What if the book was actually printed upside down? On purpose? And the publisher said, "OK." Publishers are very into trying new things, in an effort to stumble upon the magical ingredient that will get people to buy books. Magazine publishers are into trying new things too, which is why *Hamodia* graciously agreed to print this article upside down as well.

Yes, it was on purpose.

My goal, with the title of each book (in retrospect at least), is to get people to ask questions. For example, with my previous books, when you told people the title, their question was, "Could you repeat that?" With this book, I want people to see you reading it upside down and go, "What is he doing? Is he even *reading* it, or is he just *pretending* to read it while eavesdropping on our conversation?" That said, I wouldn't recommend reading this book in an airport.

And now you're suddenly aware that everyone else in the room thinks you're reading this upside down. All they see is the cover, and they're probably judging you for being a person who reads upside down. Well, they judge people by the cover of the books that they're reading. That's what type of people *they* are. So there.

So, as I am doing with the book, *This Side Up*, I urge you to write in with stories of what people said when they saw you reading this upside down, what you replied, the faces they made, and any prospective *shidduchim* that were ruined. But for now, don't make

How to Publish a Book in Twelve Months or Less, Jewish Time

any sudden moves. Just quietly flip the book back over, and move on to the next article.

YOUR TURN[8]

TO THE EDITOR:

I read the letters columns every week, and I have to say that you have a lot of intelligent and insightful readers. But in real life, I find that most of the people I know are insane. Can you run letters written by some of your more insane readers, even if you have to make them up?

CHAIM ARUCHIM
BALDIMORE, MD

---

8. This article is a Purim spoof of a "letters to the editor" column that I did for *Hamodia*, which may have partly inspired my *Jewish Press* advice column. For legal reasons, I should mention that all names are made up, as far as I know, and any resemblance to people who have exactly these names is purely coincidental. Even though, as Jews, we don't believe in coincidence. But lawyers do. I hope.

Your Turn

TO THE EDITOR:

I always enjoy reading your magazine, but nothing cheers me up as much as the recipe section. When people see me reading your magazine and laughing with delight, they say, "He must be reading the recipes again!"

Anyway, a few weeks ago, in one of your recipes, you mentioned ginger. This brought back memories of growing up on a ginger farm in Southern Missouruh. I remember planting the baby gingers and waiting for them to blossom. This was quite boring, because most of the action happens under the ground. And we always had to walk around gingerly, so as not to disturb them.

But once we harvested all the gingers, we would make them into snaps and ales and bread cookies. We would also turn them into tiny pink slices that looked like lox and sell them to sushi restaurants. Boy, was that a great prank! And sometimes we sold them wasabi root and told them it was avocado.

IZZY FINE
CANARSUH, BROOKLYN

TO THE EDITOR:

I just wanted to thank you for your wonderful paper. I move around a lot, for business, and the one constant, wherever I am, is *Hamodia*.

BARUCH HABBA
FROCKAWAY, NY

WHAT IS THIS — SOME KIND OF JOKE?

TO THE EDITOR:

As a *gadol hador*, I greatly enjoy articles that shed light on the lives of *gedolim*. Can you shed light on mine?

ANONYMOUS
BARA POCK, BROOKLYN

TO THE EDITOR:

I just thought of a name for Mr. Schmutter's new book that just came out. Is it too late?

CONFUSED,
SHEKAHGO, ILLINOISE

TO THE EDITOR:

I just wanted to thank you for your wonderful paper. I move around a lot, for business, and the one constant, wherever I am, is *Hamodia*.

BARUCH HABBA
LAKEVOOD, NEW JOIZY

TO THE EDITOR:

I just read Mr. Schmutter's article about technology that makes our lives harder, and I have something to add. Whenever I go to a hotel, I am deathly afraid of the alarm clock. It always has a million buttons and I can never figure out how to set it, so I always unplug it in case the guy before me set it to go off at three o'clock in the

Your Turn

morning. Then I have one of my friends call to wake me up. But I'm slowly running out of friends.

I.M. LATE
BAWSTIN, MA

TO THE EDITOR:

Please don't run this letter. I'm begging you. Don't run this letter. I don't even know why I wrote it in the first place. In fact, throw this away as soon as you get it.

ADAM ANT
ANONYMOUS, NJ

TO THE EDITOR:

I invited the Weissmans over for a Shabbos meal. Is that OK? Also, where do we keep the ice cream?

YOUR HUSBAND
BP, BROOKLYN

EDITOR'S RESPONSE:

We're going to my parents for Shabbos, remember? But if you want, we can make some food for the Weissmans and leave our key under the mat. And don't you dare eat the ice cream!

READER'S RESPONSE:

How about we send the Weissmans to your parents, and we stay home? Also, please don't broadcast to all of your readers that the key is under the mat.

WHAT IS THIS — SOME KIND OF JOKE?

TO THE EDITOR:

Listen, we don't want to be an inconvenience. We can always come a different Shabbos.

THE WEISSMANS
BP, BROOKLYN

P.S. It sounds like your husband wants to come to *us* for the meals.

EDITOR'S RESPONSE:

Look, I don't have time to talk about this right now! I'm trying to edit some letters!

TO THE EDITOR:

I'm writing in response to an article that Mordechai Schmutter wrote a few months back making fun of people who talk in shul. I personally talk in shul, and I was deeply offended by this article.

In his article, Mr. Schmutter argued that if what I had to say was really important, the person I was talking to would make time to hear it outside of *davening*. Well, I'll have you know that the stuff I talk about in shul is not important at *all*. It's like I was saying to my friend in shul the other day — if we weren't going to talk in shul, then why not just *daven* in shuls where we don't know anyone?

Also, my friend said that he was offended by the part of the article that commented on people who pace back and forth the whole *davening*, because he himself is a pacer. Sometimes it's hard to talk to him because he's pacing so much. He even wears a pedometer during the week, and, on Mondays and Thursdays, he can sometimes walk over two miles. By the time he takes off his *tefillin*, they're already loose!

Your Turn

Well, I have to go. The *chazzan* is starting *Kedushah*.

RUSH DAVENING
LONDON, ENGLAND

TO THE EDITOR:

I just wanted to thank you for your wonderful paper. I move around a lot, for business, and the one constant, wherever I am, is *Hamodia*.

BARUCH HABBA
HONOLULU, HAVAII

TO THE EDITOR:

I don't think any of your writers exist. I think they're all just made-up names. I also don't believe that there are any so called "readers" writing in to the editor. Please don't publish this letter.

M.T. YARMULKE
LAKEWOOD, MISSISSIPPI

TO THE EDITOR:

I just moved again, and for some reason, I haven't gotten *Hamodia* yet. Do you have my address right? Also, thanks for your wonderful paper, blah blah blah.

BARUCH HABBA,
DEMOYN, IOVA

WHAT IS THIS — SOME KIND OF JOKE?

TO THE EDITOR:

I have something I wanted to add to Mr. Schmutter's "irritating technology" piece from last week. I think it's annoying when I go to a hotel and find that the guy before me unplugged the alarm clock. I can't imagine why he does that. Some of us have to wake up at three in the morning, you know.

CRAWLING BEHIND THE BED,
BAHSTON, MA

TO THE EDITOR:

My friends and I are collecting for our yeshivah, and the doorman won't let us into the *Hamodia* building. Can you send down some money? And also a mop.

BARUCH BEER
DOWNSTAIRS

TO THE EDITOR:

I was so offended by one of the letters on the previous page, I can't even tell you.

ADAM ANT
ANONYMOUS, NJ

OK, so I'll tell you. I was the one who wrote the letter asking you not to publish said letter, and you published it anyway. Why would you do that? You think I just wasted my time, writing you

Your Turn

that letter for no reason? I'm also surprised you didn't include the whole second half of the letter, where I said something that, now that I read it again, doesn't seem to make a whole lot of sense. I can't even read half of it.

Please don't publish this letter.

TO THE EDITOR:

I want to start off by saying that I'm not Jewish. I live way out in the Midwest, and I have no idea why, but your paper keeps showing up at my doorstep. So I started reading it, and I have to say that I'm impressed. I'm picking up bits and pieces, and even though I have no idea how to pronounce any of these words because I've never heard any of them out loud, I do enjoy sharing some of your *divrei tchizuk* with my friends down at the hardware store.

My question is this: In your *dvar Torah* on *Parshas Bo*, you seem to completely contradict the Beis Halevi on *Parshas Ki Savo*. My friends at the hardware store had a similar concern.

Also, they wanted to know how you guys can publish a paper that has the word "Ham" in the title. Is this named for the food, or the son of Noah?

What a bunch of *shkotzim*.

POTIFAR JONES[9]
DEMOYN, IOVA

---

9. I feel like there are very few gentiles named *Potifar* anymore.

THE MAILBAG

In honor of my 200th humor article in *Hamodia*, I've decided that we should all take a minute to catch our breath and go through my mailbag. There's also cake, but that doesn't translate well into an article. And actually, if you want to get technical, the cake isn't really in honor of my 200th article. I just really like cake. But I do get a fair amount of mail, both snail and E, and I don't always respond to all of it in a timely manner.

Maybe it would be more efficient if I didn't keep it all in a *mailbag*.

> Dear Mordechai Schmutter,
>
> I love your column in *Hamodia*, and I read it religiously. (Get it?) Anyway, I was wondering: is your name really Mordechai Schmutter?
>
> Signed,
> Almost everyone who ever sends me a letter

The Mailbag

Dear Almost,

To tell you the truth, I honestly don't even know anymore. You know how sometimes you think you know the answer to a question, but the more you get asked that same question, the less sure you are of the answer? Like sometimes my wife will ask me six times in a single night whether I locked the back door, and even though I knew the answer the first time she asked me, by the sixth time I find that I have to go downstairs to check. So yes, I've been asked about my name so many times that I don't even know anymore. These days, when I'm filling out a credit card application and I get to a space that says "Name," I just give up. Does Nachman Seltzer ever have these problems?

My friend Sholom was telling me the other day that he has a niece in a high school in Brooklyn, and that one of her teachers was trying to explain the concept of pseudonyms.

"Like for example, Mordechai Schmutter," she said. "*Obviously* a fake name."

So my friend's niece raised her hand. "Um," she said. "Mordechai Schmutter's a real name."

"No, it's not," the teacher said. "It's a pen name. Think about it."

"Actually," the girl replied, "he's a good friend of my uncle. He lives in Passaic."

"No, no!" the teacher said, more adamantly this time. "You might *think* it's his real name, because that's what he *wants* you to think. A good writer can do that."

So to add insult to injury, I'm not even a good writer.

Finally, the girl had to stop arguing, because she didn't want to get thrown out of class.

WHAT IS THIS — SOME KIND OF JOKE?

"Mrs. Weinstein, thanks for coming in. Today in class, your daughter would not stop insisting that Mordechai Schmutter is a real name."

"Mordechai Schmutter? He's friends with my brother-in-law."

• • •

Dear Mordechai,

I read your column this week. LOL! Were you in my house?

B.L.

Dear B.,

Yes I was. I came in while you were out shopping. You're out of cold cuts, by the way.

• • •

Dear Mordechai,

The best part of your articles is that we feel like you're sitting at our kitchen table when you write.

S.B.

Dear S.,

Yeah, I really get around. One of these days there'll be a story in the news: "HUMOR COLUMNIST ARRESTED FOR COMING INTO PEOPLE'S HOUSES AND WRITING ABOUT THEM."

• • •

Dear Mordechai,

Are you funny in real life?

S.S.T.

The Mailbag

Dear S.S.,

In many ways, my columns *are* real life. There was a day last year when I was trying to explain to my students why they need to learn grammatical terms. "After all," I said, "it's not like, in real life, your wife is going to come over to you and say, 'Quick, name ten adjectives or we're not going to be ready in time for Shabbos!'"

And one kid raised his hand and said, "Um, Mr. Schmutter, isn't *this* real life?"

"Ah, Rabbi Z., I'm glad you came in. Your son would not stop insisting that this was real life."

"This *is* real life."

The truth is, though, that in real life, I have "on" days, when I'm feeling funny (and I mean that in the best possible sense), and I have "off" days, when the stresses and worries of life are weighing me down and I've spent all afternoon getting off on a deeper and deeper tangent with my students over whether or not this is real life. ("In real life, no one drops your lowest grades." "Yeah, but Mr. Schmutter, *you* don't drop our lowest grades!" "Well, *I'm* trying to prepare you for *real life*!" "So how is this *not* real life?")

No one's in a funny mood all the time, and I'm just a regular person. I put my pants on one leg at a time, just like you and me. My basic goal is to hopefully at least have one "on" day per week, and I have to make sure to squeeze out a column that day. So in general, if you bump into me on the street (or inside your refrigerator), then I'm obviously not at home writing my column, which means that, statistically, I'm not going to be "on."

• • •

WHAT IS THIS — SOME KIND OF JOKE?

Dear Mr. Schmutter,

Why don't you write about your students more often? I love when you write about your students.

One of Your Students

Dear One,

I don't make a habit of writing about my students, because then they feel the need to do crazy things in the hopes that they'll make it into an article, and most of those things are disruptive.

I find that in general, there are two types of people in my life. There are the people who know me and are always afraid that I'll write about them in an article, and to those people I say, "Why? I'm not going to use your real name anyway!" And then there are the people who don't know me that well, or only know me as a teacher, and they really *do* want to get into an article. And to them I say, "Why? I'm not going to use your real name anyway!"

And even if I did use their real names, no one believes that MY name is real — they're going to believe that all the *other* names are real? No one's going to come up to one of my students on the street and go, "Hey! You're the guy who said, 'Fine! If this isn't real life, then I can do *this*!' and then jumped out the window!"

• • •

Dear Mordechai,

My friend lent me one of your books, and it was awesome! When are you putting out another book?

Everyone

Dear Everyone,

As soon as enough people buy my previous books. *Frum*

The Mailbag

humor is still a very experimental genre, and borrowing books from your friends doesn't net the publishers as much money as you think it does.[10]

• • •

>Dear Mordechai,
>
>A few months ago, you talked about working out at the gym. How's that going?
>
>Your father

Dear Your,

Pretty good. The gym is actually the one place I can go where people don't ask me if I work there. I had a whole exercise regimen put together by a personal trainer named Brad, and my strategy, every time I go, is to do my best to avoid Brad.[11] I generally just come in and head for whichever machines I feel like heading for, such as the water fountain, and figure that it's better than sitting around at home and coming up with excuses not to go to the gym. And so far I've lost twenty pounds! OK, so it was the same four pounds five times. I keep gaining and losing them, like clockwork. So now my strategy is to try to schedule a doctor's appointment for the low part of the cycle.

• • •

>Dear Mordechai,
>
>A couple of weeks ago, you wrote about a single housefly that you couldn't get rid of. Is he still bothering you?
>
>R.R.

---

10. *Ahem.*

11. It's not easy. He runs pretty fast.

WHAT IS THIS — SOME KIND OF JOKE?

Dear R.,

Yes, he's still here, even though flies are supposed to live for only about 3–4 weeks. If flies did news reports, they would definitely do one about the fly in my house that has lived so far to the ripe old age of five weeks.

"What's the secret to your longevity?"

"I keep active. I bother this one guy all day long. Also, you wouldn't believe the kinds of food I land on. There's cake!"

I hope Brad doesn't watch that report.

ABOUT THE AUTHOR

Mordechai Schmutter is not above hiding the covers to all his previous books on the cover to this one. (Can you find them all? There are four.) Nor is he above plugging all the other things he does:

He currently writes a weekly humor column for *Hamodia*, which is syndicated in *The 5 Towns Jewish Times*; *The Jewish Link of New Jersey*; *The Jewish Link of the Bronx, Westchester, and Connecticut*; *The Queens Jewish Link*; *The Lakewood Shopper*; *The Middlesex County Jewish Times*; *The Jewish Local Pages of Passaic*; and Aish.com.

He also writes a monthly humorous question-and-answer advice column for *The Jewish Press*, which is syndicated in *The 20s and 30s* of Brooklyn twice a month, even though the math on that is impossible.

He also writes some original content for Aish.com, and an eventually-to-be-collected comic strip for *The 20s and 30s* called "*The Bunny Rabbi*," who is also on the cover of this book. (*The Bunny Rabbi* is illustrated by Yishaya Suval, who also drew the cover.)

Mordechai also writes and edits speeches, web pages, articles, cards, letters, poems, resumes, scripts, and ad copy for whoever calls, as long as they sound like they're actually going to pay him.

In addition, Mordechai dabbles in stand-up comedy for *simchos*, dinners, and so on, which, as it turns out, is all about memorizing up to a solid hour of jokes, word for word, and hoping he doesn't lose his place when people laugh.

He is also a high school teacher, in case you weren't paying attention.

You can contact him at MSchmutter@gmail.com and he will forget to get back to you in a timely fashion. He's also on Facebook, for some reason.

He will now wrap this up, because he knows you didn't spend an upward of twenty-five bucks for a business card.